THE CONGRESSIONAL BUDGET OFFICE

Selected Titles in the American Governance and Public Policy Series
Series Editors: Gerard W. Boychuk, Karen Mossberger, and Mark C. Rom

THE CONGRESSIONAL BUDGET OFFICE

*Honest Numbers, Power,
and Policymaking*

PHILIP G. JOYCE

GEORGETOWN UNIVERSITY PRESS / WASHINGTON D.C.

Georgetown University Press, Washington, D.C. www.press.georgetown.edu
© 2011 by Georgetown University Press. All rights reserved. No part of this
book may be reproduced or utilized in any form or by any means, electronic
or mechanical, including photocopying and recording, or by any information
storage and retrieval system, without permission in writing from the publisher.

Library of Congress Cataloging-in-Publication Data

Joyce, Philip G., 1956-
The Congressional Budget Office : honest numbers, power, and policymaking /
    Philip G. Joyce.
        p. cm. — (American governance and public policy series)
    Includes bibliographical references and index.
    ISBN 978-1-58901-757-3 (pbk. : alk. paper)
    1. United States. Congressional Budget Office. 2. Budget—United States.
    I. Title.
    HJ2051.J69 2011
    336.73—dc22
                                                        2010037040

♾ This book is printed on acid-free paper meeting the requirements of the
American National Standard for Permanence in Paper for Printed Library
Materials.

15 14 13 12 11   9 8 7 6 5 4 3 2
First printing

Printed in the United States of America

To Rita, Chris, Mariah, and Samuel—
who both inspire me and
make my world a more fun place to be

Contents

Acknowledgments

I WAS A relatively new PhD working at the University of Kentucky in mid-1990 when my telephone rang. It was Marvin Phaup from the Congressional Budget Office (CBO). Roy Meyers was leaving CBO, and CBO was looking for someone who had an interest in (and could analyze) budget process reform issues. Because my wife had just taken a job in Washington, I was looking to move. Little did I know, even after starting at CBO in 1991, that this phone call would forever change my professional life. I had even less reason to believe that it would lead to this book.

In 1996 I left CBO to return to academia, at the Maxwell School at Syracuse University. The longer I was away from the agency, the more I itched to tell the story of CBO. It seemed to me (and still does, as you will discover if you read on) that a story of this small institution, trying to be nonpartisan in the middle of the most partisan environment imaginable, was one that needed to be told. Because I had access to a lot of the players, it seemed that I might be able to learn just enough to do the story justice.

For a number of years, because of various professional and personal commitments, the itch remained unscratched. After moving to The George Washington University in 1999, however, I began to develop a plan. It involved figuring out what story to tell, figuring out who I needed to talk to, and what other information was needed to tell the story. At the time I had no idea that it would take more than ten years from active planning to final manuscript.

Over the course of time the project evolved into more than a history of CBO. The more I got into the research, a chronological history seemed a less effective way to tell the story than to focus on particular functions and events that would illustrate what I think are its main two points. Those points—that objective analysis is important to the effective operation of democracy, and that the capacity to provide such objective analysis is the result of the establishment of a culture that itself results from conscious managerial decisions—are what this book substantiates. In choosing this approach, I necessarily had to leave some things out and fail to highlight other contributions that may seem just as worthy of mention. I am sorry if the specific approach that I took to the story appears to slight any individual or event. This is not my intention or wish—just a by-product of time and page limitations.

A project of this magnitude can never be done alone. It is the product of a great deal of support, both intellectual and personal. In this case, however, I add to this the large number of people who were active participants in the process, because they talked to me about it, they agreed to be interviewed both on and off the record, they provided information, they agreed to read sections and comment. It's not that the book would be lessened without them. Rather, it simply would not exist. For this reason, it is a pleasure to acknowledge their contributions here and to simultaneously absolve them of any responsibility for errors and omissions.

First were the six past and former CBO directors interviewed for this book. Alice Rivlin, one of the true giants of American public service, was incredibly generous with her time—agreeing to be interviewed three times. Each of these conversations provided gems of insight that enabled me to more fully understand what had been happening, whether in the initial years of CBO, or in the Clinton White House, or (as she remains incredibly engaged) even in the last year. Bob Reischauer, whose personal devotion to nonpartisan analysis and effective public policy were an inspiration when I worked for him, agreed to talk to me three times as well. Bob was particularly forthcoming in helping me sort out details of the agency's role in the Clinton health plan. Doug Holtz-Eakin also talked to me three times—once during his tenure as CBO director and twice afterward—and encouraged the project beyond simply filling in details on issues like dynamic scoring and CBO versus the GSEs. Rudy Penner, a crucial figure in fostering the agency's nonpartisan culture, helped illuminate the mid-1980s, from Gramm-Rudman to the start of the S&L crisis. June O'Neill, who was CBO director at a time when the agency was perhaps more vulnerable that any time in its history, was able to provide details on the challenges of leading the agency during a period when Republicans were flexing their muscles after forty years out of power (at least in the House). And the current director, Doug Elmendorf, generously agreed to be interviewed twice, and was particularly helpful in sorting out CBO's role in the health care reform that eventually was signed into law in early 2010.

These people, however, represent just the tip of the iceberg. In all more than sixty people were interviewed for the book. Some are quoted, but all added to the substance of the book. Listing them recognizes but does not do justice to their contribution: Gordon Adams, Barry Anderson , Priscilla Aycock, Jim Bates, Linda Bilheimer, Jim Blum, Linda Blumberg, Ron Boster, Len Burman, Paul Cullinan, Bill Dauster, Sandy Davis, Bob Dennis, Everett Ehrlich, Doug Elmendorf, Dick Emery, Pete Fontaine, Bill Frenzel, Bill Gale, Teri Gullo, Bob Hale, Jim Hearn, Roger Hitchner, Bill Hoagland, Doug Holtz-Eakin, Jim Horney, Sue Irving, Chris Jennings, Thomas Kahn, Richard Kogan, Jeanne Lambrew, Jeff Lemieux, Jack Lew, Rosemary Marcuss, Rick May, Bruce Meredith, Roy Meyers, Gail Millar, Joseph Minarik, David Moore, Richard Morgenstern, Len Nichols, Michael O'Hanlon, June O'Neill, Van Ooms, Leon Panetta, Rudy Penner, Marvin Phaup,

Paul Posner Wendell Primus, Deb Reis, Bob Reischauer, Alice Rivlin, Shirley Ruhe, Art Sauer, Ray Scheppach, Austin Smythe, Michael Telson, Ken Thorpe, Paul Van de Water, Bruce Vavrichek.

I wish I had the space to say something to acknowledge the specific value-added of each who contributed to the book through these interviews, but a few need to be singled out for extraordinary contributions. Jim Blum (who earned the nickname Mr. CBO during his almost twenty-five years in the organization) talked to me at length twice, and read early drafts of some chapters. Roy Meyers, my predecessor at CBO but who I subsequently have collaborated with on other projects, is simply one of the most intelligent and insightful observers of budgeting, and I always came out of conversations with him wishing that I had been smart enough to have thought of it myself. Marvin Phaup, who is really responsible for all of this, also read chapters and encouraged particular lines of inquiry. Pete Fontaine, Teri Gullo, and Leo Lex provided useful data for chapter 5; Pete and Teri also helped me better understand the arcane world of cost estimating. My former CBO colleagues Jim Horney and Gail Millar helped me think the project through initially and agreed to share their insights later. Three people—Irene Rubin (who also read some early chapters), Paul Posner, and Susan Willie—read virtually the whole manuscript (chapter 7 was added later). These people all encouraged the project, and offered tremendously helpful suggestions for its improvement.

Many academic colleagues helped to make this happen. Fellow faculty at GWU—Kathy Newcomer, Joe Cordes (a former CBO employee himself), and Lori Brainard—were especially helpful. A parade of graduate assistants at GW sought out sources, transcribed interviews, formatted chapters, and generally wondered, I'm sure, where all this was leading. Among these were Andrew Huddleston, Matt Johnson, Jennifer Javier, Charlotte Kirschner, Robin McLaughry, Kate Musica, and Nathaniel Taylor. Budgeting colleagues from other universities were good role models and provided necessary distractions, among them Tom Lauth, Bill Duncombe, Dan Mullins, Rosemary O'Leary, Mike Pagano, John Bartle, and Marilyn Rubin.

Thanks are also due to my editor at Georgetown University Press, Don Jacobs, for his encouragement throughout the process, and to the series editors in the American Governance and Public Policy series. I am happy to have found a good home for the book at Georgetown Press and they, along with others throughout the editorial and marketing process, have facilitated a very smooth process.

Beyond the people who contributed to the book specifically, I owe a debt of gratitude to various others who encouraged my love of learning, and my developing interest in budgeting. Among these are the "three Bobs." Bob Olson, my professor at Thiel College for twenty-four credits worth of classes (I used to say that I majored in Bob Olson), was an inspirational teacher who instilled in me a love of history as well as an appreciation of how much difference a good teacher could make. Bob Lee, who was my budgeting professor at Penn State, introduced me to budgeting as an academic field. Bob Mandeville, who was my first boss at the Illinois Bureau of the Budget, showed me that budgeting is a profession, and that professional budgeteers provide an immense public service.

More than anything else, however, I have discovered in this process that there is a reason that people—at significant points in their lives—recognize the contributions of their families. My parents encouraged me to pursue my dreams, even if they were not sure where they were headed. My children are constantly bemused that their dad teaches and studies budgeting for a living ("That's a job?") but they provided necessary distraction, helped me maintain good humor, and put up with Dad disappearing periodically to write. I am most grateful for my partner, Rita Hilton. She has always been my best editor, and dropped everything to edit and format the manuscript. Her greatest contribution, however, is in keeping the family focused on the big picture, and keeping me grounded. I don't know how anyone could complete any significant work without this kind of support, but am extremely thankful that I don't have to find out.

Acronyms

AMT	Alternative minimum tax
BAD	Budget Analysis Division
BEA	Budget Enforcement Act of 1990
BETS	Budget Estimates Tracking System
BOB	Bureau of the Budget
CBO	Congressional Budget Office
COB	Congressional Office of the Budget
CBPP	Center on Budget and Policy Priorities
CMS	Centers for Medicare and Medicaid Services
CRS	Congressional Research Service
DOD	Department of Defense
EPA	Environmental Protection Agency
FAD	Fiscal Analysis Division
FBI	Federal Bureau of Investigation
FHA	Federal Housing Administration
FHLB	Federal Home Loan Bank
FICO	Financing corporation
FSLIC	Federal Savings and Loan Insurance Corporation
GAO	Government Accountability Office (previously General Accounting Office)
GRH	Gramm-Rudman-Hollings
GSEs	Government-sponsored enterprises
HHR	Health and Human Resources Division
HHS	Department of Health and Human Services
HUD	Department of Housing and Urban Development
JCT	Joint Committee on Taxation
JSC	Joint Study Committee
LAO	Legislative Analyst's Office
MAD	Macroeconomic Analysis Division
MBS	Mortgage-backed security
NPR	National Public Radio
NPRO	Nonpartisan research organization
NRA	National Rifle Association

NSD	National Security Division
OFHEO	Office of Federal Housing Enterprise Oversight
OMB	Office of Management and Budget
OTA	Office of Technology Assessment
PAYGO	Pay-as-you-go
RTC	Resolution Trust Corporation
SLCEA	State and Local Cost Estimate Act
SSA	Social Security Administration
SSD	Special Studies Division
TAD	Tax Analysis Division
TSA	Transportation Security Administration
UMRA	Unfunded Mandates Reform Act of 1995

Chapter 1

Truth, Power, and Consequences

I N MARCH OF 2010 President Barack Obama signed two bills that codified a goal the Democratic Party had sought for sixty years—the passage of a comprehensive guarantee of health coverage. The specific provisions of the new law were heavily influenced by a set of principles established by the president, which had to do not only with expanding health coverage, but also with controlling costs. Because of the costs, and because of general anxiety in the country about the expanding role of the federal government in the economy, a crucial focus in the legislative debate on health care reform had to do with the effects of these bills on the federal budget.

In the US political system, presidents tend to initiate policy and Congress to respond to such proposals. Presidents have to live with the reality of congressional power, however, particularly in the budget process. The US Constitution gives Congress the "power of the purse," and this power expanded greatly with the Congressional Budget and Impoundment Control Act of 1974. Not only did this law create new committees—the budget committees—in each house of Congress, it also set up a nonpartisan analytic arm, called the Congressional Budget Office (CBO).

Over time, CBO has become a powerful and influential arbiter of the economic and budgetary effects of policies. In fact, in anticipating President Obama's desire to enact comprehensive health care reform, Senator Ron Wyden (D-OR) was quoted as saying that "the history of health reform is congressmen sending health legislation off to the Congressional Budget Office to die."[1] As if on cue, a major stumbling block to enacting health care reform emerged in the summer of 2009 when CBO director Douglas Elmendorf (who had been appointed by the Democratic congressional leadership) caused a major stir by suggesting that the bills moving through Congress at that point would do little to bend the cost curve—that is, to lower the long-term cost of health care in the overall economy.[2] Opponents of the Obama health care reform proposal jumped on this conclusion as evidence that more work was necessary before taking action on health care reform. The CBO analysis, as much as anything, contributed to the decision by the congressional leadership to delay action until later in 2009. In fact, syndicated columnist Charles Krauthammer said in a *Washington Post* column that, if health care reform was to fail, it would not be (as popularly believed) the congressional Republicans or "Blue Dog" Democrats that killed it, but "the green eyeshades from the Congressional Budget Office."[3] This was not the first time that a CBO analysis had gotten in the way of an Obama proposal. Early on, House Republicans used CBO estimates of the effect of the president's economic stimulus proposal as justification for opposing it.[4]

Ultimately, of course, CBO did not kill health care reform. It passed and became law, but the process by which this occurred and the final content of the legislation was heavily influenced by CBO's analysis of the budgetary effects of various provisions. If CBO said that a particular idea would not save money (or enough money) or would cost too much, it was tweaked until it came back in line with President Obama's spending and deficit goals. In the days leading up to the vote, the president convinced some reluctant members of Congress to vote for the bill because it was fiscally responsible. His evidence? CBO said that it reduced the deficit.

Senator Wyden's view of CBO's role in health care reform almost certainly has its roots in the efforts of another new president, Bill Clinton, who had proposed a massive health care reform sixteen years earlier. This proposal, like the Obama plan, attempted to succeed in simultaneously reducing health care costs and providing insurance for the uninsured. This controversial proposal dominated the US political agenda in 1993 and 1994. Many other health care reform proposals were also proposed by members of Congress over the same period. Neither the congressional nor the Clinton proposals ultimately became law. They fell victim to a combination of the desire of those vested in the status quo (primarily the insurance industry) to block any changes, and the resolve of many Republicans not to give Clinton a victory that might ensure his reelection. But—then and later—one of the most important factors cited as killing Clinton health care was a February 1994 CBO analysis arguing that the plan would both add to cumulative deficits (the administration had said it would save money) and, rather than regulating private activity, represented a vast new expansion of the federal government.

In writing about this latter case, Theda Skocpol found the importance of CBO in this debate more than a little disturbing. "The CBO, it is worth underlining," she wrote, "has by now become virtually a sovereign branch of the U.S. federal government, comparable in clout in relation to the executive and the Congress to the courts back in the Progressive era and the New Deal."[5] Skocpol argues that, similar to cases in the past where legislative proposals were drafted with court review in mind and where legislation would often be struck down by "a few unelected judges," by 1994 "a comparable process occurs with the CBO, an expert-run agency that the Founding Fathers certainly never imagined when they wrote the Constitution! Today's drafters of legislation live in fear that the CBO will, ultimately, reject their proposals as not 'costed out.'"[6] Similarly—and, significantly, six years before the Clinton health care reform—journalist Hedrick Smith wrote that "the CBO represents the most important institutional shift of power on domestic issues between the executive branch and Congress in several decades."[7]

Even this was not the first time that CBO had become embroiled in a controversy over its response to a major presidential economic proposal. Twelve years before the Clinton reform, when Ronald Reagan became president in 1981, he and his budget director David Stockman proposed a number of substantial changes affecting the federal budget. Reagan had advocated massive increases in defense spending, large reductions in the personal income tax, and significant reductions in domestic spending. All of these changes together were proposed to result in the first balanced budget since fiscal year 1969. But in a report issued in September 1981, CBO, which had not existed the last time the budget was balanced, expressed its view that, far from balancing the budget, the Reagan changes would result in a federal deficit of more than $100 billion by fiscal year 1984. Reagan dismissed CBO analyses as "phony numbers."[8]

The preceding arguments both overstate the importance of CBO (the Skocpol claim seems particularly overblown) and misunderstand the source and significance of CBO's influence. It is unquestionable that CBO analyses have a powerful effect on both the drafting of and the prospects for legislation. It is perhaps surprising to many and obviously disturbing to some that a group of unelected bureaucrats, working in an agency that is only about thirty-five years old, now plays such a significant role in the system of US policymaking. This reality raises two critical questions. First, how did this happen? Second, is it good for the country?

Policymaking, Budgeting, and Choice

It was once famously said that "if you laid all economists end to end, they would fail to reach a conclusion." Virtually all economists do agree, however, on one thing. Resources are scarce, and therefore opportunity costs exist. Using resources for one purpose necessarily makes these same resources unavailable for other purposes. This may seem obvious, but this one simple concept—scarce resources—has enormous implications for public policy and for the role of analysis in framing choices underlying that policy.

The concept of scarce resources is not peculiar to government. It is confronted as well by businesses and individuals. It crystallizes the problem of making choices, specifically, where resources will come from and how they will and will not be used. Individuals choose between consumption and investment. Businesses choose between capital and labor. In the public sector, choices are made are about taxes and spending. Given that some revenues will need to be raised to finance government, where will those revenues come from? Will the government tax sales, income, or property, or all three? Will those with higher incomes pay a larger proportion of their income in tax than those with lower incomes? On the spending side, how much money will go to domestic programs and how much to national security concerns (guns versus butter)? Within the domestic arena, how much will be spent on health care, or education, or transportation? If resources were unlimited, we would have to worry about neither the distribution of taxes (between either sources or income groups) or the distribution of spending (over different priorities of spending).

Because resources are scarce, the public sector has derived a decision process—called the budget process—to resolve arguments about relative priorities. In the budget process, typically a chief executive will propose a tax and spending plan. A legislative body will respond to this plan, often by substituting its priorities for those of the executive. Eventually, though, agreement must be reached on a set of tax and spending decisions for the government. Either as a part of this or separately, new legislation may be proposed that will have its own fiscal and economic effects, and will need to be considered in light of these effects.

There is more than just a political dimension to all of this. It is one thing to say that you need to make trade-offs between different uses of resources. It is quite another for those different policy choices to be illuminated by analysis, so that policymakers know what the effect of various choices might be. That is, a government could say that it needed to choose between two policy goals—providing health care for everyone or providing enough defense capacity to be able to fight two major wars simultaneously. But to have a real grasp of the costs involved in that choice, two questions must be answered. First, how is each of these goals translated into particular programs or activities that the government will undertake make them happen? Second, what are the effects of those programs, in terms of both the costs involved and the results that will be achieved? The classic formulation of this is the guns versus butter model. In reality, the debate is often about education versus transportation versus health security. This same analysis must be done, however, even if a decision has already been take to pursue universal health care and the need is simply to compare different ways of getting there.

These are important and complicated analytical questions. If the decision-makers are to select the best option among alternatives, those choices must be informed. That is, they must be illuminated by analysis of costs and probable effects of each possible alternative. This is the main reason for the existence of budget controllers. Controllers exist to counter the desires of spending advocates, whose primary goal is procuring more resources for favored programs and agencies. In the US government, the budget control function is decentralized and fragmented.[9] Most federal agencies (at least at the cabinet level) have budget controllers, whose role it is to force proposals for resources to be justified. This agency control largely exists, however, because of constraints imposed on agencies from central government controllers. In the executive branch, this budget control is most closely associated with the president's budget office—the Office of Management and Budget. In Congress, direct budget control is exercised at a macro level by the budget committees and at a micro level by the appropriations committees. These congressional committees, however, are supported by CBO, which since its creation in 1974 has attempted to provide Congress with an analytical counterweight to the Office of Management and Budget (OMB) in pursuit of true budgetary independence for Congress.

So You're Not a Policy Wonk, Why Should You Care?

This book started as a history of CBO—a chronology of the life of a relatively high-profile (at least inside the Beltway), but not terribly well understood, agency of the Congress of the United States. As I delved into the story, however, it became clear that there is much more to the CBO story than simply a tale of technicians doing a technical job. The CBO story is, at base, about the importance of analysis in helping to frame political debate. Analysts, and agencies designed to provide neutral analysis, can do little to ensure their outputs are given proper weight. Sometimes that analysis takes on too much importance. Other times it is ignored. How analysis enters the political debate—and why it is important—is a significant tale in its own right.

CBO's story is not just about technocrats and analysis but also, to use Wildavsky's famous phrase, about "speaking truth to power."[10] This dimension is intrinsically relevant to those interested in the U.S. budget process and issue-specific policy. It is also relevant to any taxpayer interested in where the money comes from and where it goes. This is clear in the current policy debate about health care reform, where disputes about basic facts (and, to be honest, ignorance—even among experts, as to what drives costs and quality) can get in the way of discussion of policy options. Because resources are scarce, and those scarce resources are allocated in an unalterably political budget process, the role of analysis is crucial to policy choices. Not all analysis is created equal. Some analyses are produced or solicited by people whose primary motivation is to make their policy proposals look better (including less costly) and others' policies look worse. It is a fact in political debate that it is relatively easy for any proponent or opponent of a particular policy to find an analysis—and an analyst—that will support a given point of view. One author has referred to this as "the rise of the 'hired gun' policy analysts ready to massage the numbers to tell their political masters what they want to hear."[11]

The CBO

Making effective choices involves more than just analysis. It involves sound, objective (unbiased) analysis. As Walter Williams put it in his book on the topic of "honest numbers," what is most necessary for "reasoned public policy making" is "policy data produced by competent researchers and analysts who use sound technical methods without the application of political spin to fit partisan needs."[12] Underlying this argument is a simple but powerful notion. Policymakers and their constituents need to be confronted with the truth—in the form of the most neutral analysis possible on budgetary and economic implications of particular policy choices. Many do not have an incentive to seek it out, because it often makes the process of making choices uncomfortable. There are certainly cases where the real effects of policies cannot be known. Nonetheless, politicians and constituents both need to know either the real effects of different policies, or that the real effects are unknowable, if they are to make judicious choices between alternatives.

Examples of strategies applied by advocates to support requests for favorable budgetary treatment of preferred policies abound in the budgetary politics literature. Three well-known books—Aaron Wildavsky's *The Politics of the Budgetary Process*, Roy Meyers's *Strategic Budgeting*, and Irene Rubin's *Politics and the Budget*—offer numerous examples of strategies that involve hiding the true cost of proposed policies.[13] Such approaches are relatively common.

- The camel's nose strategy, which relies on a slow phase-in of a program to hide the substantial future commitments being made.
- Accounting tactics, among them creation of costly nonbudgetary entities that actually open the door to large future payouts—such as Fannie Mae and Freddie Mac, characterized as costless when established as government-sponsored enterprises, but ultimately bailed out at an estimated cost of $283 billion.
- Explicitly creating future costs, in other words, avoiding counting costs when commitments are made to pay them, such as loan guarantees or lease-purchase agreements—such as the effort to provide Boeing with funds to purchase a fleet of refueling tankers, which were to be purchased over a number of years through operating leases, in an attempt to obscure the ultimate cost to the federal government.
- Misestimating the macro-budgetary effects of policies—such as occurred when President Reagan underestimated the deficit effects of his tax cutting policies in 1981, and George W. Bush did the same twenty years later.

Enter the CBO. In 1974, in response to President Richard Nixon's continued efforts to ignore Congress in making budgetary policy, Congress decided to create its own process for making overall budget decisions, rather than dealing with the budget piecemeal. Part of that effort involved the creation of a new agency—the CBO—to provide Congress with analytical capacity independent of the executive branch. A surprising feature of the legislation was that it established that the new agency was to operate in a nonpartisan manner. Here was perhaps the most partisan institution imaginable—the United States Congress—and it was explicitly requiring nonpartisan analysis from its own staff.

The result has exceeded the wildest expectations of those who conceived and established the institution. CBO has developed a clear and sustained reputation for counteracting the natural tendency of the political system to sugarcoat the fiscal news. This did not just happen. Rather, it occurred first because Congress decided (for reasons still not completely clear) to make CBO nonpartisan. This would have been a hollow promise, however, were it not for leadership decisions made by the first director, Alice Rivlin, in the organization of CBO, the development and maintenance of analytical capacity within the institution, particular flash points where CBO credibility was enhanced by coming into conflict with the executive branch over particular policy or budget issues, and dumb luck. There is a necessary connection between CBO objectivity, credibility, and influence. In short, if players in the policymaking process did not believe that CBO was an unbiased referee when making the tough calls, the agency would lose credibility, and become viewed as yet another partisan voice. No agency of roughly two hundred people could remain influential in such a context.

Research

The story of CBO is important because the mission of CBO puts it squarely in a position to make major contributions to the policy debate by providing honest numbers (i.e., those employing nonpoliticized assumptions). The agency's work can have direct implications for the shape of public policy. Further, there is at least some suggestion that the CBO has succeeded spectacularly in that mission, perhaps achieving too important a status, given the tendency of some to defer to CBO on major policy questions.

Although there is some discussion of CBO in the public finance and policy literatures, there is no book that focuses exclusively on the organization. Both Haynes Johnson and David Broder and Theda Skocpol in their analyses of the Clinton health care reform include substantial discussions of CBO in that context.[14] Bob Woodward's *The Agenda* and George Hager and Eric Pianin's *Mirage* devote attention to CBO's role in the larger budgetary politics of the 1990s.[15] Joel Havemann's early book on the establishment of the congressional budget process includes an entire chapter on CBO and its early history, as does Allen Schick's classic *Congress and Money*, written in 1980.[16] Walter Williams's *Honest Numbers and Democracy* includes a chapter titled "Congress and Policy Analysis," much of which is devoted to discussing CBO. Irene Rubin's *Balancing the Federal Budget* includes a chapter devoted to OMB and CBO.[17] Roy Meyers has written at least two brief pieces on CBO and the agency plays a prominent role as a budget controller in his book *Strategic Budgeting*, and James Blum contributed a chapter on CBO to Carol Weiss's *Organizations for Policy Analysis*.[18] In addition to these, articles in the academic literature have appeared periodically that analyze particular aspects of CBO, such as its forecasting accuracy compared to other analytical institutions.[19]

These are all significant works. Indeed, they have all been used as source materials for this volume. None has told the story in the kind of detail that this book does, however. In contrast, there have been at least four book-length treatises on OMB (and its predecessor, the Bureau of the Budget), at least four on the Government Accountability Office (GAO), and one—Frederick Mosher's *A Tale of Two Agencies*—that is a comparative analysis of the two.[20]

This omission is significant. CBO has been at the center of budget debates for thirty-five years, and its experience is important because of what it may tell us about the significance of honest numbers, about faceless but neutral and dedicated civil servants, about organizational culture, and about the importance of careful, informed analysis. Some presidents—and many members of Congress— have eschewed analysis. Others have been openly hostile to it. Yet effective democracy requires analysis, because effective democracy exists only under conditions of informed choice.

What This Book Does

It is in this context—that is, competition between the branches and between different policy choices—that this book makes the case for the importance of understanding the role CBO has played. CBO would not be important if it was the norm for public policy to be informed by nonpartisan and objective analysis concerning its effects. In a world where neutral analysis is not the norm, however, any attempt to provide such analysis is worth serious study.

Organization of the Book

The book is organized into eight chapters. This first one presents the case for the importance of objective, nonpartisan analysis in the context of public policymaking. Chapter 2 presents the historical and institutional context for CBO, starting with a justification for the Congressional Budget Act, and therefore the CBO. It discusses the competing views of Congress regarding CBO, and ends with the selection of Alice Rivlin as the first director, a fateful choice that embraced—intentionally or unintentionally—a fairly broad mandate for the organization. This mandate, and Rivlin's vision in response to it, shaped CBO's early institutional culture. The remainder of chapter 2 discusses how that institutional culture was sustained over time, sometimes despite substantial institutional and political challenges.

The Congressional Budget Act gave CBO three main responsibilities. The first, to be discussed in chapter 3, was to support the macrobudgetary decisions of Congress. This includes the development of the CBO baseline (a current services estimate) and the provision of assistance to the budget committees in establishing the budget resolution, which had been created by the 1974 Budget Act as the device that set out the budgetary framework for Congress. The responsibility to support Congress in discharging its responsibilities has frequently brought CBO into conflict with the executive branch and one or the other party. This occurred in 1981, as has been discussed, when conflicts with the Reagan administration put CBO on the map, establishing its independence and its credibility. It also occurred in 1995 and 1996, when Congress demanded that the Clinton administration present a balanced budget using CBO numbers for Congress to agree to end the government shutdown, which had been precipitated by budgetary conflict between the president and Congress. Indeed, this conflict between the branches is an ongoing theme in the federal budget process. When President Bush submitted his fiscal year 2008 budget proposal, promising the balance the budget by 2012, immediately comparisons were made between the president's assumptions and those of CBO in an effort to determine the credibility of the Bush plan. President Obama's pledge to cut the deficit in half during his first term has been (and will continue to be) subjected to similar scrutiny.

The second responsibility was to support the day-to-day work of Congress by providing cost estimates of legislative proposals and keeping budgetary score of legislation in Congress to ensure that Congress lived within legal and procedural budget constraints. This responsibility forms the basis for chapter 4.

Third, the Budget Act, at least as interpreted by director Rivlin and her successors, gave CBO the role of performing broader and longer-term policy analyses, normally in anticipation of issues that were facing the country, and therefore Congress. Chapter 5 reviews the development of this capacity, which because the statute was less clear and the demand less acute, took longer to develop than the responsibilities related directly to ongoing annual activities in Congress. A part of this story is about how the CBO created the demand for its work, first because of its analysis of the Carter energy policy, which established CBO's capacity to undertake policy analysis. This capacity has proved quite valuable, particularly when clarifying issues—such as the financial risks associated with government-guaranteed financial institutions (such as savings and loans and government-sponsored enterprises) and health care financing—requires detailed technical analysis.

Chapters 6 and 7 are two comparative case studies that perhaps best exemplify the intersection of these three broad sets of responsibilities—informing budget policy, cost estimating, and policy analysis. Both chapters deal with health care reform. The first addresses the Clinton reform proposal in 1993 and 1994. By the time the Clinton health care reform plan was introduced, everyone assumed that CBO would play an important role, but were at the same time not quite comfortable with that role. The story of CBO's involvement in the Clinton health plan is both an internal story (how did CBO organize to provide the type of useful, consistent information that the Congress needed to tackle an issue as complex as health care reform?) and an external story (was the role that CBO played in this debate, in retrospect, greater than is appropriate for a staff agency that is self-consciously trying to inform policy, rather than change its course?).

In chapter 7 we have the opportunity to revisit health care reform, this time with a different outcome. In 2009 President Obama, learning from earlier Clinton experience, proposed a reform of the health system that followed a different, more decentralized path than the Clinton reform but had similar goals. Because in 2009, as in 1993, there was substantial concern about the budgetary effects of health care reform, CBO played an important role. This chapter explains the Obama approach, and how the role CBO played affected the process and the legislative outcome.

The concluding chapter looks back over the thirty-five-year history of CBO and draws lessons concerning what we know about the impact of CBO and the neutral analysis it has supplied on policymaking. In closing, chapter 8 suggests answers to the following questions about CBO—each addressed over the course of the book:

- Has CBO assisted Congress in countering the trend toward greater executive branch dominance in budget process and allocation that existed before 1974? What has the creation and growing importance of CBO meant for the ability of Congress to compete with the executive branch in the policy arena, and for presidential-legislative relations in general? More broadly, to what extent is there evidence that CBO has significantly influenced public policy—that is, are there policies that might be different had CBO not existed?
- What is the role of leadership (particularly, the leadership of CBO directors) in establishing a vision and a continuing culture for the agency?
- Has CBO in fact engaged in nonpartisan analysis? That is, to what extent has CBO produced honest numbers?
- How has CBO assisted Congress in the congressional budget process, and assisted the public (through the media or independently) in understanding the choices that face the country, and the effects of those choices?
- Given the importance director Rivlin placed on policy analysis, what can we say about CBO's performance and its effects in this area?
- What role has CBO played in educating Congress and the general public, and what difference has this made?
- What, if anything, do these lessons tell us for the future of CBO, for policy analysis in general, or about policymaking in the federal government?

More broadly, this concluding chapter takes the historical experience of CBO and attempts to draw some conclusions concerning the role of expertise generally, and nonpartisan expertise specifically, in the policymaking process. The political science literature has seen a spate of works on how legislatures use information in the policy process, including some studies that focus on the use of objective information by legislative bodies. Keith Krehbiel focuses on the organization of legislatures explicitly as an attempt to explain this organization in light of the need legislators have for information in order to do their jobs—either making policy or getting elected, depending on how one sees it.[21] In the same vein, David Whiteman has studied communication in Congress, and argues that the flow of information is essential to the ability of Congress, and individual members, to make decisions.[22]

Although Whiteman's book focuses mainly on individual member offices, it does devote a chapter to the role of policy analysis in informing members of Congress as policymakers and whether policy analysis makes a difference. In this context, he describes the process by which congressional staff interact with CBO on cost estimates as one with a certain amount of asymmetrical power; the congressional committee wants a CBO cost estimate, and the analyst controls when they get it and what it says. More broadly, however, Whiteman describes the idiosyncratic use by members and committees of CBO and other support agencies. Sometimes support agency staff help with markups; sometimes reports are used as resource for speeches or floor statements.

Further, in *The Political Economy of Expertise*, Esterling argues that interest group expertise, far from being anathema to political goals, is actually critical to achieving them. In short, he notes that "research-based analytical ideas and empirical evidence matter in lobbying politics."[23] He argues that policymakers seek out expertise not because they are somehow more interested in broader public policies than in their own interests, but because it is not possible to know what is in their own interest without knowing the effects of policies. He presents evidence that leads him to conclude that "the state of knowledge itself is exogenous to the political process."[24] The more complex a policy, the more important research and expertise are. This means that, even in an environment where the decisions themselves may be motivated by crass self-interest, value is nonetheless placed on objective analysis.

John Hird comes even closer to our current interest with his book on state nonpartisan legislative institutions. In his preface he includes what is probably an unintentionally ironic statement: "when I was in graduate school in the 1980s, the state Legislative Analyst's Office (LAO) had an outstanding reputation, and was known to be the state's equivalent of the Congressional Budget Office."[25] This is ironic because, as explained in chapter 2, the California LAO was the model for CBO, as opposed to the other way around. Hird reviews these legislative think tanks as they operate in several states, referring to them as nonpartisan research organizations (NPROs). His focus is on legislators' perceptions of the important of these NPROs, as well as the extent to which they are influential in policymaking. He finds that legislators both value and use the products of NPROs, particularly in those states where the organizations are larger and more analytical. He also argues that they create these institutions, not so much for their written products, but to have an in-house source of expertise on policy matters. Existing research on the influence of such institutions misses the mark, according to Hird: "scholars have missed the potential for the substantial influence of individuals and organizations quite apart from their written products. That is, policy analysts qua professionals, who develop personal relationships, policy networks, and the trust of policymakers, may have greater influence than previous analyses of written products suggest."[26]

All this points to a question on which it is important to focus: to what extent is CBO analysis, in all of its forms—valued by Congress, under what circumstances, and to what end? This leads to more specific questions that are touched on throughout the book: that is, is democracy better informed because of CBO; does this result in a more efficient use of scarce resources; if not, does it make any difference?

Methodology

The book relies on two main sources of data. The first is archival research. Although the academic and book-length literature on CBO is not substantial, I did have access to the numerous newspaper and magazine articles that chronicled both key events in the agency's history and the political events that dominated that history. The following publications are particularly helpful in this regard— the *Congressional Quarterly Weekly*, the *National Journal*, the *New York Times*, the *Wall Street Journal*, and the *Washington Post*. Reviewing thousands of articles that have appeared in these publications over the thirty-five years of CBO history assisted me in getting the policy context for CBO since 1975. Additionally, numerous CBO publications as well as internal CBO documents housed at the National Archives were used in the research.

The other primary source of information was key informant interviews with more than sixty people central to national budget debates over the past thirty-five years. A book about CBO, I felt strongly, should not be written only from the perspective of CBO. I have, therefore, used as sources three broad groups of people.

First, I talked to past and present CBO staff, including six of the eight CBO directors. Second, I interviewed congressional staff and former members of Congress, mainly from the budget committees, who have or had substantial interaction with CBO. Third, I sought out executive branch staff who have had contact with CBO. This last group ranged from OMB staff whose contact with CBO may have been more constant, to individuals whose contact has been related to a particular legislation, such as the Clinton health care reform.

What Is the Point?

In the end, the CBO story is important for a number of reasons I hope will become clear in the pages that follow. First, it is a story of excellent sustained leadership and shared commitment to a vision—of large numbers of people putting the mission of an organization over their personal preferences, often placing themselves in the uncomfortable position of telling powerful people things that they did not want to hear.

It is also a story about why understanding policymaking requires understanding not just what appears on the surface but also the story behind the scenes. An aspect of the backstory I hope to illuminate concerns the extent to which unelected staff members in this particular staff agency influence public policy. Why does this happen, and what are the implications for democracy and democratic choice? Both are important to know, but it is also important to understand the limitations of policy analysis. There are limits. Policy analysis does nothing but inform those with decision-making power—it does not make the choices. If analysts appear to have too much power in a particular circumstance, it is worth asking not only whether this is perception or reality, but also whether it occurred because that power has been legitimately delegated to them.

But, in the end, if CBO matters it will be because honest numbers matter. It will be because a world in which policymakers and constituents alike have reliable data and transparent analysis is a world in which informed choice is possible. CBO does not have the market on truth cornered. If its numbers have credibility—if they are honest—it is because they have developed a culture where honesty is valued, and where it makes a difference.

Notes

1. Ezra Klein, "The Number-Cruncher-in-Chief," *The American Prospect*, January 14, 2009, www.prospect.org/cs/articles?article=numbercruncherinchief.

2. David Clarke and Edward Epstein, "CBO Raises Health Care Cost Concerns," *CQ Today Online News*, July 16, 2009, www.cq.com.

3. Charles Krauthammer, "Obamacare: The Coming Retreat," *Washington Post*, July 24, 2009.

4. Minority leader John Boehner's official website, http://gopleader.gov/News/.

5. Theda Skocpol, *Boomerang: Clinton's Health Security Effort and the Turn against Government in U.S. Politics* (New York: W. W. Norton, 1996), 67.

6. Ibid.

7. Hedrick Smith, *The Power Game: How Washington Works* (New York: Random House, 1988), 290.

8. "Don't Punish the Economic Messenger," *New York Times*, April 7, 1981, A18.

9. For a more detailed discussion of advocates and controllers, see Roy Meyers, *Strategic Budgeting* (Ann Arbor: University of Michigan Press, 1994).

10. Aaron Wildavsky, *Speaking Truth to Power: The Art and Craft of Policy Analysis* (Boston, MA: Little, Brown, 1979).

11. Walter Williams, *Honest Numbers and Democracy: Social Policy Analysis in the White House, Congress and in Federal Agencies* (Washington, DC: Georgetown University Press, 1998), ix.

12. Ibid.

13. Aaron Wildavsky, *The Politics of the Budgetary Process* (Boston, MA: Little, Brown, 1964); Roy Meyers, *Strategic Budgeting* (Ann Arbor: University of Michigan Press, 1994); Irene Rubin, *The Politics of Public Budgeting*, 4th ed. (New York: Chatham House, 2000).

14. See Haynes Johnson and David Broder, *The System* (Boston, MA: Little, Brown, 1996); Theda Skocpol, *Boomerang: Clinton's Health Security Effort and the Turn against Government in U.S. Politics* (New York: W. W. Norton, 1996).

15. Bob Woodward, *The Agenda* (New York: Pocket Books, 1995); George Hager and Eric Pianin, *Mirage* (New York: Random House, 1997).

16. Joel Havemann, *Congress and the Budget* (Bloomington: Indiana University Press, 1978); Allen Schick, *Congress and Money* (Washington, DC: The Urban Institute, 1980).

17. Irene S. Rubin, *Balancing the Federal Budget: Trimming the Herds or Eating the Seed Corn?* (New York: Chatham House, 2003).

18. Roy Meyers, "CBO: The Agencies' Indispensable Adversary," *The Public Manager* 25, no. 2 (1996): 11; "The Congressional Budget Office," in *Encyclopedia of Public Policy and Administration*, edited by Jay Shafritz (Boulder, CO: Westview Press, 1998): 486–92; and *Strategic Budgeting*. See also James L. Blum, "The Congressional Budget Office: On the One Hand, on the Other," in *Organizations for Policy Analysis: Helping Government Think*, edited by Carol Weiss (Newbury Park, CA: Sage Publications, 1992), 218–35.

19. See, for example, Mark S. Kamlet, David C. Mowery, and Tsai-Tsu Su, "Whom Do You Trust? An Analysis of Executive and Congressional Economic Forecasts," *Journal of Policy Analysis and Management* 6, no. 3 (1987): 365–84.

20. On the executive budget office, see Charles Dawes, *The First Year of the Budget of the United States* (New York: Harper, 1923); Percival Brundage, *The Bureau of the Budget* (New York: Praeger, 1970); Larry Berman, *The Office of Management and Budget and the Presidency: 1921–1979* (Princeton, NJ: Princeton University Press, 1979); Shelley Tompkin, *Inside OMB* (Armonk, NY: M. E. Sharpe, 1998). On GAO, see Harvey Mansfield, *The Comptroller General: A Study in the Law and Practice of Financial Administration* (New Haven, CT: Yale University Press, 1939); Joseph Pois, *Watchdog on the Potomac: A Study of the Comptroller General of the United States* (Washington, DC: University Press of America, 1979); Frederick Mosher, *The GAO: The Quest for Accountability in American Government* (Boulder, CO: Westview Press, 1979); Roger L. Sperry, Timothy D. Desmond, Kathi F. McGraw, and Barbara Schmitt, *GAO 1966–1981: An Administrative History* (Washington, DC: U.S. General Accounting Office, 1981). For a comparison of OMB and GAO, see Frederick Mosher, *A Tale of Two Agencies: A Comparative Analysis of the General Accounting Office and the Office of Management and Budget* (Baton Rouge: Louisiana State University Press, 1984).

21. Keith Krehbiel, *Information and Legislative Organization* (Ann Arbor: University of Michigan Press, 1992).

22. David Whiteman, *Communication in Congress* (Lawrence: University Press of Kansas, 1995).

23. Kevin Esterling, *The Political Economy of Expertise* (Ann Arbor: University of Michigan, 2004), 243.

24. Ibid.

25. John Hird, *Power, Knowledge, and Politics: Policy Analysis in the States* (Washington, DC: Georgetown University Press, 2005).

26. Ibid., 2.

Chapter 2

Organizing for Nonpartisan Analysis

THE CBO WAS born out of controversy between the executive and the legislative branches of the federal government. Part of this controversy involved a frustration among some with a lack of fiscal responsibility, particularly in Congress. This lack resulted from the decentralized nature of Congress—the notion that budget-making by committee was by its very nature not confronting the problem of overall resource scarcity. Moreover, Congress itself became frustrated with what it perceived as its domination by the executive branch in the budget-making process.

Congress is currently viewed as a more or less equal partner to the president on budgetary policy, but this has not always been true. Most analyses of the period between 1921 and 1974 suggest that the president was in the driver's seat. In fact, Allen Schick refers to the period explicitly as one of "presidential dominance" in the budget process.[1] This ascendancy had been ushered in by the enactment of the Budget and Accounting Act of 1921, which increased both the visibility of the executive budget and the capacity to produce it by requiring an annual presidential budget submission and the creation of the Bureau of the Budget.

Toward the end of this period, Congress, which had never been completely comfortable in an acquiescent role, became much more hostile to what it viewed as heavy-handed presidential budgetary tactics. This dissatisfaction first surfaced in the Johnson administration, largely in reaction to the budgetary pressures brought about by the Vietnam conflict. Although President Johnson had insisted in his 1967 budget message that the Vietnam War and the Great Society could be financed simultaneously, just one year later he called for a tax surcharge to finance both priorities.[2] This, coupled with the growth of entitlement spending associated with the Great Society (particularly fueled by Medicare and Medicaid), put additional pressure on the budget. As an example, whereas in 1962 mandatory spending (mainly entitlement spending, such as Social Security, Medicare, and Medicaid) came to only 6.1 percent of GDP (about one-third of overall federal spending), by 1975 it had risen to 10.9 percent (more than half of the overall federal budget).[3]

Budgetary conflict escalated further during the Nixon administration. President Nixon openly challenged congressional prerogatives in two ways. First, he engaged in substantial impoundments, refusing to spend money appropriated for various social programs. Second, in response to the decentralized nature of congressional decisions, he insisted that Congress enact spending ceilings. Because no congressional committee had jurisdiction over the entire budget, assigning responsibility for annual budget outcomes was difficult. Further, although Congress controlled (to varying degrees) the pieces of the budget, no one controlled the totals. The recurring budget deficits that began to appear in the late 1960s required Congress to take the unpopular step of raising the limit on the public debt on a frequent basis.[4] Several of these became law between 1968 and 1971.

The conflict over spending limitations came to a head in the context of the fiscal year 1973 budget. First, in July 1972 Nixon challenged Congress to enact a $250 billion limitation on outlays for fiscal year 1973, which had already begun.[5] This limitation was below the amount Nixon argued would be spent in the absence of such a ceiling. The president reiterated his request in September; this request was, at Nixon's request, attached to a bill raising the limit on the public debt. The dispute was not over the size of the limited budget, but about who—Congress or the president—would have the power to enforce the limitation. The president wanted substantial discretion to cut the programs that he wanted—a de facto line item veto—but did not specify what those programs would be.[6] Separate spending limitations passed the House and Senate, but the resulting impasse over the specifics of the limitation led to language in the conference agreement both establishing the $250 billion limitation and voiding it after one day. But, though "the conflict over spending priorities ended in stalemate, it did spur a search for new methods of budget control."[7]

As a part of the same bill, Congress established a Joint Study Committee on Budget Control (JSC). This committee, made up of thirty-two members from the House and Senate, was to "propose procedures for improving congressional control over budgetary outlay and receipt totals and to assure full coordination of an overall view of each year's budgetary outlays with an overall view of the anticipated revenue for that year."[8] The committee issued two reports—an interim report on February 7, 1973, and a final report on April 18, 1973.

In the interim report it outlined the scope of the budgetary problem facing the United States—mainly that a trend toward large annual federal deficits had been in part the result of "the failure to arrive at congressional budgetary decisions on an overall basis."[9] This resulted, in their view, from various factors, including the separation of tax and spending decisions, the rise of uncontrollable (backdoor) spending, and the resulting reduction in the percentage of federal spending under the jurisdiction of the appropriations committees.[10] Ultimately, the JSC issued a series of detailed recommendations for budget reform:

- committees on the budget should be formed in both the House and the Senate, with responsibility for consideration of a budget resolution to provide

overall budgetary limitations, and a simultaneous consideration of both the revenue and spending sides of the budget;
- joint staff for the two budget committees should be headed by a legislative budget director and "the director and the staff would be highly trained, professional and nonpartisan."
- rules and timetables would be set for budget resolutions and the relationship between these resolutions and other budgetary actions.

The legislative budget director and staff were to be direct staff to the budget committees, and no separate budget support agency was envisioned: "The director and the joint staff in this case, in a sense, will give Congress its own center of congressional budgetary operations, much along the lines of the Legislative Analyst and staff of California's Joint Legislative Budget Committee who provides the legislature in effect with its own budget director. The director and staff not only would provide assistance to Congress in developing its priorities, but also would provide the service to Congress of listing the effect of existing and proposed legislation (appropriations and authorizations) on budgetary expenditures of up to three to five years ahead."[11]

Note the relatively narrow scope of responsibilities here—the staff was to be staff only to the budget committees, and was to support the annual budget process by doing baseline estimates and cost estimates for proposed legislation. The new staff agency was not envisioned as an independent source of analysis, and its analytical products were fairly narrowly circumscribed. Indeed, Schick notes that "the new staff would have been primarily a 'numbers' operation, producing the data and reports necessary for the budget process."[12]

Budget reform was ultimately handled by three committees. This narrow scope for legislative budget staffing was incorporated into the House budget reform bill—H.R. 7130, which was under the jurisdiction of the House Rules Committee. Two Senate committees—government operations and rules and administration—had jurisdiction over the proposed legislation. These committees added several provisions to the legislation, including a reconciliation process that would become a significant procedure in future years (see chapter 3).

Notably, the Senate reform legislation also recommended that a Congressional Office of the Budget (COB) also be established. According to the Senate report, "the COB is the result of the Committees' belief that Congress needs a highly competent staff to guide it in fiscal policy and budgetary considerations, similar in expertise to the President's Office of Management and Budget."[13] The report noted that it believed that this new agency should staff the entire Congress, rather than only the budget committees. The committee noted that, although COB might be expensive, "the critical objective of providing Congress with the expert help it needs to regain its control over the Federal budget process is overriding."[14]

The Congressional Budget and Impoundment Control Act of 1974 (hereinafter the Budget Act), the compromise bill, was signed into law by President Nixon on July 12, 1974. Its most significant features were the creation of the budget resolution, the budget committees, the impoundment control procedures, and the CBO.

Legislative Provisions Governing CBO

Title II of the Budget Act specifies the staffing and responsibilities of the CBO. Included in details of the legislation are the following significant provisions:[15]

- CBO was to be headed by a director and a deputy director (who would act as director in the event the director position was vacant, or if the director was absent or incapable of performing his or her duties). The term of the first director was to expire on January 3, 1979. Subsequent terms would expire at four-year intervals.
- The director would be appointed by the Speaker of the House and the president pro tempore of the Senate,[16] upon recommendations from the budget committees "without regard to political affiliation and solely on the basis of his fitness to perform his duties."[17] The director could be removed by either House by resolution.
- The director was empowered to appoint all other CBO personnel, who should likewise be appointed without regard to political affiliation. The director was given wide latitude in terms of organizing CBO and establishing the "duties and responsibilities" of CBO staff.
- CBO could obtain data needed to conduct its analyses from the relevant executive branch agencies, and was instructed to coordinate with other congressional support agencies so as to avoid unnecessary duplication.[18]
- The law specified a pecking order for CBO assistance to Congress. Its first responsibilities were to the money committees—budget, appropriations, ways and means, and finance. It did not specifically work for other committees or for individual members, but was instructed to provide these other committees and members with the information collected in the course of serving the budget, appropriations, and tax writing committees.
- Only one report was required to be completed on an annual basis. The CBO was required, on or before April 1 of each year, to provide the budget committees with a report providing information intended to inform the work of the budget committees. This information would include "alternate levels of total revenues, total new budget authority, and total outlays," the level of tax expenditures under current law, and major spending broken down by major functional category.

- CBO was further given an opening for providing other information to the Congress, as a result of the following language: "The Director shall from time to time submit to the Committees on the Budget of the House of Representatives and the Senate such further reports (including reports revising the report required by paragraph [1]) as may be necessary or appropriate to provide such Committees with information, data and analyses for the performance of their duties and functions."
- Finally, in a separate section of the Budget Act, CBO was instructed to prepare cost estimates of proposed legislation. These estimates were to provide Congress with information on the five-year cost of legislation reported by a congressional committee. The law specified that the cost estimate should be included in the committee report accompanying such reported legislation.

Five aspects of CBO's statutory guidance are of particular interest when viewed in the context of subsequent developments. First, it is significant that at no point was there provision for the entire Congress, or either House of Congress, to vote or ratify the choice of director; this responsibility was to reside solely with the budget committees and the leadership. Second, the law did not use the word *nonpartisan* to describe CBO as an institution, but said that the director should be appointed "without regard to political affiliation." Third, Congress expected the CBO director to have the same relationship to CBO staff that a typical member of Congress has to his or her personal staff. CBO staff were not to be civil service personnel, and nothing in the law would prevent wholesale dismissal of staff by a given director. This made CBO staff substantially different from GAO staff, most of whom are explicitly civil service. Fourth, the law gave CBO important cover by specifying that its primary relationship was to the money committees; this made it different than GAO or the Congressional Research Service (CRS), which worked for all committees and all members. Finally, the combination of the wide latitude provided the director to establish the duties of the staff and to produce other reports left significant freedom for CBO leadership to define additional scope of CBO activities.

Selecting the Director and Organizing CBO

Practically, the most critical early decision involved the selection of the first director. Section 905(b) of the Budget Act had provided that CBO would not come into existence until the date of the first director's appointment.[19] The differences between the House and Senate visions for CBO clearly came to a head over the selection of this director.

The House Budget Committee, led by Representative Al Ullman (D-OR), was interested in selecting someone who would support the annual budget process, but not extend the scope of the agency's mission beyond relatively narrow budget-related work. In short, the House expected that CBO would perform the tasks specifically mentioned in the law, that is, cost estimates, scorekeeping, and baseline projections. They did not expect CBO to carve out a broader role for itself by analyzing issues not directly related to the annual budget process.[20] As Robert Reischauer, a special assistant to the first CBO director and later director himself, observed, "The characterization of what the House wanted was basically a manhole in which Congress would have a bill or something, and it would lift up the manhole cover and put the bill down it, and you would hear grinding noises, and twenty minutes later a piece of paper would be handed up, with the cost estimate, the answer, on it. No visibility, (just) some kind of mechanism below the ground level doing this . . . noncontroversial, the way the sewer system is."[21]

This vision led the House to support the appointment of Deputy Comptroller General Philip S. (Sam) Hughes. Hughes was a highly regarded career civil servant who had previously worked for the Bureau of the Budget, rising through the ranks to become deputy director.[22] With his combination of budgeting experience and work for a congressional support agency, he was viewed as ideally suited to head CBO. He was also considered nonpartisan because he had worked in both Republican and Democratic administrations.

The Senate anticipated a much broader scope of activity for the new legislative budget agency. Chairman Edmund Muskie (D-ME) agreed that Hughes could do a "competent administrative job," but said that he desired "somebody who can grasp the dimensions of the global problem that this committee is going to be struggling with."[23] This alternate vision led Senator Muskie to support a candidate with a different profile. His choice to lead the new agency was Alice Rivlin.

Rivlin shared some of Hughes's strengths, including knowledge of the budget and a reputation as a straight shooter. She was, however, seen as having a bit more of a point of view, and a higher profile, than Hughes. She had a track record both in government service (in the well-respected Office of Planning and Evaluation in the Department of Health, Education, and Welfare in the Johnson administration) and in policy debates from her time at the Brookings Institution.[24] At Brookings she had been responsible for the annual publication *Setting National Priorities*, a widely read and clearly written volume of policy options.[25] She envisioned CBO not only as an institution that would provide budget numbers, but as one that would help the budget committees "help frame difficult policy choices by providing analysis of the budget implications of various program and policy options, called 'program analysis'."[26] Unlike Hughes, who was a career government official, and an accountant by training, Rivlin was a PhD economist.

Rivlin was one other thing that Hughes was not. She was a woman being considered for a job in one of the greatest bastions of male domination to be found anywhere—the United States Congress. Reportedly, Representative Ullman was less than enthusiastic about the prospect of naming a woman, and even the Senate Budget Committee had not considered her until Senator Alan Cranston (D-CA) asked, "Is the only reason that we are not considering Alice Rivlin is that she is a woman?"[27] The deadlock was eventually broken when Ullman left the House Budget Committee to chair the Ways and Means Committee, and the new House chairman, Brock Adams (D-WA), gave in to Muskie.[28] According to Nancy Kates's research, "to save face for Adams, the two chairmen spread the story that they had flipped a coin to name the director; those involved say the coin toss never took place."[29]

On February 25, 1975, Alice Rivlin was sworn in as director of CBO, and CBO officially came into existence. She was, at that point, practically a staff of one. The only real employees were the staffers of the former Committee on the Reduction of Federal Expenditures, who had been transferred to CBO as a part of the Budget Act, and this group eventually settled in to run the scorekeeping function (see chapter 4). Other than that, however, Rivlin had a somewhat fuzzy mandate and little else. Congress had not mandated how the CBO was to be organized. Various congressional estimates put the projected size of the staff at somewhere between fifty and two hundred (the most specific number had been in a Senate Budget Committee memo that estimated a staff of 118), but she was not bound by any of these estimates.[30] She would, of course, need to obtain appropriations to fund whatever level of staff she ultimately determined appropriate.

Although there was no explicit model for CBO, several organizations were clearly influential. The first was Brookings, where Rivlin had spent a good deal of her career. Certainly her vision for policy analysis was based on the kinds of applied policy studies done at Brookings. There was also an important model—the California Office of the Legislative Analyst—at the state level. According to Rivlin, "that organization was started by a legendary character named Alan Post, who had recently stepped down. We invited him to Washington . . . and we certainly had a conversation with him."[31]

Wisely, Rivlin set out to convert legislative ambiguity into functional reality by consulting with key players who had views about the new organization. A meeting on March 8, 1975, less than two weeks after her appointment, included several people who would go on to play important roles in the organization, including Reischauer, James Blum (a former OMB official then working at the Council and Wage and Price Stability), Frank DeLeeuw from the Urban Institute, David Mundel from the Kennedy School of Government at Harvard, and Alfred Fitt, a lawyer who had worked for the Department of the Army.[32] In fact, this meeting was apparently partially intended to allow Rivlin an opportunity to observe some people that she might decide to hire for CBO.[33]

Notes from the meeting suggest a number of important concerns on the minds of the participants. To begin with, Rivlin is quoted as saying that CBO's goal is to become highly respected by both parties; building the image of nonpartisanship is high on the agenda for the new agency. Herbert Jasper, who had worked at OMB and GAO and who had helped draft the Budget Act, noted that CBO was crucial to the intent of the Budget Act; that is, CBO would enable

Congress to act from a position of strength. It could do this through analysis, because the White House would cease to be the only game in town.[34] To demonstrate how lofty the expectations were, one participant added that CBO "has the task of presenting materials that will lead to rational decision making by Congress."[35]

The most important decision to come out of this meeting had to do with how CBO was going to organize itself to handle its two primary functions: supporting the budget process and doing policy or program analysis. There were two competing models. The first was to organize CBO along functional lines, such that, for example, the people doing cost estimates for defense or Social Security were in the same divisions as those doing policy analysis in the same functional area. The potential advantage to this model was efficiency. The second was to organize along product lines, separating budget analysis from policy analysis in distinct divisions. The major advantage to this model was that it protected the policy analysts from getting drafted into budget work.[36]

The House and Senate Budget Committees had advocated the functional model because they considered it to be the most efficient organization.[37] Nonetheless, the product model was eventually chosen because it offered the kind of dedicated resources for policy analysis that Rivlin viewed as essential for the agency to be able to build constituencies for its analytic work. She had a pronounced concern, shared by Blum, Reischauer, and other early architects, that budget analysis would invariably drive out policy analysis if both were carried out in the same offices. The organizational chart set up by Rivlin as a result of that March 1975 meeting remains the model for CBO, with very few changes.

The model envisioned the following organization. There was to be

- a Budget Analysis Division (BAD), which would do cost estimates and otherwise support the annual budget process;
- a Fiscal Analysis Division (FAD), to do macroeconomic forecasting;
- a Tax Analysis Division (TAD), to do policy analysis relative to taxes;
- three other program divisions organized along functional lines (Natural Resources and Commerce, Human Resources and Community Development, National Security and International Affairs); and
- an Office of General Counsel and an Office of Intergovernmental Relations (which would handle internal management issues, such as budgeting, personnel, and computers). These would be attached to the director's office.

The March 1975 initial planning meeting included substantial discussion about the CBO policy analysis role. Informing Congress in a way that would permit more rational decisions was an open cry for policy analysis. The story of GAO, which had to that date attempted to use its analysis to influence policy with limited success, was viewed as cautionary. Rivlin herself noted that she believed that

CBO should help Congress engage in "longer-range thinking" on issues such as energy.[38]

Other important questions remained:

- *Office space.* CBO had been housed in temporary quarters in the Carroll Arms Hotel, which had been converted to a Senate office building and was, in any event, slated to be demolished. In a tight market for congressional office space, where would CBO sit?
- *Policy recommendations.* CBO had to decide whether it would offer policy recommendations or simply present options. The GAO had long presented recommendations in its reports. Would CBO reports mimic the GAO style, or forge its own?
- *Hiring.* The most immediate issue, however, was hiring staff. The most important initial decisions concerned who would head the new divisions. The good news was that the new CBO attracted much attention from job-seekers. Stacks of resumes were coming in for staff positions, and assistant directors were still needed for the new divisions. Rivlin set Bob Reischauer and David Mundel to vetting and organizing staff resumes, and she concentrated on assistant director positions.

Arguably, the most important initial hires was the assistant director of the budget analysis division. The work of this division most interested Congress, because it would generate the numbers that would enable Congress to successfully counter those coming from the other end of Pennsylvania Avenue, specifically OMB.

Jim Blum was tapped to head BAD. He reports having been pleased to be selected to head BAD because he thought that's where the action would be. He recalled, "I remember thinking about CBO and . . . going through the Budget Act and underlining in red everything that involved CBO—everything that CBO had to do . . . I wanted to do the budget part."[39] Further, Blum knew that for Rivlin's vision for the program divisions to be fulfilled, it was important for BAD to begin producing analytical products almost immediately. This would relieve some of the pressure from the rest of the organization, which had no established constituency.

As her first deputy director, Rivlin chose Robert Levine, who had worked for the RAND corporation, a national security think tank. Other divisions were staffed, in large part, with PhD economists, reflecting Rivlin's view of the mission of the organization, which was to provide information on the economic effects of policies, rather than to engage fully in the political process.[40] In terms of the line employees, BAD was also staffed first because of the more immediate need for its products. The program divisions were staffed later. Rivlin tapped DeLeeuw to head the Fiscal Analysis Division, Douglas Costle (later head of the

Environmental Protection Agency under President Carter) to head Natural Resources, William Fischer to head Human Resources, Charles Davenport to head the Tax Analysis Division, and John Kohler to head National Security. Alfred Fitt was named general counsel.

Staffing CBO and Developing Its Culture

Once CBO had space (albeit temporary), and at least some people, it remained for the organization to start providing output to Congress in support of the annual budget process. The creation of CBO did not guarantee its success. There were many details that needed to be filled in by Rivlin in setting up the new organization. She quickly became aware that members of Congress as a whole had neither a clear nor a consistent view of the organization's structure and role. Further, an organization such as CBO was destined to both be ever-present in the operations of Congress and to annoy members of each party from time to time. Decisions Rivlin and her staff made in the first two years ultimately determined the organization's path. The story of these early choices is thus revealing because they set the stage for CBO's future credibility and influence.

CBO had begun hiring staff immediately on the appointment of Rivlin, and was permitted to do so without receiving a regular appropriation from Congress. Accordingly, by the time CBO first testified, it had "already hired or made job commitments to 193 persons, and it requested funds for 259 positions, a level it considered appropriate for the full array of services contemplated by the Budget Act."[41] The House Appropriations Committee did not support that number, and Rivlin was subjected to intense questioning in two days of hearings in November 1975. The House ultimately approved funding for the 193 positions for which commitments had already been made. After the Senate restored 35 positions, the House held firm in its position, and CBO was appropriated enough to fund 193 positions for fiscal year 1976.[42]

Not only was it necessary to fill all positions provided by Congress, but CBO also needed to develop a policy on how it would respond when people had been recommended by members of Congress and congressional committees. On Capitol Hill, of course (then and now), patronage hiring is the norm. In this environment, CBO needed to decide how it was going to handle referrals from Congress. Alice Rivlin has noted that the budget committees shielded her from much of this pressure. She recalled that the only real issue was with House majority leader Jim Wright, who wanted to place particular individuals at CBO.[43] Ultimately, the decision was made that being recommended by a member of Congress or congressional staff would neither disqualify nor advantage in the hiring process; potential staff would be evaluated strictly according to their qualifications.

Five issues dominated the first years of CBO's history:

- whether CBO was going to work solely for the budget committees, or had a broader mandate;
- whether CBO was to be analytically independent, or was to have its agenda set solely by Congress or congressional committees;
- whether CBO's work duplicated the work of other congressional support agencies or committees;
- the extent to which CBO reports and analyses should include policy prescriptions, and the general partisan posture of CBO; and
- the manner in which CBO was to make its findings known, and the general relations among CBO, congressional committees, and the media.

For Whom Did CBO Work?

The creation of CBO was accompanied by a tug-of-war within Congress for control of the agenda of the new entity. Two of the other three congressional support agencies—the GAO and the CRS—had a rather broad mandate and broad constituency. Each served both congressional committees and individual members of Congress. The third, the Office of Technology Assessment (OTA), tended to serve specific committees and was generally constrained to studying issues related to technology by the nature of its mandate.

By statute, CBO was to follow a certain hierarchy of access to its expertise. The money committees (budget, tax, and appropriations) had priorities. Next in line were other committees, then individual members "to the extent practicable." Although this offered protection to CBO, records from the early years show evidence of confusion among members of Congress concerning how CBO was to prioritize its workload.

It was very clear from the outset that the budget committees would have preferred that CBO be viewed as their staff (and theirs alone). Rivlin was having none of that. A July 1975 SBC memorandum, in fact, indicated that "many of the Committee staff believe that the CBO should be more in the posture of an 'employee' with respect to the Budget Committee."[44] But Rivlin knew that being under the direct control of the budget committees would impede her ability to do many of the things that she envisioned as critical to the success of the new organization—interacting independently with members of Congress, responding to requests from other committees, taking on requests for analyses in substantive areas not under the jurisdiction of the budget committees. In short, embracing such an artificially narrow mandate would have ensured a relatively minor role for CBO. It would have done little else but support the annual budget process.

The hearing record from this early period includes a striking number of instances in which Rivlin asserted her vision of this broader role for CBO, often in the face of attempts from budget committee members to articulate a narrower role. She stated the organization's multifaceted role explicitly (more clearly than the statute did) at an oversight hearing before the SBC in October of 1975: "The CBO, as you know, is the analytical arm of the new budget structure. It is our job to provide you with analysis and with budget information that will help make the budget decisions easier and to show you as clearly as we can what the choices are and what the consequences would be of adapting various alternative policies. . . . In saying that, I must remind myself and you, that the CBO was not set up to work solely for the Budget Committees. I work for the whole Congress and have responsibilities to all committees and indeed to all members."[45]

Not only did she have to be careful to assert the organization's position as working for the entire Congress, but she needed to be constantly vigilant not to be viewed as serving one House at the exclusion of the other. This even applied to CBO's physical location. CBO had been housed in temporary quarters on the Senate side of the Capitol. This had caused some friction with the House; the Carroll Arms location was, according to Reischauer, viewed as "the 'in-law apartment' of the Senate Budget Committee."[46] Their eventual permanent location (where they remain to this day) happened to be in an abandoned FBI fingerprint warehouse on the House side, which did not necessarily sit well with the Senate, leading to the following tongue-in-cheek exchange:

> RIVLIN: On the organization of the CBO . . . we have now moved into a larger building on the House side. . . . It is the old FBI Files and Records Building, down sort of between the Rayburn Building and the railroad, is the only way to describe it.
>
> MUSKIE: The FBI association creates no problems?
>
> RIVLIN: Well, it creates a sort of peculiar atmosphere. There are bars on the ground floor windows, but we are on the fourth.
>
> MUSKIE: What kind of bars?
>
> RIVLIN: Not the right kind.
>
> CRANSTON: I think the first bad thing you have done is leave the Senate to go to the House.
>
> RIVLIN: I would like to stress that we have not left the Senate to go to the House, that just happens to be where we are housed.[47]

There was also some discussion of having CBO arbitrate between the inevitable differences between the bodies on budget resolutions and appropriations. Senator Pete Domenici (R-NM) recognized the potential for CBO to be placed in a compromising situation, suggesting that "it is a bit dangerous in terms of how much we ask the CBO to reconcile that problem. . . . it is precarious for their long-term well-being that they not be the negotiator with the committees like Appropriations."[48]

An additional dilemma for CBO involved the extent to which CBO was to work for individual members. At least two of the other support agencies—CRS and GAO—explicitly worked for both committees and members. CBO did not believe that it had the resources for such coverage. Further, the budget committees became concerned that if CBO worked for individual members, it would substantially dilute the support that could be provided to the new budget process. By January 1976, CBO had worked out a statement that essentially became (and remained) its policy with regard to individual member requests, articulated by Rivlin to the House Budget Committee.

> The first conclusion we came to, in consultation with both Budget Committee chairmen, was that we should be very strict in our interpretation of the law regarding Member requests. The law as we read it does not require the CBO to furnish to Members any information other than what it has already produced. Therefore we have worked out a policy statement in consultation with the Budget Committee chairmen in which we inform Members that if they request information from CBO, they may have copies of work already done by us which are pertinent to the request. Alternatively, they may reformulate their requests through a committee chairman as a committee request. If the committee chairman signs off on it, we are then authorized to undertake the study.[49]

Perhaps in part because of CBO's effort to define its mission more broadly, there was some dissatisfaction among the budget committee staffs concerning the quality of CBO's work during this early period. A 1976 study on congressional support agencies noted that CBO had failed, given expectations and the budget committees' interpretation of the mandate, "to provide strong support and backup to the two Budget Committees."[50]

How Independent Was CBO?

A related but clearly separable issue during these early years was the extent to which the CBO would be setting its own agenda as opposed to following an agenda set by Congress. Of course, the organizational decisions that Rivlin made were critical in maintaining analytical independence. Because the policy analysis divisions were institutionally independent of BAD, they would have the flexibility to seek out clients and outlets for their services. Clearly CBO would need a larger staff under this model than if budgeting and policy analysis had been in the same division, but this was intentional. In fact, in the original staffing plan, only about fifty of the 259 requested positions would have been in BAD, less than half the number intended for the program divisions and about the same as the staff of the fiscal and tax policy divisions combined.[51] By 1977, CBO had 208 staff, the Budget Analysis division staff accounting for one-third of that, or 66 people. This stood in contrast to Rivlin's original notion that Budget Analysis would make up only 20 percent of the agency.[52]

Clearly Rivlin believed that if Congress were to truly be able to challenge the executive branch in budgeting and policymaking, it must use its independent judgment to anticipate issues that would be the subject of congressional policy-making. This meant that CBO needed wide latitude to study issues on which it believed Congress needed information in order to support its decision processes, whether Congress requested the analysis or not. As Allen Schick summarized, CBO "wanted to decide what to study . . . it wanted to select the assumptions used in its studies, and the alternatives considered."[53]

In fact, Senator Bob Dole (R-KS) took the agency to task in an early oversight hearing for its tendency to initiate studies rather than wait for Congress to request them. He noted that, as of that time (October 1975, about seven months into CBO's organizational life) CBO was working on thirty-eight studies, twenty-two of which had been self-initiated.[54] Dole noted that resources might not be available to the budget committees because "you have them all wrapped up in your own studies." He went on to suggest that there might be places where the budget committees could tell CBO to avoid certain topics. Rivlin was unequivocal (and courageous, it must be noted) in her response: "if you wanted to veto our looking into something, I would want to resist that. The report is our report, as stated in the statute."[55]

The budget committees were not alone in decrying these self-initiated reports. The House Appropriations Committee (recall that the appropriations committees had every incentive to keep CBO as weak as possible) repeatedly challenged Rivlin about the justification for self-initiated studies. Rivlin's suggestion that the requirement to produce an annual report justified looking into a wide range of allocative options was greeted with concern that this implied no resulting limits to CBO's ability to address questions, even if Congress were not interested in the answer or were embarrassed by it.[56] By the late 1970s, almost all of CBO's products had a nominal sponsor. This was in large part because of organizational learning. CBO absorbed what other support agencies already knew: that sponsorship was necessary to identify an interested constituency, and therefore to gain political cover. This was true even in cases where the initial impetus for the study came from within the agency. In other words, if CBO really wanted to do a study, and no one had asked for it in advance, it was advisable to sell it to a requestor.

How Would CBO Remain Nonpartisan?

The Congressional Budget Act clearly stated that the director of CBO and CBO staff should be appointed without regard to political affiliation. This clearly implies that the organization is nonpartisan, but it is no small challenge to forge a culture of nonpartisanship in a highly partisan atmosphere.

Although no one seriously argued (at least publicly) that CBO should be partisan, many members of Congress were understandably interested in using CBO to serve their own purposes. In addition, Congress was not accustomed to staff organizations that both were expressly nonpartisan and had substantial discretion in setting their own agenda. Rivlin herself noted that she was "rather pleased by the fact that we have been attacked by both sides, both from the right and from the left."[57] This was significant in part because of the perception in some circles that Rivlin's background suggested that she occupied ground somewhat to the left of center.[58]

The appropriations committees, which were concerned about the power that had been acquired by the budget committees, seemed particularly interested in gaining control over CBO. At a November 1975 Senate Appropriations Committee hearing, Senator John McClellan offered the following admonition: "I don't think the Budget Office of the Congress is designed to make policy. I think the purpose of it is to acquire information, and make analyses and advise the Congress of the facts as it finds them and as it sees it."[59] In fact, the committee report on the CBO appropriation for fiscal year 1976 reads in part: "In the legislative branch, debate over public policy must be conducted by elected officials. Neither the Congressional Budget Office, nor any of its employees, should initiate, or take positions on, individual policy recommendations."[60]

As early as October 1975 Rivlin was articulating a clear strategy for how CBO could remain somewhat above (or below) the fray: "First, let me say strongly and loudly that CBO wants to be fair and nonpartisan, and to be perceived as and to be an analytically straightforward professional organization that calls issues as we see them, without any bias in any political direction. Now that is not easy to achieve."[61]

She then drew a specific distinction between policy recommendations, which CBO would not give (CBO would "assiduously refrain" from these), and "technical" recommendations, which would be acceptable, if asked for (on budget presentation, for example). "It is not that the law precludes us from that," she went on, but "once we started making policy recommendations there would be no way to resist political pressure or the perception that we succumbed to political pressure."[62] She considered it inevitable that CBO analyses would be used for partisan purposes, but wanted CBO to do whatever it could to ensure that it did not conduct itself so as to brand the budget office as partisan.[63] In fact, even though CBO tried very hard to avoid making recommendations, conclusions were often implied by the media, which were not comfortable with reports that did not reach a clear conclusion. A headline in the *Washington Star* in June 1975 mistakenly reported, for example, that a CBO report had "urged" a $15 billion tax cut, which it had clearly not.[64]

It was also in the interest of the budget committees to have CBO refrain from policy prescriptions, because the very existence of these new committees generated animosity from other committees in Congress. At a January 1976 hearing, Representative Herman Schneebeli (R-PA) reminded Rivlin that "we are both on the spot" and requested the House Budget Committee chairman to "abide by and continue to pursue the policy of the firm no-policy position by the CBO, because not only will they be in trouble but we here on the Budget Committee will also be in trouble."[65]

Eschewing policy recommendations was not the same thing as avoiding policy questions, however. CBO was advised that, despite the fact that a given president's budget proposal would be viewed as partisan, it was within the purview of CBO to analyze and comment on any given president's proposal: this would not constitute prima facie evidence of partisanship. Rivlin and several committee members agreed that CBO could (indeed should) reasonably evaluate presidential proposals, but needed to be careful in terms of not straying too far into making judgments on matters of policy, rather than trying to somewhat neutrally evaluate the effects of proposed policies.[66]

Duplication of Effort

As a new congressional support agency, CBO entered an environment in which the existing three support agencies—OTA, CRS, and GAO—had already established constituencies and mandates. One of the primary concerns raised in the first couple years of CBO's existence was the extent to which CBO duplicated the efforts of other support agencies or indeed even committees in Congress.

One of these concerns had to do with duplication between CBO and the budget committees. House ranking member Delbert Latta (R-OH) raised this issue specifically at an oversight hearing, and Rivlin responded that the law clearly envisioned different responsibilities for the two entities. Although CBO was to be a "nonpartisan analytical group," she conceded that the budget committee staff would also be doing some analysis. She emphasized that the primary way to avoid duplication was through communication between budget committee staffs and CBO.[67]

Questions of duplication between CBO and the other support agencies were more pervasive, and more difficult to lay to rest. Senator Richard Schweiker (R-PA), who was on the Senate Appropriations Committee, likely expressed the concern of other senators (and an even greater number of House members) when he noted that while providing economic projections and budget information were clearly core functions of CBO, "I think we are really getting into a problem in the research area."[68] He noted specifically that CBO might do transportation studies when OTA was already doing such studies, and that CBO might do studies in the health area, when either OTA or the health committees were already involved in studying health programs. This led to a long, and not very illuminating, discussion between Rivlin and the Senate appropriations subcommittee, to the effect that duplication was a bad thing, that it should be avoided, and that CBO would take the initiative to try and avoid duplication before they took on a study.[69] Ultimately, the conference report on the fiscal year 1976 appropriations bill included language specifically forbidding CBO to duplicate the efforts of these other agencies.[70] In fact, in response to this admonition, the support agencies initiated a Research Notification System in early 1976; this required the support agencies to share information concerning ongoing and planned studies.[71]

CBO, the Media, and Congress

One area in which CBO was sort of wading into uncharted waters was in its relationships with the media. Congress was not accustomed to having its own employees have contact (at least for attribution) with the media, and certainly did not expect the media to find out about the content of CBO analyses before Congress did.

CBO had one of its first, and most controversial, experiences with media attention in response to its first (June 1975) report on the economy. Rivlin had granted an interview with Lee Cohn, a reporter for the *Washington Star*, in advance of the issuance of the report. She had told Cohn that the report was embargoed, because she knew that the budget committee chairs, Senator Muskie and Congressman Adams, would want to release it themselves. The next day, before the budget committee chairs had an opportunity to release the report, the results of the CBO analysis appeared in the *Star*, much to the displeasure of Rivlin's employers.[72] Rivlin reported later that "Muskie called me from the floor, fit to be tied."[73] The reaction was similar in the House. At a House Budget Committee Oversight hearing, Congressman James O'Hara (D-MI) sarcastically noted that "I think the CBO report on the economy issued June 30 is even better than I thought it was when I read about it in the paper several days before."[74] Indeed, although the report was well received, it added to a problem that had already existed—that is, that Rivlin was perceived as having—and desiring—a higher profile than her congressional masters. Congress, in short, was not used to being upstaged by its staff.[75]

Another budgetary issue that received attention in that early period was Rivlin's alleged desire for a vehicle for the office. Apparently, the considerable movement of CBO staff back and forth from Capitol Hill had required CBO staff to be transported for testimony and other business in Rivlin's personal vehicle. To address this, CBO requested funds to purchase a vehicle—a station wagon—that CBO staff could use instead as transportation to Capitol Hill. What seems in retrospect to have been a quite reasonable—or at least routine—request provided an opportunity for congressional staffers and members who wanted to knock the director—and perhaps the budget process—down a peg or two. Illustrative of the extent to which this story took on a life of its own was the December 1975 article in *U.S. News and World Report* that reported as fact that she had angered House appropriators by asking both for more staff and "a chauffeured automobile to carry the staff from the office to the Capitol." The article quoted a congressional staffer as saying, "She's building a beautiful empire here."[76] The only real problem with the story is that it wasn't true. The request had never been for a chauffeured vehicle. In any event, language was placed in the CBO appropriation (that persisted until fiscal year 2005, after which it was finally removed) prohibiting the use of any funds "for purchase or hire of a passenger motor vehicle."[77]

Perhaps the highest profile example of Rivlin "not behaving like a staffer" was related to a press conference called by CBO to release its report on the Carter energy policy. This policy was the centerpiece of President Carter's first year in office (see chapter 5 for additional analytical details), and CBO had done a detailed analysis on the economic and energy conservation effects of the policy. Rivlin publicized the results at an off-the-record briefing for the press, which had been cleared in advance by the budget committees and the Ad Hoc Energy Committee. According to a staffer from the Ad Hoc Committee, however, the difference between a backgrounder (where embargoed information might be shared and any quotes were off-the-record) and a press conference were somehow not clearly understood by the press, or CBO, or both.[78] Congressman Robert Giaimo (D-CT), the chair of the House Budget Committee, was very concerned about the impact of both the report and the press conference not only on the Carter policy, but on the budget committees. The budget committees were still trying to establish themselves within Congress, and this kind of high-profile press event was not well received by the Democratic leadership, who tended to take it out on the budget committee chairs rather than directly on the leadership of CBO.[79] Giaimo was quite direct in a June 1977 *Washington Post* article, saying of Rivlin, "She has to maintain a lower profile. If she doesn't, she could be threatening the budget process. Not everybody is happy with us, with the budget process or with CBO. When they get unhappy with her, they come crying to me."[80]

In fact, the next day there was a scheduled House Budget Committee oversight hearing of CBO, during which Congressman Giaimo took Rivlin to task for the process of releasing the CBO findings.

> THE CHAIRMAN: I would like to know a little more about the ground rules under which you operate, because if they are not proper ground rules, we can have some difficulties on the floor of the House. And the one who will carry the brunt of those difficulties will be the chairman of the full committee.
>
> DR. RIVLIN: I appreciate that.
>
> THE CHAIRMAN: The problem is this. In the matter of your energy report that was in the paper earlier this week, do you see the role of the Congressional Budget Office as making final conclusions and judgments, which by definition are really political and not economic?[81]

Rivlin then proceeded to outline for Chairman Giaimo the process through which the report had been requested and prepared, and the analysis of the effect of the Carter plan on energy savings. She noted that the report had concluded that perhaps some of the energy savings in the plan were overestimated. Giaimo then got to the point:

> THE CHAIRMAN: Do you consider it your function, as head of CBO, to have a press conference on that report and to issue conclusions?

DR. RIVLIN: I didn't issue any conclusions.

THE CHAIRMAN: "'The Carter energy proposals,' CBO Director Alice M. Rivlin told a press conference, 'would slow, not reverse, the increase in national energy consumption. . . . There has been a lot of talk of "sacrifice"
or of the "moral equivalent of war," but one doesn't see it in this plan,' Dr.
Rivlin said." Now, are you speaking for the Congress in this instance?

DR. RIVLIN: No, sir.

THE CHAIRMAN: For whom are you speaking? That is what I am trying to get
clear in my own mind.

DR. RIVLIN: I was explaining what the conclusions of the report were and
how we got the numbers and where we differed from the administration
and where we concurred.[82]

The discussion continued at some length, trying to nail down ground rules
concerning how far CBO could go in releasing its findings, and to whom. In the
end, Rivlin stated what she would and would not do: "I have been very careful
never to make a recommendation on what the Congress ought to do. That is not
easy because members keep asking me to do it. I have been very careful not to
make recommendations, and not to make any personal judgments. What I do do
is to explain what CBO studies are about, what the options are that are contained
in the study, and what the conclusion is, and how we arrived at it."[83]

The perception that CBO was media hungry was so pervasive that an otherwise favorable 1977 internal congressional report on the organizational effectiveness of CBO started with the sentence, "The Congressional Budget Office maintains too high a profile."[84] Admonishing CBO for its "willing visibility" and its
"public declarations on economic policy questions, without prior sanction and
clearance by the responsible Congressional committees," this report suggested
that CBO needed to keep in mind its appropriate role as subservient to Congress and its committees. The report specifically suggested that the decision of
whether and when to release a CBO report needed to come from the requesting
committees. It noted that, among the support agencies, it found "only CBO to require this admonition against 'going public' without adequate clearance."[85] This
problem apparently did not go away immediately. A 1980 *National Journal* article
notes that members were annoyed with the level of publicity enjoyed by Rivlin,
including an April 1980 appearance on the CBS program *Face the Nation*.[86]

Of course, there is an inherent tension in all of this. When Congress decided
to hire a policy analyst of Rivlin's stature to direct CBO, they (intentionally or
unintentionally) bought a certain visibility for the office (to be fair, the House
did not intend to do this at all, as we have seen). This type of visibility would not
have been present if, for example, Sam Hughes had been chosen as director. Even
if they knew that they were choosing someone who might garner publicity in
theory, however, that did not make the reality of Rivlin's profile easy to accept in
fact.

CBO Establishes Itself

These growing pains were perhaps inevitable for an agency that was attempting to do what CBO was doing. By the late 1970s, CBO cost estimates and baseline estimates, and indeed the budget process itself, were well established on Capitol Hill. In fact, a 1979 *Washington Post* article noted matter-of-factly that CBO was "thorough—and as skilled as [President] Carter's own budget makers—on basic economic and budgetary computations."[87] Republicans, who had seen CBO as just a tool of the Democratic majority at the outset, were thrilled at the criticisms of President Carter's policies. The policies of Ronald Reagan, however, brought new criticism by CBO of a Republican president, thus turning the tables on the Republicans (see chapter 3).

As CBO developed over time, its key challenges would be associated with at least three kinds of key events. First, shifts of party control in either the executive or the legislative branches: when such key political shifts occurred, such as the election of presidents of different political parties (such as Reagan or Clinton), or the shift of party control in Congress, CBO would find itself under pressure to respond to proposals to substantially change the federal role in the economy. Second, and related, whenever major policy initiatives came out of the White House, CBO increasingly would need to analyze these proposals and comment on their cost, which had the potential of making some people very happy and of displeasing others. Third, when there were leadership transitions at CBO—that is, when CBO directors' terms expired—there was frequently difficulty in naming replacements, which created institutional and political challenges for the agency.

In September 1982, having privately notified congressional leaders over several months, Rivlin announced publicly that she would not seek a third term.[88] This was a critical time for CBO. An agency that had had only one director in its first seven years—and that had been created out of that director's vision—would have a new leader. This new director might or might not continue the policies Rivlin had initiated. The new director could either cement the reputation that CBO had built for nonpartisan analysis, or shift CBO's focus so that it would be just one more partisan voice on Capitol Hill.

The first step was to identify the new director. Rivlin was considered the Senate's person. The House, and particularly the House Budget Committee, felt that it was their turn to lead the process of identifying a director. That Senate and House control were split between the parties (Republican and Democratic, respectively) complicated the selection by creating real constraints on the potential candidate pool. Candidates viewed as too far to the left would have a very difficult time obtaining Senate concurrence, and those further to the right would have difficulty gaining House approval. Identifying a mutually acceptable candidate was critical because the CBO director is appointed jointly by the Speaker of the House and the president pro tempore of the Senate.

James Jones (D-OK), the House Budget Committee's new chairman and a moderate Democrat, was conscious of his challenge—to find a director who would simultaneously be acceptable to both the Senate Republicans and to House Speaker Thomas 'Tip' O'Neill (D-MA), one of the most liberal members of the House. This meant, in reality, that any successful candidate would need to be a moderate, regardless of whether the individual was a nominal Republican or a nominal Democrat.

In this context, Jones turned to Rudolph Penner, a Republican who was a senior fellow at the American Enterprise Institute, a highly credible but somewhat right-leaning think tank. Penner explains that he "came to the attention of Jim Jones because as a Republican I was saying some critical things about the prospect of deficits and the Reagan fiscal policy."[89] Penner accompanied Jones and other members of the House Budget Committee on a trip to the United Kingdom, where Penner "got to know him and other members of the Budget Committee quite well and I think Jones thought it would be nice to have a Republican director that was somewhat critical of the Republican president, and the Republicans didn't object to it in any way."[90]

Jones had found his director. The choice of Penner was ratified by a vote of the bipartisan House-Senate selection committee and a vote of the full House Budget Committee.[91] Convincing Tip O'Neill was another matter. Several House chairmen had lobbied O'Neill to appoint a Democrat.[92] According to Penner, "it was extremely difficult to get Tip O'Neill to go along with the idea. I don't know if [O'Neill] had ever appointed a Republican in his life . . . and it took quite a delegation—a whole bunch of people from the House Budget Committee went to argue on my behalf—Jim Jones and Leon Panetta, I think, were in the group. . . . The Republicans were in control of the Senate and they seemed quite pleased that Jones would accept a Republican."[93]

Rivlin remembered that Jones had asked her to approach O'Neill about the Penner appointment. She recalled that O'Neill, who was very political, "didn't like the idea and Jim Jones knew he didn't like the idea. . . . I remember Tip O'Neill saying . . . he said if it has to be a Republican it should be a real Republican not a Mugwump. . . . He is a very partisan person and he never quite got the nonpartisanship."[94]

The process of selecting a director dragged on. In the meantime, Rivlin stayed on, eventually sporting buttons she wore up to Capitol Hill that said "Free Alice Rivlin."[95] According to Penner, "one of the funny sort of anecdotes related to this whole thing was that till the last minute I don't think that Howard Baker [R-TN, the Senate Majority Leader] really believed that Tip O'Neill would go along with this, so Baker would not let my letter be signed on the Senate side until Tip O'Neill had affixed his signature."[96]

This process took about a year. Penner had been contacted about the job in September 1982 and did not formally take office until September 1983, at which point Rivlin had served a full eight months past the end of her second term. Penner inherited an organization with some established procedures and institutions, and some anxiety about a change in leadership, and made few changes. He believed in particular that he did not want to create the impression that other top positions in CBO were partisan appointments. He was quoted soon after the appointment as saying that he did not have "any intention of reorganizing this place. It's a tremendous staff that Alice has built over there."[97]

Rivlin had left some positions open, including the deputy director, which Penner filled first with Eric Hanushek and later with Edward Gramlich, and assistant director for tax analysis, which he filled with Rosemary Marcuss.[98] He also did not change in any fundamental way the organizational structure of CBO. In particular, although from the outside he had questioned the wisdom of separating budget and policy analysis, he eventually was convinced that this was a better model because if everything were together "cost estimating would have driven out policy analysis. After the first week I was there, I had no doubt about the wisdom of separating them."[99] The continuity that could be expected under Penner was emphasized by economist Alan Greenspan who referred to him at the time as "in certain respects a Republican Alice Rivlin."[100]

Although he made no significant changes in organizational structure or personnel, Penner differed in both style and interests from Rivlin. Rivlin had spent a lot of time trying to establish the fledgling policy analysis function (leaving much of the budget analysis work to be supervised by Jim Blum). Penner instead focused on the macroeconomic forecast and becoming familiar with the cost estimating function. On the other hand, the staff was impressed with how easy the transition was, and quickly became comfortable with Penner: "the continuity was as good as it could have been. Also Penner in his first testimony . . . won the staff. He sounded right, sounded good, he was good on his feet, and everybody, having test driven the director once, felt a lot better."[101]

By the time of Penner's appointment, the budget committees had ceased doing formal oversight hearings, concluding that neither CBO nor the committees benefited particularly.[102] Nevertheless, some issues brought out in early hearings continued to be sources of controversy for the new director. Penner noted that he spent the most time confronting questions related to duplication. "The thing that I continually got harassed about was duplication of the work of GAO and the OTA, etc. . . . which was a very annoying issue because very frequently Congress would ask all three for the same studies and moreover on a lot of these important issues it is OK to have more than one study."[103] Criticisms seemed to be driven by concerns on the part of the appropriations and budget committees saw the policy analysis work as coming at the expense of what they really cared about, which was the scorekeeping."[104]

The most significant result, from an organizational perspective, of the Penner directorship is that nothing really changed. In fact, by the time of Penner's departure, it was generally understood that the language in the statute that said that

CBO directors should be selected (but more importantly should behave) without regard to political affiliation was an established practice.

Unlike Rivlin, however, Penner made it clear that he would leave when his term expired, and not wait for a successor to be appointed. Thus, in October 1986, Penner announced that he would not seek another term, noting at the time that he did not want to commit to another four years. His departure set the stage for one of the most difficult periods in CBO's history. It would be almost two full years before Congress was able to agree on a new director. The consensus of people who were there is that the main reason for the delay was simply that the choice of a CBO director was not a very significant priority for Congress. Although the two individuals who ran the agency in the interim were highly respected and by all accounts did a good job, operating for two years without a permanent leader is a significant event in the life of an organization. Penner's deputy, Edward Gramlich, ran the agency for eight months. When he departed, because of a need to return to his tenured academic position at the University of Michigan, he left long-time Budget Analysis chief James Blum in charge. Blum remained in the acting director position for more than fourteen months.

During this period CBO continued to provide its day-to-day support to the budget committees and to Congress as a whole, but its profile was relatively low. The uncertainty over who would be the new director took its toll on the organization. The *Washington Post*, in a December 1987 editorial, urged Congress to get on with the business of naming a new CBO director without succumbing to pressure (notably from House Speaker Jim Wright) to name a partisan Democrat.

> Because Congress won't make up its collective mind on a director to run it, the Congressional Budget Office is now in some considerable danger . . . The last director of the CBO, Rudolf (sic) Penner, announced four months ago that he was leaving. . . . His Deputy, Edward R. Gramlich, became act-ing director, but, last week, after another 10 months of procrastination by the Congressional leaders, he returned to his teaching job at the University of Michigan. . . . Sen. Lawton Chiles, the chairman of the Budget Committee, does not intend to pursue reelection. Perhaps he might consider, as an endur-ing service to Congress, taking an active role at last in resolving this standoff in a way that will be seen to preserve the CBO as an institution above political manipulation.[105]

Neither this editorial nor a similar one that followed in January 1988 had much effect. The dispute dragged on for another year. Part of the delay reportedly had to do with the House Budget Committee's advocacy of long-time House Budget Committee chief economist Van Ooms to be CBO director.[106] Although there was general agreement that Ooms was well qualified, the Senate was not inclined to accept someone coming directly from the House, and it was their turn to pick a director, given that Penner had been Jones's choice. Therefore, when the Senate

Budget Committee advocated Robert Reischauer, it had little effect on breaking the stalemate. Moreover, a March 1988 article indicated that Reischauer was vetoed by Wright because of his role in "a study by the Congressional agency of President Carter's energy proposals that the Speaker did not like"[107] (see chapter 5).

Ultimately, Speaker Wright dropped his objections and the House and Senate agreed on Reischauer as director. Asked what finally led to an appointment, Jim Horney, who was at that time a House Budget Committee staffer, responded "my memory is that what broke the impasse was just 'we had to do something.'"[108]

A former CBO assistant director and deputy director who had been associated with both the Urban Institute and the Brookings Institution since leaving CBO in 1981, Reischauer was very familiar with the organization. Although a nominal Democrat, he was also acceptable to both political parties. New House Budget Committee chair Leon Panetta advocated his selection. In addition, Senator Pete Domenici and his longtime budget aide Bill Hoagland, who had worked for Reischauer at CBO, continued to support his nomination.[109] Later both the Senate and the House took credit for his appointment; no one seemed to remember whose turn it was. It had in fact been the Senate's, but that might not have mattered by the time two years had passed. Reischauer did not formally appoint a deputy director for the remainder of this term, but Robert Hartman, who had been a special assistant at CBO since 1982, occupied the deputy director position on an acting basis until 1991.

CBO during the Era of Republican Control

The 1994 midterm congressional elections gave the Republican party control of both houses of Congress for the first time in forty years. This ultimately had two effects on CBO. First, the House Republican Contract with America set much of the CBO agenda for the next two years. Second, the antipathy of the House leadership (particularly Speaker Newt Gingrich) to the CBO meant that it was improbable that Reischauer would be reappointed when his term ended in January 1995. Although the Republicans had been pleased that Reischauer had not caved to pressure on President Clinton's health care reform proposal (see chapter 6), they believed that CBO's adherence to static economic models would get in the way of the policies Congress would be pursuing under a Republican regime. These static models, particularly according to House Republicans, did not give enough credit for the positive economic effects of Republican policies, such as tax cuts. Speaker Gingrich in particular made it clear that he was in the market for a new CBO director, and that wholesale staff changes were needed as well. A *Washington Post* editorial expressed alarm at the prospect, noting that "to pack [CBO] now for short-term purposes with people of a particular point of view would do an enormous disservice, not least to Congress itself."[110]

Unlike the previous transition, when it had taken two years, the selection in 1995 was quick, for at least two reasons. First, because Republicans controlled Congress, partisan fights between the House and Senate were less likely. Second, although there had sometimes been disagreements concerning whether it was the House or Senate that would take the lead in selecting a director, it was clear in this case that the House would do so. Speaker Gingrich, frequent CBO critic and Majority Leader Dick Armey (R-TX), and new House Budget Committee Chairman John Kasich (R-OH) had strong views concerning the CBO directorship, and thus would be initiating the process.

Many candidates were named in the press. Some accounts gave front-runner status to former OMB director James Miller. Economists John Taylor and David Bradford were mentioned repeatedly in press accounts.[111] As late as December, the *Washington Post* reported that the leading candidate, Stanford University's John Cogan, had dropped out of consideration, and that House Republicans might even be convinced to reappoint Reischauer.[112] It was rumored that he would be acceptable if he was willing to develop what Armey described as new "work skills," in other words, to embrace dynamic scoring.[113]

Finally, in January 1995, three new candidates emerged: Kathleen Utgoff, former head of the Pension Benefit Guarantee Corporation; David S. C. Chu, a defense expert from the Rand Corporation; and June O'Neill, an economist at Baruch College in New York City. This was the first that any of these three had been named in public press accounts.[114] Chu and O'Neill were former CBO staff members.

O'Neill recalled almost ten years later that the process proceeded in two waves. She had been on the original list of candidates put together by a task force appointed by Speaker Gingrich, and the House had agreed on her. However, Senator Domenici insisted that the Senate Budget Committee have a say in the process. At that point O'Neill went to visit Domenici and found that "he was concerned about wholesale dismissal of people at CBO. He said did I plan to do that. And I told him I really didn't have any intention of doing that because it was very hard to get people to do this . . . and I'd been a CBO unit chief in the 1970s, and I knew a lot of the skilled analysts, and I wasn't about to start firing people and start replacing them with Republican hacks, which I think was his concern."[115]

Eventually Domenici was convinced that June O'Neill had no intention of gutting CBO and on February 11, 1995, she was appointed as the agency's fourth director. Congress had once again not filled the vacancy until after the previous director's term had expired, but the transition was lightning fast compared with the eight months between Rivlin and Penner and the twenty-six months between Penner and Reischauer. At a news conference announcing her selection, O'Neill was praised by Kasich for "her willingness to change the way the budget office makes estimates."[116] O'Neill herself was more guarded, saying simply, "I expect I'll be dynamic when that's called for and static when that's called for."[117]

Despite the public pronouncements that had been made concerning both replacing CBO staff and dynamic scoring, O'Neill insists that no one ever made either one a precondition of her appointment. She noted that the furthest Gingrich went was to repeatedly say to her, "all I want from you are honest estimates," and that no one gave her any instructions to replace any CBO staff.[118] In fact, she made only one staff replacement (several others left voluntarily within the first year or so), and went so far as to retain Blum, who had been Reischauer's deputy director in the second term, as her own number two person. O'Neill had worked for Blum in the late 1970s, and said later that she kept him in place because "I thought that it would be a good balance because Jim knew a lot more about budget details than I did. . . . I didn't really know all the technical scoring issues as he did. And since he had headed budget analysis for so many years I thought it would be a good division of labor."[119]

Nonetheless, some Democratic members of Congress were nervous about the O'Neill appointment, because they perceived it as a part of an attempt to "cook the books" at CBO. Both James Exon (D-NE), the ranking Democrat on the Senate Budget Committee, and Martin Sabo (D-MN), the ranking Democrat on the House Budget Committee, expressed concern about the O'Neill appointment. The Democratic view was perhaps best summarized in the comment by Senator Byron Dorgan (D-ND), who said of the Republicans that "because they have not gotten the answers they would like, they decided they want to make a change in the people who give the answers."[120] Other observers, including the *Washington Post* editorial page, were not concerned. Harking back to the role of CBO as "the skunk at the congressional picnic," a *Post* editorial noted that "Mr. Reischauer was an excellent skunk, as were his Democratic- and Republican-appointed predecessors and as his successor will likely be too."[121]

As if to underscore the point, CBO did not offer much assistance to either side in the budget battles over implementing the Republican Contract with America. Within six months of her appointment, stories began to appear suggesting that CBO was not providing scoring favorable to Republican balanced-budget plans. Kasich was quoted in September 1995 as saying that CBO and CBO staff had a "very stupid way of doing things."[122] Later that year, a separate article noted that Democrats were concerned that O'Neill was behaving as a tool of the Republican majority when CBO forecast that $400 billion more in spending reductions would be necessary for the administration to make good on their pledge to balance the budget by 2002.[123]

In October 1998 O'Neill announced that she would not seek a second term but would return to academia when her term expired in January 1999. There was at least some speculation that she would not have been reappointed, but O'Neill insists that she never had any intention of remaining for more than one term.[124] The *Washington Post* noted that "after four stormy years in which GOP leaders repeatedly complained that CBO's analyses and recasts were hampering their budget and tax policy initiatives, there was little doubt that O'Neill would be replaced when her term expires in January."[125] The same article suggested that O'Neill had maintained the integrity of the organization, noting that the institutional culture of CBO would, at any rate, resist any efforts by any new director to make it more politically responsive.[126]

As was true of the choice of O'Neill, the choice of an individual to succeed her came relatively quickly. On January 14, 1999, congressional Republicans named Daniel Crippen director of CBO. Crippen, who was clearly the Senate's candidate (the Senate had taken the lead this time, because the House had identified O'Neill), came to CBO with a different profile than any of his predecessors. He had been a White House staffer under President Reagan, a Senate aide to Majority Leader Howard Baker in the 1980s, and a Washington lobbyist. His background was also more overtly political. He was also the first CBO director without a PhD in economics, although his doctorate in public policy (specifically public finance) was obviously highly relevant. Democrats decried the appointment as a politicization of CBO, and some Republicans were displeased because they viewed his association with Baker as evidence that he was not conservative enough.[127]

There also were suggestions that members of Congress wanted Crippen to shake up CBO, something that O'Neill had been expected to do but had not done. An article announcing his appointment noted that "some conservative Republicans have complained that the agency is dominated by what they see as the old-fashioned liberal views of career civil servants in senior positions."[128]

The early Crippen tenure was in fact unique among CBO transitions in that it was characterized by more substantial personnel turnover at high levels within CBO than had been associated with any other change in director. Within the first year of his arrival, several long-time CBO staffers had departed, including Deputy Director Blum (who had been there from the beginning), Budget Analysis Division head Paul Van de Water, Projections Chief Jim Horney, and General Counsel Gail Del Balzo. At the same time, Crippen hired longtime OMB official Barry Anderson to be his deputy, and brought several other officials—most of whom had substantial executive branch experience—with him. For the first time in the agency's history, a relatively large cadre of officials was connected to the front office. They in effect occupied the same sort of position as political appointees in the executive branch, transmitting directions from the agency leadership to the career staff.

Interviewees are unanimous in their assessment that Crippen and Anderson were not seeking to replace liberals at CBO with conservatives, but it seems likely that they did view CBO as in some need of shaking up. Anderson noted later that they believed that CBO had lost touch with the client, and that many long-time CBO staff were apparently not as aware as they should have been of the needs and interests of the Congress. [129] Whether or not it was the intent, the staff turnover—and the emphasis on expanding the front office staff—struck many long-time CBO staff as an implicit indictment of the career staff and the nonpartisan tradition of the agency. This impression was given more credence when the new director began making statements that some (inside and outside CBO) viewed as policy advocacy, if not outright partisanship. For example, Crippen appeared to advocate partial privatization of Social Security. This was a break from practice, because it would have been considered inappropriate for the CBO director to express a position on such a controversial issue.

An article from the *New Republic* that appeared not long after Crippen's appointment highlighted several events in the early part of the Crippen tenure that indicated highlighted the differences between Crippen and past directors. Unlike his predecessors, who the article said had "ben[t] over backward to avoid any hint of favoritism," Crippen was seen as taking positions on many of the significant issues facing the Congress, including Medicare and Social Security. The article suggested that Crippen was attempting to ingratiate himself with the Republican majority, perhaps mindful of a return to lobbying when his tenure as CBO director had ended.[130]

Despite some internal disquiet, by the end of the Crippen tenure none of the worst fears expressed at the outset came to reality. He served in the tradition of past CBO directors. If there was a drift toward policy advocacy in the first year, there was also a noticeable difference between the first year and those that followed. For example, there had been early concerns that Crippen would advocate dynamic scoring. Those expectations were not borne out, and Crippen became an articulate opponent of changing CBO's methods of analyzing legislative proposals.

One striking example of the Republican dissatisfaction with CBO at the time was the reaction of House Budget Committee chairman Jim Nussle to CBO scoring decisions that he did not agree with. In uncharacteristically intemperate language, he had the following reaction in a closed-door meeting with his Republican colleagues: "The CBO sucks, and you can quote me on that."[131] In this case, the apparent immediate cause of Nussle's displeasure was the fact that a second estimate of a farm bill that had already been approved by the House had emerged from CBO. This estimate showed higher costs than the earlier estimate, which might have assisted Republicans in garnering opposition to the bill, had it been received earlier. This was the culmination of several years of frustration among Republicans, especially for what they viewed as a failure of CBO to follow Republican orthodoxy concerning dynamic scoring.[132] Although many Republicans did not necessarily revise their general view of CBO, Nussle did eventually—at a conference organized by CBO two years later—publicly apologize for the comment.[133]

One thing is clear. By the end of Crippen's tenure, it was the Republicans, not the Democrats, who were his main detractors.[134] This followed a fairly well-established pattern. Democrats turned on Rivlin and Reischauer (over Carter energy and Clinton health proposals, respectively), and it was Republicans who were most disappointed with June O'Neill. By the time Crippen left, the concerns expressed at the outset—that he was chosen to be a tool of the Republicans—seemed a distant memory.

Crippen's term expired in January 2003. There was much speculation about his replacement, particularly given that House Budget Committee Nussle had not been a fan of CBO in the past. Some feared that he would take this opportunity to bring someone in as CBO director who would, at long last, use the director's position to assist the party in power—the Republicans—in pursuing their agenda.

Again, this concern was ill placed. None of the three finalists—then deputy director and longtime budget professional Barry Anderson (whom Crippen publicly identified as his personal choice, going so far as to predict his selection),[135] Urban Institute economist Eugene Steuerle, and Syracuse University economist Douglas Holtz-Eakin—were viewed as extremists. None seemed likely to lead the agency in a substantially different direction than their predecessors.

There was a catch. Holtz-Eakin concerned many observers, not because of anything in his academic record, but because he was currently on leave from Syracuse as chief economist in President Bush's Council on Economic Advisors. In this position, he had helped craft many of Bush's economic policies—policies he would now be asked to comment on if he were named CBO director. Some observers viewed this apparent conflict of interest as sufficient to consider him unqualified to be CBO director. There was no precedent for someone coming directly from an administration to the CBO directorship. Recall that many (for example, in 1987 and 1988) viewed having served in a partisan position within Congress as disqualifying an individual from serving as CBO director. Presumably this sort of concern would extend to someone coming from the current administration, particularly given that CBO is so frequently called on to comment on executive branch proposals.

From Holtz-Eakin's perspective, the CBO director search was "a fairly normal search process." It was clear, he thought, that the House Budget Committee was running the show, and that the Democrats were not very influential in the process.[136] There seems to be consensus among both knowledgeable Republicans and knowledgeable Democrats that House Budget Committee Chairman Nussle was interested in choosing a CBO director who, far from cooking the books to support Republican ideas, would clearly operate in the agency's tradition of nonpartisanship. Nussle's deputy staff director, Jim Bates, argued that "had a candidate come in and shown that he or she wasn't capable of being independent of the administration, it is unlikely that that person would have been selected" by the House Budget Committee.[137] Nussle, however, presumably had issues with the Republican leadership, where Majority Leader Tom Delay and other conservatives would have been more comfortable with someone who would clearly favor orthodox Republican policies. In this context, choosing someone who was a reputable economist but came directly out of the Bush administration might have been the only way to meet Nussle's objective of getting a high-quality CBO director. According to one observer, "it was brilliant of Nussle. It was the only way I think conceivable to get a director as good as Doug was to do what he did—which was to appoint a guy straight out of this administration . . . how could Delay and [Speaker Dennis] Hastert and [House Ways and Means Chair Bill] Thomas complain about it?"[138]

The fears, particularly among Democrats, about Holtz-Eakin were not borne out by experience. Many, both inside and outside Congress, seemed impressed that he gave little support to Bush administration policies, some of which were drafted when Holtz-Eakin worked in the White House. A dynamic score of the president's fiscal year 2004 budget, conducted soon after the new director took over, gave very little credence to any notion that there would be substantial economic feedback from the president's policies. House and Senate Budget Committee Democrats were surprised by the extent to which Holtz-Eakin played issues down the middle. Holtz-Eakin himself noted in an interview in mid-2004 that much of the early criticism seemed to have died down, relating a story that Senator Kent Conrad had said, "I didn't think you could do this, but you've done a very good job. Thank you."[139] In fact, Alice Rivlin, when asked whether having a string of three consecutive Republican directors was a cause for concern, replied, "until Douglas Holtz-Eakin, I might have been concerned. But he seems to be playing the role so well and being so explicitly nonpartisan and objective that I've stopped worrying. It really doesn't have to do with politics—it has to do with his being a strong person who's running it well. I think it would be nice if there was another Democrat but I would like it to be a nonpartisan, scholarly, Holtz-Eakin-like Democrat."[140]

In late 2005 Holtz-Eakin announced that he would be leaving his post as CBO director at the end of December 2005, just short of three years into his term. Donald Marron, who had been appointed deputy director in October 2005, took over as director on an acting basis. Marron's background included stints both in the White House (like Holtz-Eakin, he had been on the staff of the Council on Economic Advisors) and the Joint Economic Committee. The Holtz-Eakin term would have expired in December 2006.

The Democrats Again

Marron managed CBO as acting director for more than a year, and the situation was largely status quo, with few organizational or substantive changes from the Holtz-Eakin directorship. During this period, the federal budget continued to be in deficit, the costly wars in Iraq and Afghanistan continued to be prosecuted, and Congress and the president did little to address either the short-term or long-term problems facing the federal budget. One significant political event did occur during this time. The Democrats, who had not controlled Congress in twelve years, were victorious in the midterm elections of 2006, and thus took charge of both houses of Congress beginning in 2007.

The next CBO director's term, starting in January 2007 to run until January 2011, was filled by Peter Orszag. Orszag had been a White House official during the Clinton administration, and spent much of the Bush administration working at the Brookings Institution, where previous CBO directors Rivlin and Reischauer had also worked. He was an expert on the federal budget, in particular health and tax policy. Orszag was a noncontroversial choice with both houses in Democratic control, and proceeded to put his own brand on CBO, particularly because he began immediately to speak out even more forcefully than past directors on the potential dangers involved in not getting a handle on health care costs. He focused the attention of the agency not on demographics (that aging baby boomers are about to increase the eligible population for Social Security and Medicare) but on the increasing cost of health care. He hired twenty more health care analysts (bringing the total to about fifty, or about one-third of CBO's analytical staff) in recognition of the fact that failure to solve problems associated with the cost of health care was more than a political problem: more profoundly, no one knew how to solve the problem.[141] This places health care reform in sharp contrast to Social Security. There are several known certain solutions to future imbalances associated with Social Security—Congress has simply chosen not to legislate to employ them. Orszag also named Robert Sunshine, a universally revered figure within CBO who had been the head of the Budget Analysis Division for almost a decade, and had been with the agency almost since its inception, as his deputy director.

Orszag, however, was destined to have a shorter tenure as CBO director than any one else who had held the post. Largely because of President Obama's commitment to health care reform, in late 2008 he chose Orszag as director of the Office of Management and Budget. In naming him, Obama said "as director of the Congressional Budget Office, he re-energized and re-invigorated the agency, while shifting its focus to control the health-care crisis that is not only a cause of so much suffering for so many families but a rapidly growing portion of our budget and a drag on our entire economy."[142] Implicit in this was the notion that health care and the future of the economy are inexorably intertwined, and that someone who understands both would be necessary as director of OMB, if the administration was to reach its goals.

This also meant, however, that CBO was again without a director, because Orszag had left fewer than two years into a four-year term. He thus became the second consecutive appointed director to depart early, and CBO would be led by an acting director for the second time in three years. This time Sunshine ran the agency while the search was conducted for a new director. There were some concerns that CBO might be in for a long period without an appointed director. First, GAO had been without a comptroller general for almost two years, with no

Table 2.1 Directors and Acting Directors of the Congressional Budget Office

Director	Tenure
Alice Rivlin	February 24, 1975–August 31, 1983
Rudy Penner	September 1, 1983–April 28,1987
Edward Gramlich*	April 29, 1987–December 22, 1987
James Blum*	December 23, 1987–March 5, 1989
Robert Reischauer	March 6, 1989–February 28, 1995
June O'Neill	March 1, 1995–January 29, 1999
Daniel Crippen	February 3, 1999–January 3, 2003
Barry Anderson*	January 4, 2003–February 2, 2003
Douglas Holtz-Eakin	February 3, 2003–December 29, 2005
Donald Marron*	December 30, 2005–January 17, 2007
Peter Orszag	January 18, 2007–November 25, 2008
Robert Sunshine*	November 26, 2008–January 21, 2009
Douglas Elmendorf	January 22, 2009–present

*Acting director

end in sight. Second, given the ambitious agenda of President Obama, and the capacity of CBO to call claims of the administration into question, the Congress might reasonably conclude that a lower-profile CBO fit the interest of the Democratic party, if not Congress. Nonetheless, Congress named Douglas Elmendorf, another Brookings economist who had been a CBO staffer in the 1990s, as the eighth CBO director in late January 2009. The Elmendorf tenure, at this writing, has been dominated by the Obama health care reform effort; chapter 7 discusses this role for CBO and Elmendorf.

Conclusion: Organizational Development

This organizational analysis of CBO yields several conclusions at this point.

1. The attention Alice Rivlin paid to establishing the culture of nonpartisanship was critical to both building CBO's reputation and providing the ability for the agency to maintain that nonpartisan profile when faced with internal and external challenges in the future.
2. It is hard to overstate Rudy Penner's influence in moving CBO from an organization created in Alice Rivlin's image to one that would maintain that kind of analytical and nonpartisan culture going forward. In fact, after the early period of Rivlin's term, Congress apparently stopped trying to change CBO's institutional role in the budget process, and resorted to fighting rearguard battles on particular issues.
3. Even though there have been concerns from time to time about CBO moving in a partisan direction, all directors have adhered to the original vision

of the organization—while simultaneously putting their stamp on the organization.

4. The end result of establishing nonpartisanship as a foundational norm of CBO is that it would be very difficult for a director or Congress to change that culture at this point. Wholesale replacement of (highly qualified and professionally respected) staff would be necessary.

5. In practice, Congress has been highly responsible in its selection of CBO directors. Even when substantial concern was raised at the time of a director's appointment, as with O'Neill and Holtz-Eakin, for example, there is no particular evidence that the Congress made specific actions a condition of selection.

6. Time and time again, directors of CBO have shown that they are more likely to upset the people most responsible for appointing them. At a minimum, this was true of Rivlin (Carter energy policy), Reischauer (health care reform), and O'Neill and Crippen (both dynamic scoring). This is by itself substantial evidence of nonpartisanship. It is probably even more specifically evidence that institutionally the organization is much more likely to upset those who propose policies, because of CBO's role in reviewing (and often throwing cold water on) those policies.

7. The Senate's initial vision of CBO clearly was ascendant over the House vision, and that has had a substantial effect on the organizational development of CBO. The Senate got their choice of director—Rivlin—in the short run, which resulted in a long-run win on organizational culture. The organization has become much more what the Senate envisioned than the budget office envisioned by the House.

8. For a number of reasons, the trend is toward single-term directors. Only Rivlin and Reischauer have served more than one. None of the last four directors (before the current one) has served more than one term, and the last two have not even completed their appointed terms.

9. With respect to its interactions with CBO, there is a difference between what Congress says and what it does. There may be times that Congress is genuinely upset with CBO over some decision. Other times CBO is a convenient scapegoat, or Congress (or the budget committees) may hide behind CBO in their effort to either challenge other committees within Congress or to stake out ground that differs from the president, even if he is from their own party. (This theme is expanded in chapter 3.)

Notes

1. Allen Schick, *The Federal Budget: Politics, Policy, Process*, 2nd ed. (Washington, DC: Brookings, 2000), 14.

2. Allen Schick, *Congress and Money* (Washington, DC: The Urban Institute, 1980), 25–26.

3. Congressional Budget Office, "Historical Budget Data, Outlays for Major Spending Categories," www.cbo.gov/budget/data/historical.pdf.

4. Schick, *Congress and Money*, 31.

5. Before fiscal year 1977, the federal fiscal year ran from July 1 through June 30.

6. A line item veto would permit the president to cut some parts of spending bills, while leaving the remainder intact (see Schick, *Congress and Money*, 32–41).

7. Schick, *Congress and Money*, 17.

8. Joint Study Comm. on Budget Control, *Recommendations for Improving Congressional Control over Budgetary Outlay and Receipt Totals*, Report, 93rd Cong., 1st sess., April 18, 1973, 1.

9. Joint Study Comm. on Budget Control, *Improving Congressional Control over Budgetary Outlay and Receipt Totals*, Interim Report, 93rd Cong., 1st sess., February 7, 1973.

10. Joint Study Comm., *Improving Congressional Control*, 1973, 4–10.

11. Joint Study Comm., *Recommendations for Improving Control*.

12. Schick, *Congress and Money*, 132.

13. Senate Comm. on Government Operations, *Federal Act to Control Expenditures and Establish National Priorities*, 93rd Cong., 1st sess., November 28, 1973, 31.

14. Ibid.

15. This list is summarized from Senate Comm. on the Budget, *Congressional Budget Reform: Public Law 93–344, Enacted July 12, 1974*, 94th Cong., 2nd sess., August 1976, 21–24.

16. The president pro tempore is the senator with the most years of seniority from the majority party.

17. Senate Comm. on the Budget, *Congressional Budget Reform*, 21.

18. At the time, the other three support agencies were the General Accounting Office, the Congressional Research Service, and the Office of Technology Assessment.

19. Senate Comm. on the Budget, *Congressional Budget Reform*, 50.

20. Joel Havemann, "After Two Years, CBO Gets High Marks from Congress," *National Journal* 9, no. 33 (1977): 1256.

21. Nancy D. Kates, *Starting from Scratch: Alice Rivlin and the Congressional Budget Office*, Part A (Cambridge, MA: Harvard University, 1989), 3.

22. Schick, *Congress and Money*, 133.

23. These quotes are taken from the transcript of a Senate Budget Committee meeting held December 19, 1974, as reported in Schick, *Congress and Money*, 133.

24. Kates, *Starting from Scratch*, Part A, 3.

25. Ibid.

26. Ibid., 4.

27. Ibid.

28. An interesting political footnote to the Rivlin selection is that Ullman only took over at Ways and Means in the aftermath of the scandal that erupted when the previous chairman, Wilbur Mills, had to resign. Mills resigned when his connection to Fanne Foxe (a stripper) was revealed: she took a well-publicized dip into the Tidal Basin while in Mills's company. Arguably, were it not for Fanne Foxe, Alice Rivlin would not have been named CBO director.

29. Kates, *Starting from Scratch*, Part A, 5.

30. Schick, *Congress and Money*, 134.

31. Alice Rivlin, interview with author, January 8, 2010.

32. Kates, *Starting from Scratch*, Part A, 6. A full list of participants is included in the notes from the Ad Hoc Advisory Comm. meeting, March 8, 1975, which can be found in the National Archives, College Park, MD, Accession Number 520-98-0003, Box 1.

33. Rivlin, interview, 2010.

34. Ad Hoc Advisory Comm. meeting.

35. Ibid.

36. A discussion of this is found in Kates, *Starting from Scratch*, Part A, 6–7.

37. Havemann, "After Two Years," 1256.

38. Ad Hoc Advisory Comm. meeting.

39. James Blum, interview with the author, February 5, 2004.

40. Kates, *Starting from Scratch*, Part B, 5.

41. Schick, *Congress and Money*, 135.

42. Ibid.

43. Rivlin, interview, 2010.

44. Memorandum from Mark Lackritz to John McEvoy, July 8, 1975, quoted in Schick, *Congress and Money*, 137.

45. Senate Comm. on the Budget, *Congressional Budget Office Oversight*, 94th Cong., 1st sess., October 6, 1975, 4.

46. Kates, *Starting from Scratch*, Part B, 7.

47. Senate Comm. on the Budget, *CBO Oversight*, 1975, 10.

48. Ibid., 20.

49. House Comm. on the Budget, *Congressional Budget Office Oversight*, Part 2, 94th Cong., 2nd sess., January 23, 1976, 10.

50. William M. Capron, "The Congressional Budget Office," in Senate Comm. on the Operation of the Senate, *Congressional Support Agencies*, Compilation of Papers, 94th Cong., 2nd sess., 1976, 81.

51. Schick, *Congress and Money*, 145.

52. Havemann, "After Two Years," 1256.

53. Schick, *Congress and Money*, 139.

54. Senate Committee on the Budget, *CBO Oversight*, 1975, 32.

55. Ibid., 35. The statute, it must be noted, was not quite that clear.

56. Schick, *Congress and Money*, 149–51.

57. House Comm. on the Budget, *Organization and Activities of the Congressional Budget Office*, 94th Cong., 1st sess., July 23, 1975, 15.

58. This view was articulated by some staffers Capron interviewed (see Senate Commission on the Operation of the Senate, *Congressional Support Agencies*, 84).

59. Senate Comm. on Appropriations, *Supplemental Appropriations for Fiscal Year 1976*, 94th Cong., 1st sess., November 12, 1975, 640.

60. Representative Delbert Latta (R-OH), ranking Republican on the House Budget Committee, quoting from the Appropriations Committee report (Senate Comm. on the Budget, *CBO Oversight*, 1975, 16).

61. Senate Comm. on the Budget, *CBO Oversight*, 1975, 25.

62. Ibid.

63. Senate Comm. on the Budget, *CBO Oversight*.

64. "They're Not the Budget Twins," *National Journal* 9, no. 33 (1977): 1260.

65. House Comm. on the Budget, *CBO Oversight*, Part 2, 8–9.

66. Ibid., 16–17.

67. House Comm. on the Budget, *Organization of CBO*, 1975, 6.

68. Senate Comm. on Appropriations, *Supplemental Appropriations for Fiscal Year 1976*, 94th Cong., 1st sess., November 12, 1975, 628.

69. Ibid., 628–36.

70. House Comm. on Appropriations, *Supplemental Appropriations Bill, 1976*, 94th Cong., 1st sess., November 7, 1975, HR 94–645, 32.

71. House Commission on Information and Facilities, *Congressional Budget Office: A Study of Its Organizational Effectiveness*, 95th Cong., 1st sess., January 4, 1977, 11.

72. Lee Cohn, *Washington Star*, June 1975.

73. Kates, *Starting from Scratch*, Part B, 8.

74. House Comm. on the Budget, *Organization of CBO*, 1975, 7.

75. Havemann, "After Two Years," 1256.

76. "Three with a Brand-New Power to Hold Down the Federal Budget," *U.S News and World Report*, December 8, 1975, 31.

77. See Office of Management and Budget, *Budget of the United States Government: Fiscal Year 2004, Budget Appendix* (Washington, DC: GPO, January 2003), 18.

78. Michael Telson, interview with the author, October 21, 2003.

79. Ibid.

80. James L. Rowe Jr., "Some Congressmen Bristle at Rivlin Appearances," *Washington Post*, June 24, 1977, E10.

81. House Comm. on the Budget, Task Force on Budget Process, *Congressional Budget Office Oversight*, 95th Cong., 1st sess., June 2, 1977, xx.

82. Ibid.

83. Ibid., 20–21.

84. House Commission on Information and Facilities, *Congressional Budget Office*, 1.

85. Ibid., 2.

86. Richard E. Cohen, "The 'Numbers Crunchers' at CBO Try to Steer Clear of Policy Disputes," *National Journal* 12, no. 23 (1980): 938.

87. Art Pine, "Hill's Budget Cutters Face Challenge," *Washington Post*, January 22, 1979, 3.

88. Victor Cohn, "Alice Rivlin Won't Seek Appointment to a Third Term as Director of CBO," *Washington Post*, September 12, 1982, E3.

89. Rudy Penner, interview with the author, April 21, 2004.

90. Penner, interview.

91. Jonathan Fuerbinger, "Officials Foresee Rudolph Penner as Congress's Top Budget Expert," *New York Times*, July 18, 1983, A13.

92. John M. Berry, "Democrats Want Own in CBO Post," *Washington Post*, May 27, 1983, D1.

93. Penner, interview.

94. Rivlin, interview, 2010.

95. Ibid.

96. Penner, interview.

97. Robert Pear, "A New Chief Espouses an Old Bipartisan Tone," *New York Times*, September 1, 1983, B10.

98. Penner, interview.

99. Ibid.

100. Jane Seaberry, "No-Label Economist," *Washington Post*, November 13, 1983, G1.

101. Everett Ehrlich, interview with the author, June 23, 2004.

102. Blum, interview, February 2004.

103. Penner, interview.

104. Ibid.

105. *Washington Post*, December 29, 1987, A14. It should be noted that Peter Milius, an editorial page writer for the *Washington Post* during this period generally took it upon himself to use his position to serve as a protector of CBO.

106. Tom Kenworthy, "Party Politics Leaves CBO Directorless," *Washington Post*, January 29, 1988, A19.

107. Jonathan Fuerbinger, "Power Struggles Leave Budget Agency Paralyzed," *New York Times*, March 31, 1988, A24. This seems to be a case of guilt by association; there is no evidence that Reischauer participated in the energy study.

108. James Horney, interview with the author, June 29, 2004.

109. William Hoagland, interview with the author, March 26, 2004.

110. "A Rubber-Stamp CBO?" *Washington Post*, November 16, 1994, A24.

111. Clay Chandler and Eric Pianin, "Budget Scorekeepers Await Changes," *Washington Post*, November 18, 1994, A25; Clay Chandler, "Hill Leaders Still Seeking CBO Chief," *Washington Post*, December 22, 1994, B9.

112. Chandler, "Hill Leaders Still Seeking CBO Chief."

113. Ibid.

114. Clay Chandler, "Congress Has Another CBO Candidate," *Washington Post*, January 13, 1995, F3.

115. June O'Neill, interview with the author, September 29, 2004.

116. "Leader Chosen for Congress Budget Office," *New York Times*, February 11, 1995, 1: 9.

117. Eric Pianin, "Professor Named New CBO Head," *Washington Post*, February 11, 1995, A4. O'Neill later recalled (in an interview with the author) that her statement had been intended as a joke, but that not everyone took it that way.

118. O'Neill, interview.

119. Ibid.

120. Eric Pianin, "Democratic Senators Seek Delay in Appointment of CBO Chief," *Washington Post*, February 15, 1995, A17.

121. "An Excellent Skunk," *Washington Post*, February 17, 1995, A24.

122. Eric Pianin, "Honeymoon Over for Kasich and Handpicked Budget Maven," *Washington Post*, September 4, 1995, A23.

123. Jonathan Peterson, "CBO Chief in Hot Seat of Budget Debate," *Los Angeles Times*, December 11, 1995, A1.

124. O'Neill, interview.

125. Eric Pianin, "June O'Neill to Depart CBO Early," *Washington Post*, October 29, 1998, A25.

126. Ibid.

127. George Hager, "Former GOP Aide Is Choice to Lead Hill Budget Office," *Washington Post*, January 14, 1999, A25.

128. Robert Pear, "Ex-Aide to Reagan Will Head the Congressional Budget Office," *New York Times*, January 14, 1999, A11.

129. Barry Anderson, interview with the author, March 10, 2005.

130. Jonathan Chait, "The Yes Man: Republicans Find a New Friend in the CBO," *The New Republic* 220, no. 22 (1999): 16–18.

131. Susan Crabtree, "Nussle Slams CBO," *Roll Call*, May 13, 2002.

132. Kelly Beaucar Vlahos, "Republicans Target CBO for Unattractive Economic Reports," *Fox News*, May 25, 2002, www.foxnews.com/story/0,2933,53679,00.html.

133. Jim Nussle, remarks at CBO director's conference, 2003.

134. John Maggs and David Baumann, "Speaking His Mind," *National Journal* 34, no. 27 (2002).

135. Ibid.

136. Douglas Holtz-Eakin, interview with the author, August 11, 2004.

137. James Bates, interview with the author, June 29, 2004.

138. Horney, interview.

139. Bob Cusack, "I'm Very Sensitive to Justifiable Criticism," *The Hill*, July 14, 2004, 6.

140. Alice Rivlin, interview with the author, October 23, 2003.

141. Ezra Klein, "The Number-Cruncher-in-Chief," *The American Prospect* 20, no. 1 (2009): 15.

142. Ibid.

Chapter 3

Macrobudgeting

THE CONGRESSIONAL BUDGET ACT identified two specific roles for CBO in support of the annual budget process—assisting Congress in establishing fiscal policy by enacting the annual budget resolution, and informing Congress on the cost of legislative proposals. In the first, which is the focus of this chapter, CBO was to support the new budget committees as they sought to set overall fiscal policy by enacting, first, the annual budget resolution and, second, the related legislation that followed. The second role—costing budgetary proposals—is covered in chapter 4.

Because the budget committees were the new kids on the block, establishing the budget process faced resistance (if not outright hostility) from both Congress and the president. On the congressional side, the existing fiscal power structure (the tax writing committees and the appropriations committees) viewed the new budget process as a threat to their exclusive power over the congressional purse strings. From the president's perspective, given that the entire point of the new structure was to strengthen the congressional role in budgeting, the new process was a clear threat. And CBO, in its effort to diminish the dominance of executive branch (particularly OMB) numbers, was clearly at the center of this effort.

The story of federal budget policy over the past thirty-five years has many subplots—from the establishment of the budget resolution in the late 1970s through the Reagan revolution, the deficit-focused reforms starting in 1985, and the eventual movement of the budget into surplus in 1998 and then back to deficit again in 2002. Those stories have been told by numerous authors in a number of books and articles over the past thirty years.[1] But CBO was at the center of all of these debates. This book attempts to tell the story of CBO's role and the ways that CBO influenced this history.

Establishing the New Budget Process

After organizing, CBO saw its most important task as developing its first economic and budget report. This report, produced in June 1975, was the first time that CBO had acquired any visibility with the press, and was released to the press on an embargoed basis. This led to one of the first major flaps that CBO had with the budget committees, because the details of the report leaked before its release. Rivlin told the story this way:

> I had a big tiff on our first report—the June '75 one that was about the economy. . . . I had established that set of rules (that the report was to be embargoed) . . . and a *Washington Star* reporter called and said he couldn't come, could I meet with him separately? And it was somebody I knew and trusted so I said OK and he broke the embargo and he said he hadn't broken the embargo because he hadn't quoted from the report, only from my conversation. . . . Well, he knew the report was embargoed, but he didn't know that our conversation was embargoed, he claimed—I found it pretty slippery.[2]

Interestingly, what caused as much of a problem as the leaking of the report was the surprise that some members of Congress felt at discovering that CBO was preparing its own economic forecast. No one within CBO questioned the necessity of this. They believed that supporting the budget committees in producing a budget resolution meant that CBO had to do something that the Congress had never done before—produce its own independent economic forecast. In short, it is not possible to have independent budget numbers without an independent economic forecast, since so much of the budget depends on the economy. Not all members of Congress, however, seemed to see it as an appropriate function for the new agency. As Bob Reischauer explained, "to underscore how new all this was, when we did our first economic forecast (news of which was published in the *Washington Star*), Ed Muskie . . . called up Alice and said 'What the hell are you doing a forecast for? We don't need a forecast . . . the administration does a forecast . . . and it had never even crossed Alice's or my mind—or Bob Levine's, that we wouldn't do an independent forecast. That just shows you how foreign this whole concept [was] of an entity which decides what is necessary to fulfill its responsibilities without getting formal approval from those that think they are the masters."[3]

As President Ford proceeded toward a hoped-for reelection, the economy was a continuing major issue. In particular, the high rates of inflation and the "deepest recession of the postwar period" threatened Ford's prospects, and CBO was asked to comment on the president's economic policies.[4] In January 1976 Rivlin remarked that the president's policies, far from stimulating the economy, would actually slow the recovery down compared to a more expansionary policy favored by some in Congress, including some on the budget committees.[5]

The Ford budget was the first of many times a CBO director challenged the estimates included in an executive budget. In an October 1975 speech to the

National Economists Club, Rivlin argued that the president's budget had overestimated fiscal year 1977 spending. She went further and challenged the appropriateness of the president's tactics in dealing with Congress. Rivlin asserted that the president was wrong in demanding that Congress adopt his budget; she believed that the president was openly threatening the new congressional budget process.[6] These remarks prompted a rebuke from House Budget Committee Chairman Brock Adams (D-WA). In an October 28 letter to Rivlin, he wrote that he did not believe that CBO should become "a policy arm of the Congress" and that elected members of Congress were "very concerned when they must defend statements for which they are not responsible." The new budget process itself was under attack and therefore "we must all be careful about our speeches given to groups other than the Congress until this process has been tested and used by the Congress."[7]

Jimmy Carter defeated Ford in the 1976 election, but it did not take long for his administration to discover that, despite the fact that Rivlin worked as a staff official in an institution run entirely by Democrats, a Democratic president was not immune from the sting of CBO analyses that placed the agency at odds with the administration on key fiscal policy issues. President Carter, who had pledged to have a budget surplus by fiscal year 1981, discovered a $30 billion difference of opinion between his administration and CBO on the size of that projected surplus. CBO officials cautioned that though both administration and CBO estimates were within a reasonable range of possible outcomes, the CBO estimate would mean $30 billion less to spend (or a need for additional taxes) on funding new programs.[8] Later the same year, Rivlin told a Senate committee that neither the 1981 balanced budget goal (recently restated by the president's budget director) nor the full employment goal was likely to be reached.[9] She repeated the assertion after the president's fiscal year 1979 budget was released.[10]

One significant indicator of the seriousness with which Congress took CBO analysis is that both budget committees, each of which had Democratic chairs, used CBO assumptions in drafting the budget resolution. For example, in the fiscal year 1980 resolution, the Senate Budget Committee used CBO's inflation and unemployment numbers, even though adopting those numbers led to a larger deficit forecast and (implicitly) more spending cuts than the president's budget.[11] Over the Carter years, CBO was consistently less optimistic than the executive branch on both economic projections and budget estimates.[12]

Clearly, the combination of the CBO analysis of the Carter energy program (discussed in more detail in chapter 5) and CBO's questioning the Carter budget projections made it uncomfortable for the president's supporters in Congress. Speaker O'Neill and especially House Majority Leader Wright were bothered by the continuing specter of one of their own employees calling the president's policies into question.[13] The *Washington Post* felt compelled to defend CBO in a December 1977 editorial, pointing out that the agency was doing precisely what

Congress had set it up to do and that its continued independence proved that Congress wanted independent counsel, regardless of how uncomfortable that counsel might be. The *Post* concluded that "in matters of economic policy, two computers are better than one."[14]

The CBO criticism of Carter policies came as a surprise to many Republicans in Congress, who had assumed that Rivlin had criticized the Ford budgets because she was herself a Democrat and because Congress was controlled by Democrats. Rivlin remembered later that the flaps about the Carter analyses were in fact "extremely helpful in establishing our bipartisanship because before that the Republicans had criticized us a lot because of similar incidents involving Ford and once we had on the record a criticism of Carter then they became our greatest supporters on both sides of the hill."[15]

The Reagan Revolution

The implication of this independence was clearly felt by the time Ronald Reagan was elected president in November 1980. By this point CBO had established itself as a clear and independent voice on fiscal issues. It had challenged both a Republican and a Democratic president, and was beginning to be regarded as perhaps the most credible source on fiscal matters in Washington. What really solidified that reputation, however, was the fiscal tsunami that accompanied Reagan's election. In particular, CBO was a counterpoint to the perception that Reagan and his budget director, David Stockman, had politicized OMB numbers.

Reagan was elected with a three-part fiscal agenda—to cut income taxes, to increase defense spending, and to eliminate the federal deficit. This last pledge was significant. The deficit for fiscal year 1980, which had ended three and a half months before Reagan took office, stood at $74 billion. Part and parcel of the Reagan economic policies was supply side economics, which essentially argued that cutting taxes had enough of a stimulative effect to reduce federal deficits rather than increase them.

Once Reagan submitted his set of budget proposals to Congress, CBO set out to analyze them, presenting a preliminary analysis that the president's proposal had underestimated spending by up to $25 billion. When released in late March of 1981, the final CBO analysis of the Reagan budget presented sharply different views of fiscal reality than those in the budget plan. CBO assumed a $22 billion higher deficit ($67 billion rather than $45 billion) than the administration for fiscal year 1981, and concluded that instead of a small surplus for 1984, the deficit would remain, albeit at a reduced level of $49 billion.[16] CBO also evaluated the effect the Reagan program would have on different income groups, focusing particularly on the poor.[17]

The higher profile CBO acquired in the wake of the Reagan program put the agency in a difficult position. The political balance of power had shifted in

Congress; the Senate was now under Republican control and CBO was seen as a possible obstruction to a popular new president whose party held the majority in one house. A CBO analysis suggesting that the Reagan program would not balance the budget by 1984 (which he had promised) led the president to accuse CBO of producing phony numbers and to calls for Rivlin's removal because she was a Democrat and hostile to the supply side mantra.[18]

The law did not make it easy to remove a CBO director. The only way was by a vote of one or the other house of Congress. Clearly the House, which was still controlled by the Democrats, had no interest in doing this. In the Senate, however, certain conservative Republicans worked actively for Rivlin's ouster.[19] They were rebuffed by the new Senate Budget Committee chair, Pete Domenici. Rivlin recalled, "when Reagan was elected, the new administration tried to get rid of me. . . . What the law said was that I could be removed by a majority vote of either house, and they starting working on the Republicans in the Senate. . . . Pete Domenici said no, that I should serve out my term, that I was doing a good job, that this was the prerogative of the Congress, not the White House. I think he got Dole's backing, and the more extreme members backed down."[20]

That CBO was by that point generally considered nonpartisan helped those who were concerned about the Reagan program. CBO's forecasts gave Congress (particularly Democrats in Congress, but also some Republicans, such as Domenici, who were concerned that the Reagan program did not add up) ammunition to use to try to fight (or at least moderate) the Reagan program. The result of the controversy was that annual CBO deficit projections, which had been virtually invisible outside of narrow constituencies, gained substantial visibility. Ultimately, the authority of the CBO (and Rivlin) to challenge administration budget estimates was supported by budget committee leaders on both sides of the aisle, including Senate Budget Committee chair Domenici and new House Budget Committee chair James Jones (D-OK).[21]

By later that year, after the passage of the large Reagan tax cut, the CBO analyses were even less optimistic. In a September 1981 report, Rivlin projected a fiscal year 1982 deficit of more than $80 billion, and a 1984 deficit in excess of $100 billion.[22] In the end, CBO's analyses of the future effects of the Reagan program were much more realistic than those of the administration, and presaged (although underestimated) the large deficits that began to emerge by the mid 1980s. CBO identified the president's 1981 tax cuts as unaffordable, in light of the failure of the administration to cut spending to make up for the lost revenues.[23] In fact, by the summer of 1982, barely a year after the president's tax cuts were enacted, CBO was projecting deficits at between $140 and $160 billion between fiscal years 1983 and 1985.[24]

CBO's challenge to the Reagan budget assumptions solidified its reputation for independence. In a feature article about Rivlin in April 1983, the British publication *The Guardian* noted that "it has been Mrs. Rivlin's quietly-offered analyses which have done the worst damage to Mr. Reagan's credibility" and that "she has demonstrated an almost surgical approach to David Stockman's (Reagan's first budget director) arithmetic."[25]

All of this perhaps papers over a bit the difficult position the CBO found itself in at the time. There is some suggestion, as Roy Meyers notes, that the agency consciously adopted a model that would lessen the differences between CBO and administration numbers because "CBO leaders felt that not doing so would make CBO vulnerable to substantial retribution from the Republican-controlled Senate."[26] Richard Kogan argued that CBO should not have held its fire at this point by using economic assumptions that were more optimistic than those projected by CBO's own internal models.[27] Van Ooms, who was a high-level staffer on the House Budget Committee at the time and for many years afterward, recalled, "I sort of said 'Alice, this looks to me like unbridled optimism,' and she said, 'No it's bridled optimism.' Alice was doing her best to not pick a fight with the Reagan administration."[28] Consistent with this view, Everett Ehrlich, who was on the CBO staff at the time, referred to Rivlin's "incredibly deft playing of that hand . . . the way that she rose to that occasion and took the rudder."[29] Rivlin herself said this later:

> That was our finest hour in some ways. We did a report, which in hindsight was entirely too optimistic. But it said that the OMB estimates of the deficit were much too optimistic and we were much "righter" than our numbers showed. But that was a huge brouhaha. But by then CBO's right to say it was not questioned in the Congress—only in the White House. And it made me a minor heroine in the Congress, especially among the Democrats, but even Bob Dole and the more sensible Republicans who didn't really believe in supply-side economics were quite supportive, such as Domenici.[30]

In the end, most agree, although CBO may have held its fire at least to some extent in 1981, this did no long-term damage to its credibility. It is likely that Rivlin's call protected CBO from retribution that might have been far more damaging. In reviewing the episode in 1998, Williams noted that "CBO did not suffer great harm to its credibility and an unyielding Rivlin stand would likely have been foolhardy."[31] In any event, the main point is that CBO had played its role; it had permitted Congress to question the projections, based on fanciful assumptions, coming out of the Reagan White House. That CBO's projections could have been "more right" seems hardly the main point. Forecasting is an art, not a science. Rivlin later disputed the notion of any intentional effort to minimize differences between the administration and CBO. "I don't think so. I think we played it straight. We as it turned out were much too optimistic. We didn't predict the depth of the recession and the size of the deficits. . . . The recession of 1981–82 was a really serious thing. Worst until now and we didn't anticipate how bad it was going to be."[32]

As chronic deficits became a fact of life, CBO began to produce a publication that would become a routine as fiscal imbalances persisted. Originally titled *Budget Options*, this annual volume became a source of data on likely savings and the possible economic and social impacts associated with various options to reduce the deficit. These ranged from the relatively small effects of replacing the dollar bill with a dollar coin to major proposals to means-test entitlement programs such as social security. Writing in 1992, Jim Blum identified the deficit reduction options book as "the most widely distributed of all CBO publications."[33] By the time surpluses arrived in the late 1990s it ceased publication. By 2004, after the return of deficits, CBO was in the business of presenting deficit options again.

If congressional Republicans believed that replacing Rivlin with Rudy Penner in 1983 signaled a change in CBO's outlook, they soon found out that they were mistaken. At a December 1983 conference, Penner noted that "the mathematics are in place for an explosion, and we cannot remain on that path forever."[34] CBO was by that point forecasting a 1986 deficit approaching $200 billion, and a fiscal year 1989 deficit in excess of $300 billion.[35] But although many analysts—from inside and outside the administration—were consistently alarmed (or at least concerned, in the case of the insiders) about the deficit, there was little political will or incentive to address it before the 1984 presidential election.

Penner noted later that CBO built greater credibility over the realism of its forecasts compared to the executive, but that the result was all relative. Although through "the Reagan era and the era of rosy scenario CBO acquired a lot of credibility. . . . if you look back at the forecasts, they were pretty awful. They were terribly overoptimistic in Alice's time, and I think every one of mine . . . turned out to be optimistic. But because we were so much closer to reality than the administration CBO had acquired a lot of credibility over that time."[36]

By the mid-1980s, some consensus had begun to develop to do something to rein in the deficits that were projected to remain at the $200 billion level for the foreseeable future. This ultimately led to the enactment of the Balanced Budget and Emergency Deficit Control Act of 1985, also known as the Gramm-Rudman-Hollings Act.

Gramm-Rudman-Hollings

An article of faith among most observers of federal budgeting holds that when political leaders are unwilling to absorb the political cost associated with controlling the budget, they try to reform the budget process. Exhibit number one for this belief is the Balanced Budget and Emergency Deficit Control Act, or Gramm-Rudman-Hollings (GRH). Needing political cover to do something as politically unpleasant as raising the debt ceiling—which was tantamount to admitting failure of prevailing budget policy—and unwilling to inflict immediate pain (by actually cutting spending or raising taxes), Congress turned to a procedural tonic.[37]

The elixir was concocted by three senators—Phil Gramm (R-TX), Warren Rudman (R-NH), and Ernest Hollings (D-SC). All were serious students of the budget, which led them to conclude that the time was right for action, resulting in what Senator Rudman referred to as "a bad idea whose time has come."[38] The Gramm-Rudman-Hollings law set fixed deficit targets designed to eliminate the deficit by fiscal year 1991, and created a complex procedure designed to reduce the deficit through automatic spending reductions should these targets be exceeded.

GRH created enormous challenges for CBO, both before it was enacted and after. The problem with it before the fact was that no one really knew how it would work. As of mid-1985 it was an idea without any specific means of bringing it to reality. Rudy Penner, in particular, was quite concerned about the power that Gramm-Rudman would bestow on the unelected CBO director. He made his views well known to the congressional leadership, many of whom did not want to hear about it. He said that some of the early versions of the proposal "were terrifying to me as CBO director because they would give me the power to impound funds. I probably reacted quite strongly to that because I thought it would destroy CBO. . . . And I should have known that . . . those things would never get into the law, but I did fight them and made myself very unpopular with the proponents of GRH. And they actually perceived me as being partisan. It was more a fight over the details and it also seemed overwhelmingly obvious to me that it couldn't possibly be constitutional."[39]

Despite Penner's reservations, CBO assisted in drafting the legislation. Staff helped Congress work out many of the specifics of sequestration, including what accounts to include and how to implement the sequestration of specific programs.[40]

Ultimately, in late 1985, GRH became law.[41] It faced an almost immediate constitutional challenge because the law had given the comptroller general (the head of the GAO) the job of ordering sequestration (the automatic target-meeting procedure established under the law); in fact, the first set of such cuts were ordered by GAO head Charles Bowsher in January 1986.[42]

The original Gramm-Rudman law was found unconstitutional by the US Supreme Court in 1986. In its decision, *Bowsher v. Synar*, the Court found that the law's sequestration procedure violated the separation of powers under the US Constitution, by vesting a legislative branch official (the comptroller general) with a fundamentally executive power.[43] Congress responded to the Court's decision by enacting a new law, the Balanced Budget and Emergency Deficit Control Reaffirmation Act, of 1987. This law gave the director of the Office of Management and Budget (unquestionably an executive official) the power to order a sequester.

As the 1980s drew to an end, the deficit continued to grow and the likelihood of meeting the deficit targets shrank. As early as 1987, only two years after the passage of GRH, CBO projected that the fiscal year 1988 budget was $45 billion short of meeting the law's target of a $108 billion deficit.[44] By the time Reischauer took over as director in 1989, he was warning Congress of a need to make cuts of almost $70 billion to meet the GRH deficit target of $64 billion for fiscal year 1991.[45]

The GRH legislation, though viewed largely as a failure by most observers, did spotlight the forecasting of CBO and OMB because of the need for these estimates to enforce the GRH deficit limits. Beyond enhancing the role of CBO in the budget process, the legislation did contribute to better communication between CBO and OMB, because both institutions had to explain the bases for disagreements.

CBO and the S&L Crisis

As if the deficit problem was not bad enough already, beginning in the mid-1980s the federal government faced a new drain on its resources. A crisis had stealthily been brewing in the financial sector for some time. Thousands of financial institutions across the country began to fail as a result of inadequate government regulation of the industry. By law, the Federal Savings and Loan Insurance Corporation (FSLIC) was on the hook to bail out failing thrifts, to the tune of up to $100,000 per depositor account.

Suddenly the CBO needed to develop the capacity—never needed before—to estimate the financial fallout from a major banking system failure. This required the ability to predict when and under what circumstances particular savings and loans would go out of business. Further, it was necessary to estimate the aggregate exposure that would result for the federal government. Consistent with its general role as the numbers truthteller for Congress, during the S&L scandal CBO was practically alone, with the notable exception of GAO, in presenting estimates reflecting the true financial extent and effect of the bailout. This particular effort to inform policymakers was cited by Richard Kogan as one of the most significant contributions of CBO over its history. At the outset of the S&L bailout, political leaders in the White House and in Congress had every incentive to understate its cost, particularly given the effect the cost would have on compliance with GRH targets. When CBO said it would add significantly to federal deficits, it became impossible to ignore that basic fact, even though "there were still people in Congress who were saying this is going to take care of itself."[46]

The CBO estimate was unwelcome news all around, implicitly putting pressure on the office to come up with a different answer. Elected officials can obtain electoral benefits from cutting taxes or from spending money on programs that will provide benefits to constituents in the future. Almost no elected official finds it beneficial to tout as an accomplishment spending billions of dollars making good on past promises to investors, particularly when most taxpayers are net payers rather than net receivers from the bailout.

The main budgeting controversy surrounding the S&L crisis fits squarely in this context. The Reagan administration and many in the Congress wanted the transactions of the Resolution Trust Corporation (RTC), which included the funds paid to bail out investors—to be placed outside the federal budget. There they believed costs would appear more or less invisible to the public, because they would not count in official deficit forecasts.

Although the revelation of the cost did force Congress to confront the fact that the S&L bailout would cost money, Congress attempted to finance the bailout through creating what was referred to in one publication as a shell funding scheme.[47] Under the bill favored by the Reagan administration to resolve the approximately two hundred failed thrifts that were expected as of 1986, a financing corporation (FICO) would have been set up for the sole purpose of loaning funds to FSLIC to permit all insolvent thrifts to be liquidated. The administration's plan called for this corporation to transfer equity, not debt, to FICO; thus FICO would have a financial interest and would be paid dividends, but would not have to repay the funds.

Both Treasury and OMB blessed the transactions as appropriate, but CBO questioned the budgetary treatment of the bailout. A CBO memorandum stated that CBO "treat[s] the debt of the funding shell as the debt of the FSLIC, because the funding shell's only source of income and only claim is on the FSLIC and because the FSLIC is committed to make payments to the shell . . . sufficient to service and retire all its debt."[48] CBO separately labeled the Reagan administration proposal as a "budgetary gimmick."[49]

Rudy Penner recalled this as one of the most uncomfortable periods of his tenure:

> The initial parts of the bailout were off-budget and I had a big fight about that and it delayed the process a bit. . . . The bill had been introduced in the House and (the bill said) it was off-budget. We had a lot of internal debate within CBO. I remember Alfred Fitt (the CBO legal counsel) saying we didn't have a legal leg to stand on in trying to keep it on-budget. . . . We fought it for a while and didn't get any support from the budget committees. I remember Domenici being particularly angry with me about it. There were really no friends. But ultimately the bailout was on budget so I like to think that our initial fight although we lost did raise all the right issues.[50]

Although the bailout was ultimately on-budget, the CBO analysis was undoubtedly ignored at the outset. In what appeared to be a face-saving but not particularly substantive change, the House Banking Committee reported out a new version of the bailout plan including "technical changes to the financing structure" suggested by the administration.[51] And though CBO blessed the bill as deficit neutral with these changes, some—including House Banking Chairman Fernand St. Germain, a Rhode Island Democrat—thought that the bill still relied a bit much on "smoke and mirrors."[52] CBO reported the transactions as off-budget as long as Congress insisted on this, and did not just ignore the law. In other words, CBO did not insist that a "law that says that black is white should be ignored for scorekeeping purposes."[53]

The 1990 Budget Summit

By the time Reischauer took over as director in January 1989, the budget process created by GRH had largely fallen apart. The target for fiscal year 1991, which was $64 billion under the law as revised in 1987, was far below the CBO projected estimate of $138 billion published in January of 1990.[54] Given that this would have required a cut of $74 billion from a budget that had already been enacted, it would be impossible to achieve the GRH target. CBO's baseline projection for the out years showed continued deficits, and the actual deficit for fiscal year 1993—the year that GRH required a balanced budget—was $255 billion.[55]

In this context, deficit hawks in both parties, including the chairs and ranking members of both the House and the Senate budget committees, attempted to draft a budget resolution that would reduce the deficit. They were hamstrung in large part by the inability to consider tax increases as a result of a pledge by President George H. W. Bush that he would not raise taxes. On obtaining his party's nomination for president in 1988, President Bush had made a campaign promise asking people to "read my lips; no new taxes!"

In May 1990, faced with the impossibility of enacting a budget resolution that would reduce the deficit by the level required by Gramm-Rudman and feeling a sense of pressure to accomplish something, President Bush's key economic advisors and congressional leaders convened a budget summit. Held at Andrews Air Force Base, the summit included high-ranking budget officials from the administration and chairs and ranking Republicans of the money committees (budget, appropriation, and tax writing). Although initially resistant to tax increases, President Bush eventually agreed that "everything" was on the table, implicitly suggesting that tax increases might be acceptable. His lieutenants, mainly Chief of Staff John Sununu and Budget Director Richard Darman, on the other hand, continued to hold out for a package that included only reductions in spending.

It was early fall of 1990 before the impasse was broken when Bush agreed to consider tax revenue increases in a broader deficit reduction package. On September 30, 1990, as fiscal year 1991 was about to begin, an agreement was reached by the summit participants. This agreement, however, was voted down by the rank and file in the House and Senate (in part, in the House, as a result of a revolt led by Congressman Newt Gingrich of Georgia), and sent the summiteers back for more negotiations.

Subsequent to this initial defeat, the negotiators returned to the table and made a number of relatively minor changes that resulted ultimately in an agreement that resulted in $490 billion in projected deficit reduction over five years.[56] These deficit-reducing actions were, at the time, projected to result in a virtual elimination of the federal deficit. In fact, a budget surplus had been predicted by the participants by fiscal year 1994; CBO, which was slightly more pessimistic, projected declining deficits, but still a small deficit in fiscal year 1995.

CBO had a significant, but low profile, role to play in the budget summit. First, CBO presented the underlying baseline estimates that, in a very real sense, led to a sense of urgency that something needed to be done. Certainly OMB agreed on the trajectory of future budgets, if not on all the details. And certainly there were political imperatives to do something about the budget problem in 1990, rather than waiting until 1992 (when the president would be running for reelection) or allowing GRH's automatic cuts to kick in.

Second, CBO had, as noted, been assembling an entire menu of options since the Reagan administration for reducing the federal budget deficit. The annually published volume containing these options listed many policy changes that Congress considered when it was attempting to come up with the specific tax changes and spending cuts to be included in the 1990 package.

Third, the CBO analyses of the distributional effects of tax and spending changes may have played some role in the outcome. Clearly, according to participants, distributional considerations entered into the deliberations at Andrews.[57] One person familiar with the negotiations referred to these as "the driver of the final shape of what was and wasn't acceptable."[58] Tax increases and reductions in spending were consistently considered in terms of which income groups would experience them. Congress was considering these changes in the context of the distributional effects of changes made in the 1980s. Here CBO provided analyses that showed that the wealthy had received more benefits from the 1980s tax policies. In particular, studies by CBO showed that the top 5 percent of families had 45 percent more in pretax income in 1990 than they did in 1980; the result was the opposite for the poorest 10 percent, whose incomes fell by an average of 10 percent.[59] In fact, one of the participants in the Andrews summit said that the final negotiated deal almost did not get enough support in the Democratic caucus because the effects were not as progressive as they had been led to believe; this mutiny was only averted when House Speaker Tom Foley argued that there were other things to consider besides just the distributional effects.[60]

Finally, one area where CBO had a clear impact during the budget summit was budget process reform. As noted, CBO had been an unenthusiastic participant in both drafting and implementing GRH. The summit participants needed to negotiate some changes to the prevailing GRH process, if only because the core—the deficit targets and sequestration—had proved so unworkable. Some of the procedural reforms ultimately included in the 1990 Budget Enforcement Act (BEA), such as the discretionary caps and the pay-as-you-go system (PAYGO), were more or less jointly drafted by the House and the Senate budget committees, with input from CBO. One significant procedural reform, credit reform, had fairly identifiable CBO parentage. CBO, and particularly the Budget Process Unit under Dick Emery and Marvin Phaup, had been studying credit budgeting in general for a number of years. There was general concern that cash-based credit budgeting was creating signals encouraging support of loan guarantees over direct loans. Response to this concern led to credit reform, the federal government's first (and really only) movement toward accrual budgeting. In fact, CBO and OMB career staff, along with the staff of the budget committees and Bush budget director Richard Darman, really drove the credit reform changes, which were highly arcane and technical.[61]

The budget summit—and specifically the BEA—was seen at the time as having shifted budgetary power substantially back from Congress to the executive, particularly from CBO and the budget committees to OMB. The new budget process established by the BEA granted the power to order a sequestration of either discretionary or entitlement programs to OMB rather than CBO. This was seen as, in effect, giving the executive branch the power to provide cost estimates during the legislative process, a power that had been reserved to CBO since the outset of the budget process.

Congress was not confident that it wanted to cede this sort of control. In fact, almost immediately after the new budget process was adopted, House leadership unveiled a plan that would have used CBO and JCT numbers to assess the actual compliance with the provisions of the BEA and the amount of any sequestration that would occur.[62]

In retrospect, the concern that the BEA would contribute to the diminution of the Congress's—and by extension CBO's—influence was ill-placed. OMB's prominence did not come at the expense of CBO and the budget committees. If anything, the BEA, with its emphasis on estimates of future effects for discretionary spending and the PAYGO process, which required costly legislation to be offset by spending cuts or tax increases, expanded the importance of all scorekeepers. A budget process focused on scorekeeping—on tracking the financial results of legislation—is inevitably going to expand the influence of those that produce the numbers. Further, even though OMB was the estimator of record with regard to sequestration, CBO continued to play its traditional role of challenging OMB estimates. It was in fact the CBO estimates that committees needed to worry about in the legislative process.

Not surprisingly, the biggest threat to the goals of the budget pact—actually reaching a balanced budget—was not procedural, but economic. The economy had already plunged into recession before the ink on the budget agreement was dry. This meant that, by the time of the 1991 CBO annual report, the economy was already in recession.[63] By the time of the 1991 summer update, CBO was projecting deficits of $234 billion in fiscal year 1994 (the year that summiteers had said the budget would be balanced).[64] The somewhat remarkable aspect of this turnaround in fiscal fortunes was that the increasing deficit did not result from any actions of the Congress and the President to undo any of the 1990 policy actions. Instead, changes in economic and technical assumptions were completely to blame; in other words, the deficit returned not because of bad decisions in 1991, but because of bad forecasts in 1990.

The 1993 Clinton Budget Plan

Bill Clinton was elected president in November 1992, running on a platform with the economy (and the budget) at the center. The unofficial mantra of the campaign was "It's the Economy, Stupid!" Coming out of the early 1990s recession, and with the unexpected ascendancy of Ross Perot (and his emphasis on deficit reduction) in the 1992 election, it was critical for Clinton to focus on the U.S. economy as the first priority of his administration. Because he had been elected with only 43 percent of the popular vote, it was considered imperative that his administration at least appear to do something about the deficit in order to appeal to the Perot voters.

CBO had already gained some prominence during the campaign. Candidate Clinton's economic missive, *Putting People First*, was published in June 1992, using the deficit forecast CBO had included in its January 1992 annual report. Based on these numbers, the Clinton plan pledged to cut the federal budget deficit in half within four years. When CBO issued a subsequent—and much more pessimistic—forecast of the deficit in August of that year, the Clinton campaign did not revise its economic plan, nor did it acknowledge that these new estimates now meant that his plan did not add up—a charge made repeatedly by the Bush campaign in the run-up to the election.[65] In January 1993, outgoing President Bush issued his budget, showing a deficit of $237 billion for fiscal year 1997, $68 billion higher than the OMB-forecast deficit of five months earlier.[66]

The deterioration in the deficit forecast, and President-elect Clinton's acknowledgment of the higher deficit numbers, occasioned a formal restating of the new administration's budget positions. The president and his budget director, Leon Panetta, both backed off the emphasis on economic stimulus that had been a centerpiece of the economic manifesto, and reaffirmed the commitment to cutting the deficit in half. But because meeting this pledge would occasion more policy changes than Clinton had anticipated, there would be less room in the budget for new spending.[67] Equally the new forecast lessened the capacity for the middle-class tax cut the president had proposed during the campaign.[68]

Despite the reported emphasis on the deficit, the first battle that Clinton had with Congress was over a $16.3 billion economic stimulus package, which Clinton expected would win easy approval from the Democratic-controlled Congress. The proposal encountered opposition, particularly in the Senate, where a group of relatively conservative Democrats such as David Boren (D-OK) questioned its usefulness. Indeed, CBO itself questioned the value of the economic stimulus. In January 1993 testimony before the Senate Budget Committee, CBO director Reischauer argued that it was unlikely that the relatively small, infrastructure-driven stimulus package would have any short-term effect on the economy.[69] Clinton himself was reportedly quite upset with the role that CBO was playing in the debate. The president, after one particular CBO analysis that disagreed with the assumptions underlying the investment plan, was quoted as fuming "we've gutted our investment program by turning the government over to Reischauer!"[70]

In the end, this was not primarily a story of CBO versus the administration. Deficit hawks within the administration were able to convince the president instead to pursue a relatively large deficit reduction package that embraced both tax increases and spending cuts. This was in part a political decision. Some within the administration believed that if Perot voters were to be courted, it could only be done by demonstrating progress on the deficit.

President Clinton released his deficit reduction plan before a joint session of Congress on February 16, 1993. In an extraordinary moment in this speech, the president pledged that he would unveil a budget plan using independent figures from CBO. This provoked howls of derision, mainly from House Republicans, who had argued for years that CBO was merely a tool of the congressional Democratic majority. This response prompted a retort from the president: "Well, you can laugh, my fellow Republicans. But I'll point out that the Congressional Budget Office was normally more conservative on what was going to happen and closer to right than previous presidents."[71]

This extraordinary budgetary moment—a president pledging to use the forecasts of the Congress's own budget office to score his proposals—was designed to take disagreements about the cost of the plan's components off the table. Considering that CBO was created in response to a concern that OMB numbers were the only budget numbers in town, the suggestion that only CBO numbers would now be used by the president as the basis for his own budget proposal seemed to suggest that Congress's budget office had exceeded all expectations in terms of its credibility and influence.

Even at the time, many key players in the administration were uncomfortable with the pledge to follow CBO numbers. In an interview, former Clinton budget director Leon Panetta explained much later that, while he found the pledge personally difficult as OMB director, "it was really a political weapon. . . . it made sense to pull the rug out from under those that might have been critical."[72] In retrospect, however, the perception of CBO as Democrat-controlled was so strong among many House Republicans by this point that there was no way that pledging to abide by CBO numbers was going to help Clinton win any Republican support for his 1993 deficit reduction plan. He chose a risky strategy that backfired on him later, both in the fight over health care reform (see chapter 6) and after the Republicans took over Congress. Alice Rivlin later argued in testimony before Congress that another reason for the use of CBO numbers was simply that OMB had not had enough time to develop its own forecast; by its midsession review six months later, it had gone back to using OMB assumptions.[73]

As with the 1990 budget agreement, CBO's role in 1993 was largely responding to the agenda by costing out proposals. Unlike 1990, when there was a budget summit, however, the 1993 process was a normal one (albeit one where the Democrats were negotiating with each other). Budgetary changes were adopted within the context of the regular budget process. It began by adopting a budget resolution, and then proceeded to enact reconciliation and appropriation bills. This meant that CBO played a central behind-the-scenes role by establishing the starting point (the baseline) and by costing out the proposals that committees were required to devise to meet their reconciliation targets. Although the final package itself was controversial, CBO's role—in contrast to the one it played when the Reagan program was enacted and during the GRH era—was lower profile.

Perhaps one of the most significant roles for CBO in this debate related to the president's promise to present a plan including at least as much deficit reduction from spending cuts as from tax increases. CBO, as a part of the debate, apparently was asked to certify that the ratio was one-to-one. In fact, in a July 1993 op-ed piece, OMB deputy director Rivlin noted that the president had proposed an exactly one-to-one ratio of tax increases to spending cuts and that CBO had certified this ratio as having been met.[74]

The Clinton plan eventually became law when the Omnibus Budget Reconciliation Act of 1993 passed Congress (without a single Republican vote) and was signed by President Clinton in August 1993. At the time the president argued that the plan was the largest in history, specifically noting that the amount of deficit reduction ($496 billion over five years) exceeded the amount included in President Bush's ($482 billion over five years) plan. In the CBO's summer update, it praised the Clinton budget deal but poked holes in these estimates, arguing that largely because some savings counted by Clinton were already assumed in the 1990 agreement, the marginal deficit reduction under the Clinton plan was actually $433 billion, which was lower in both nominal and real terms than the Bush package had been.[75]

If the first year of the Clinton presidency was dominated by the broader economic package, health care reform dominated the agenda in the second. CBO had a significant role to play in the health care debate, particularly given the president's pledge to lower health care costs while ensuring coverage to those Americans without health insurance. CBO's role in the Clinton plan is outlined in great detail in chapter 6. Basically, it centered on the cost of the legislation and the extent to which the president was proposing a government or private-sector solution. The White House considered it essential for the health plan to exist within the larger goal of reducing the deficit. The health plan failed to become law, and many believe it set the stage for the major defeat experienced by the Democratic party in the 1994 congressional midterm elections.

Arguing over Assumptions and Shutting Down the Government

In November 1994 the American people went to the polls and voted for the most significant change in congressional control in forty years. They returned the Republicans to majority position in the Senate for the first time since 1986. More important, they reversed party dominance in the House of Representatives, which Republicans had not controlled since the 1950s. This had immediate effects on both economic policy priorities and forecasting assumptions in Congress. There were also big implications for CBO.

The Republican agenda was driven by the so-called Contract with America, a wide-ranging set of policy prescriptions that had been signed by virtually all Republican would-be House members. This agenda included many economic and budget issues: for example, a balanced budget constitutional amendment, a line-item veto for the president, rules to make it more difficult to enact tax increases, and regulatory reform measures. More generally, it flipped the focus of debate. In the first Clinton administration, economic policy had focused on tax increases and expanding entitlements. In the second, Congress was interested in curtailing entitlement spending and ultimately decreasing taxes.

As explained in chapter 2, the most immediate consequence for CBO was the selection of June O'Neill as the new director. During the first year of Republican return to majority status, expectations that CBO would embrace dynamic analysis predominated. Republican advocates of tax cuts viewed it as a method that would facilitate enactment of revenue reductions. Dynamic scoring is the intellectual heir of supply-side economics. Advocates theorize that revenue reductions can generate enough economic growth to offset many (if not all, in some cases) revenue losses. New Speaker Gingrich and many of his House colleagues had decried prior CBO and Joint Committee on Taxation estimates as socialist, and looked for a dramatic change in analytic practice in the agency. However, some Republican senators, including Domenici and Dole, were less supportive of dynamic scoring changes.[76]

Sympathy toward dynamic scoring had been seen as a necessary qualification for a new CBO director. In addition, the House Republicans reportedly wanted any new director to make significant staff changes. Long-time staff, including the incumbent deputy director, Jim Blum, were seen as sympathetic to Democrats and hostile to Republican notions of good policy. This was more than an academic argument. Because large federal deficits persisted, even after the Bush and Clinton deficit reduction deals, static analyses of tax cuts threatened their viability. Ultimately, the selection of O'Neill, who was clearly the choice of the House Republicans (and particularly Newt Gingrich, because House Budget Committee chair John Kasich was not familiar with her), mollified the right wing of the party. They believed that she would both shake up CBO staff and make the CBO analyses more favorably disposed towards supporting Republican tax-cutting policies.

The new Congress and President Clinton were at odds over two key components of the Republican policy. First, the Republicans had pledged to eliminate the federal budget deficit in seven years, using CBO assumptions. The administration, which had long since returned to using more optimistic OMB assumptions, had wanted to do so in ten years. Second, Republicans (particularly House Republicans) had promised to cut taxes, which would put extra downward pressure on expenditures and might make the elimination of the deficit even more difficult, dynamic scoring notwithstanding.

Largely ignoring the president's fiscal year 1996 budget, Congress immediately set out to adopt a budget resolution that met their goal of achieving a balanced budget within seven years. Operating from a position of political weakness, Clinton eventually responded to the plan by offering one he argued would achieve a balanced budget at the end of ten years.[77] In offering such a plan, he reversed course by acknowledging that the twin goals of deficit reduction and cutting taxes could be achieved simultaneously, alienating some within his own party.[78] Clinton's new proposal, however, still used OMB numbers. When it was subjected to a CBO analysis, that analysis argued that, far from achieving a balanced budget within ten years, the deficit at the end of that time under the Clinton plan would be $209 billion.

This foreshadowed what turned out to be the major conflict of the fiscal year 1996 budget debate, played out through the rest of calendar year 1995 and into 1996. Whereas the White House insisted on using OMB baseline estimates as a starting point for any balanced budget plan, Congress wanted the administration to use CBO numbers. The political difference between the two options was substantial. Because the OMB baseline was more optimistic, the president could achieve balance with far fewer spending cuts than would need to occur using congressional assumptions. This, coupled with the fact that the ten-year path was easier than a seven-year path no matter whose assumptions were used made it a matter of some consequence for the president that he use his own budget office's numbers.[79] Baseline differences between the two budget offices were actually relatively small, but were magnified when extended for ten years and viewed in the context of meeting a particular target in a particular year.[80]

At this point in the negotiation, Congress ignored the president, working out a conference agreement on a seven-year balanced budget plan (using CBO assumptions) and adopting that plan on June 22, 1995.[81] This set the stage for the drafting of a mammoth reconciliation bill for Congress to consider later in the summer. It effectively relegated the executive branch to a bit player role at this point, but everyone understood that it would be necessary to gain presidential assent on the reconciliation bill, a difficult prospect at best.

To achieve a balanced budget by fiscal year 2002, including a tax cut, Congress was relying on what CBO referred to as a fiscal dividend. The existence of this potential dividend had first been raised in testimony by outgoing director Reischauer in January 1995. He had argued then that a balanced budget would lead to lower interest payments and higher economic growth, and therefore higher revenues. He put the value of the dividend at $140 billion over seven years (later revised to $170 billion).[82] The estimated dividend equaled approximately two-thirds of the tax cut that was included in Congress's balanced budget plan.[83] The fiscal dividend is a dynamic concept. The logic posits broader economic benefit from a proposed policy—balancing the budget—that feeds back into the budget in the form of lower spending and higher revenues. There is an obvious irony here. This dividend had first been identified by Reischauer, not O'Neill. Despite this clear evidence to the contrary, many congressional Republicans continued to insist that the CBO did only static analyses and did not factor in the economic effects of policies when estimating their effects.

The budget battle continued through the summer and into the fall. Congress and the president agreed on a series of continuing resolutions designed to keep the government operating. Both sides braced for the possible train wreck that would come when Congress presented the reconciliation bill to the president, which was almost certain to result in a presidential veto. The veto would then result in a threatened government shutdown, because congressional Republicans were holding up most of the appropriation bills pending the president's approval of the reconciliation legislation.

Then something remarkable happened—remarkable at least in the real world, but perhaps not in the sometimes surreal world of federal budgetary politics. Significant portions of the federal government were actually shut down because of political dispute over whether the balanced budget plan produced by the president would be scored as achieving balance by CBO (as Congress wanted) or OMB (as the president advocated). The specter of ceasing federal activity over whose budget assumptions to use seems odd enough on its face. It appears particularly absurd when examining what this means about the evolution of the Republican and Democratic party positions in a little less than three years. The Republicans in Congress, who had laughed at Clinton's intent to use CBO numbers in 1993, *now demanded that he do so*. Clinton, who in 1993 said that CBO numbers had been historically more accurate than OMB numbers, *now insisted on using OMB numbers*.[84] Why this change? The Republican Congress could not have spending cuts at the level desired if OMB numbers were used. The corollary was that the budget would not be balanced without greater spending cuts than the president desired unless relatively more optimistic OMB numbers were used. Further, of course, the norm was well established that administrations used OMB numbers; the previous use of CBO assumptions had been a rather uncomfortable departure from this, according to Leon Panetta.[85]

These differences between the administration and Congress had been illustrated earlier that summer during a remarkable hearing of the House Budget Committee, where OMB director Alice Rivlin (founding CBO director, to add to the irony) was repeatedly raked over the coals for failure to use CBO assumptions. Chairman Kasich chastised the administration for the lack of a serious plan, which was defined as "something that withstood the rigors of CBO." He argued that the president had broken his own pledge, made in 1993, to use CBO numbers.[86] To make his point, he replayed a tape of the portion of the president's speech to Congress when he had promised to do so. One after another, Republican members of the House Budget Committee grilled Rivlin over what they argued was a reversal by the Clinton administration, and that the failure to use CBO numbers was designed intentionally to cook the books. Rivlin countered that the differences between the two were small, that both were credible, and that working out a baseline was a possibility. She further argued that in fact the administration had used CBO numbers only once, in the context of their original deficit reduction plan. All subsequent presidential budget submissions had used OMB numbers. This revelation occasioned the following exchange between Rivlin and Representative Jim Kolbe (R-AZ):

MS. RIVLIN: I think the portion of the tape implies that the President promised he would use CBO numbers forever. In fact, we only used CBO numbers once, in February 1993. Since then, without any objection from Congress, we have used, as administrations must, our own forecasting and estimating capabilities.

MR. KOLBE: Now I must interrupt you. I mean we may have unearthed here today what may be the greatest monumental flip-flop in the Clinton administration. Now we are hearing that we only promised to use CBO for one year. I do not remember on that tape saying that this was going to be used for one year. I do not remember anything of that sort being said.

CHAIRMAN KASICH: Maybe we can go back and replay the tape.

MR. KOLBE: Well, we could if we need to replay the tape here. But this strikes me as we have unearthed a whopper here today. This is like a double, triple, off-the-diving-board flip here, as we go into the water here.

MS. RIVLIN: Absolutely not. Did you not notice when Leon Panetta came to present the "Mid-Session Review" in the summer of 1993, or when he came back to present the 1994 budget, or when I was presenting the last budget, that we were using our own numbers? Did you not notice that?[87]

Ultimately, Congress and the administration did not reach agreement in time to avert a partial government shutdown that began on November 16. Several portions of the government were shut down, but Congress did finally pass the seven-year balanced budget bill, preparing to send it to the president. The first government shutdown ended on November 19, 1995, when Congress and the president agreed on a continuing resolution that would keep the government operating until December 15. The resolution included language requiring a CBO-scored balanced budget plan, specifically, that Congress and the president come up with a plan by the end of the year to balance the budget, using CBO numbers.[88]

Specific text of the relevant sections of the resolution follows (emphasis added):

(a) The President and the Congress shall enact legislation in the first session of the 104th Congress to achieve a balanced budget no later than fiscal year 2002 *as estimated by the Congressional Budget Office*, and the President and Congress agree that the balanced budget must protect future generations, ensure Medicare solvency, reform welfare and provide adequate funding for Medicaid, education, agriculture, national defense, veterans and the environment. Further, the balanced budget shall adopt tax policies to help working families and to stimulate future economic growth.

(b) *The balanced-budget agreement shall be estimated by the Congressional Budget Office based on its most recent current economic and technical assumptions, following a thorough consultation and review with the Office of Management and Budget and other government and private experts.*[89]

This seemed to resolve the issue. However, both sides immediately began debating what these words meant. The White House said that it only meant that CBO would evaluate the deal after-the-fact. Republicans argued that it meant that OMB needed to use the CBO baseline to craft its plan.[90]

CBO's new economic forecast issued in mid-December actually made the prospects of reaching agreement a bit brighter. The revised budget projection made the balanced budget goal marginally easier to achieve. The seven-year baseline projection improved by $135 billion, but most of this improvement came in the early years, with year six and year seven numbers virtually unchanged.[91] Nevertheless, more optimistic numbers made an agreement easier to reach, provided the sides had an interest in reaching an agreement.

Unfortunately, it was not enough. On December 18, 1995, a second federal government shutdown began. Again, the sticking point was the failure of the president to put a budget proposal on the table that used CBO assumptions and balanced the budget in seven years. The day after the shutdown took effect key congressional leaders from both sides of the aisle indicated that Clinton had said that he would be willing to use CBO assumptions. Indeed, a December 18 floor vote provided a sense of Congress that the president should use CBO numbers; in an indication of how politically weak the Clinton administration was, the vote was 351 to 40, with 115 Democrats crossing over and joining virtually all Republicans in voting for the resolution.[92]

Clinton took until January 7, 1996, when he ended the shutdown by presenting a seven-year plan based on CBO assumptions. CBO certified that its baseline had been used throughout. There was a big difference, however, between using agreed-upon economic assumptions to meet this condition and reaching agreement on details, and a wide gulf between the two plans. The president's plan balanced the budget by both cutting taxes and spending less than the Republican plan.[93]

In a highly unusual development, while preparing this new plan, Clinton administration staff came to CBO specifically to discuss economic assumptions with CBO staff. This meeting had been brokered by the White House and Speaker Gingrich. According to June O'Neill, "we had this session where everyone came—Joe Stiglitz, and Larry Summers, and Joe Minarik were there—the administration sent all their big guns and we had this long debate about economic assumptions and what they should be."[94] In the end, this meeting was more notable for being held than for the result; no changes to CBO's forecast resulted.[95]

In the end, of course, there were no more government shutdowns and no balanced budget plan, at least in 1996. Congress ultimately decided that further government shutdowns were not in its interest, in large part because opinion polls showed that it was blamed for them more than the president was. The president decided that it was not in his interest to reach agreement on a balanced budget plan, but rather to use the battle to show his sharp differences with the Republican nominee in the 1996 presidential election.

The country had been treated to the rare spectacle of two government shutdowns, precipitated by arguments over whose budget assumptions—CBO's or OMB's—to use in the debate. If doubts lingered that the 1974 Budget Act had made Congress full partners in the budget process, they were eliminated by the 1995 and 1996 budget debacle. It seems impossible to consider such a showdown taking place under the pre-1974 process.

The 1997 Balanced Budget Plan

Clinton was reelected in 1996, as was a majority Republican Congress. Both sides pledged to continue to focus on eliminating the federal deficit. Further, neither side saw a repeat of the 1995–96 government shutdown as in their interest. Therefore, the odds of reaching some kind of a balanced budget accord were vastly improved as the president took office for his second term. Details of such a plan, however, remained elusive.

The environment was seemingly improved when CBO revised, substantially, the economic forecast that would underlie its January 1997 annual report. In a somewhat unusual move, CBO presaged the improvement in its forecast in

November (after the election).[96] This had the effect of also easing the environment surrounding the president's budget for fiscal year 1998. Clinton had pledged to rely on CBO estimates in presenting a balanced budget plan, one that had the federal deficit falling to 0 by fiscal year 2002.[97]

The president submitted his budget in February 1997, arguing that if it were enacted, a balanced budget by fiscal year 2002 would be possible. In its annual review of presidential budgets, CBO questioned this conclusion. The March 1997 CBO analysis, which used the president's policies but CBO economic and technical assumptions, concluded that the president's proposed plan would instead result in a deficit of $69 billion by 2002. In fact the differences between CBO and OMB numbers were small, but the rhetorical significance of "getting to 0 in 2002 using CBO numbers" was so substantial by that point that even small differences tended to be magnified in debate.

Throughout the spring of 1997, as the budget resolution was being drafted on Capitol Hill, the House and Senate leadership negotiated with the White House on the fundamentals. They eventually narrowed the gap between them on a plan to balance the budget by 2002 to as little as $50 billion over five years. Then something happened that changed the character of the entire negotiation. In a letter written to members of the House and Senate Budget Committees, CBO director O'Neill revealed that, based on more recent economic data, CBO had concluded that it had significantly underestimated federal revenues, to the tune of $45 billion annually over five years. In effect, this resulted in a five-year windfall of $225 billion for budget negotiators.[98] This was extraordinary not because CBO changed its forecast—this, as we have seen, happens frequently. It was unusual because CBO's revised forecast would not normally come out until August. O'Neill made a conscious choice to release its estimates early. This was done because CBO knew that negotiations were ongoing, and that if the new forecast changed the underlying baseline on which those negotiations were based, the White House and Congress should know that.[99] The new figures therefore came out at precisely the moment they were most likely to influence the ongoing budget negotiations. As Irene Rubin recounted, the timing was a bit suspicious to some: "The seeming magic of the last-minute found money made some observers skeptical of what underlay the estimates for the out-years."[100]

According to CBO participants, what was referred to as the May surprise was not the by-product of any conscious effort to make life easier for the negotiators. Rather, it resulted from the supposed discovery of new revenues from a normal and relatively routine process. Each month, CBO deputy director Jim Blum and assistant director for tax analysis Rosemary Marcuss reviewed the Treasury Department's monthly statement for evidence of any deviations from trends in revenue or spending assumed in the baseline. The analysis of the February and March statements had suggested the possibility of a revision, but had not concluded that such a revision was inevitable. When their review of the April 1997 statement (April being, of course, an important month for federal revenues) confirmed the higher-than-expected revenues, this seemed to make it all but inevitable that the revenue figures in the August update would be revised significantly upward.

There was little doubt about the fiscal year 1997 numbers. The debate concerned whether the trend was likely to continue for the next four years, and whether these increased revenues were likely to be reflected in CBO's August update. In the end, CBO decided that they were, and decided that the only responsible thing to do was to release them early. This was viewed as particularly important because the CBO analysis of the monthly Treasury statement was routinely made available to the House and Senate budget committees, other interested committees in the Congress, OMB, and others in the executive branch. Therefore the option of sitting on the information did not exist; the only question was whether to publicize the information even more widely.[101] O'Neill noted that she "felt quite strongly that we should give some public recognition to the fact that this [the changes in the economy leading to increased revenues] had happened."[102]

This budgetary windfall was not universally viewed as helpful. It came as an agreement was imminent, and was viewed by some with skepticism because of concern over potential adverse effects. Because Congress was interested in cutting spending more than the president, the lessening of pressure to cut spending could have resulted in congressional Republicans backing away from a deal. There was a precedent for this from 1995. Some had concerns that more positive forecasts took pressure off policymakers to address the long-term problems associated with entitlement spending.

Barry Anderson, at the time the top civil servant within OMB (later deputy director of CBO), recalled receiving an angry phone call from OMB director Franklin Raines, who was upset because the sudden appearance of more revenue had the effect of disrupting the delicate negotiations between the White House and Congress. Once the assumptions that had governed the negotiations changed, pressure to reopen the entire debate mounted. Blum recalled receiving a call from Bill Hoagland, the Senate Budget Committee staff director, saying in effect, "what are you doing, don't you know this is going to upset the negotiations?"[103] On the other hand, some Democrats may have been happy because the discovery of additional cash obviated the need to make cutbacks in some benefit programs, particularly by modifying the consumer price index in a way that would decrease some government benefits.[104]

Whether the CBO revision made an agreement temporarily difficult to achieve, the result was that the White House and Congress were able to craft a deal that had a little bit for everyone. There were tax cuts, against the administration's wishes, but not as many or for as many people as the Republicans wanted. There were spending cuts, more than the administration wanted to support but also not nearly as many as the majority in Congress wanted. What had eluded both sides in 1995—a compromise—finally was achieved, but only with the help of an improving economy that made the budget-balancing job much easier. By the time of CBO's summer update in August 1997, the agency had certified that the Balanced Budget Act of 1997 would indeed result in a $32 billion surplus in fiscal year 2002.[105] By the time of the president's fiscal year 1999 budget and the CBO January 1998 annual report, both OMB and CBO were forecasting a return to surplus not by 2002, but by much sooner than that. Both analyses showed only small deficits for fiscal year 1998, and forecast surpluses for 1999 and beyond.[106]

Ultimately, O'Neill's tenure as director coincided with a significant turnaround in federal budgetary outcomes. When she took office, the federal budget was still projected to show a large structural deficit. A combination of legislation (the 1990, 1993, and 1997 deficit reduction agreements) and continued improvement in the economy yielded a balanced budget in fiscal year 1998. This balance came a full four years earlier than projected after the 1997 agreement.

Even this major accomplishment, however, carried with it some controversy for CBO. What proved to be underforecasting of revenue by CBO (and others) angered some Republicans. They believed that the 1997 tax cut could have been larger had they known that the underlying revenue situation was more positive.[107] The agency continued to come under attack—mostly from Republican circles— because of the inaccuracy of its forecasts. Some House Republicans wished to seize on an improved budgetary picture to engineer another tax reduction before the 1998 midterm elections. They were counting on a further improvement in the outlook to be presented in the agency's summer update, hoping that this change would pave the way for these larger tax cuts. When this did not occur, they threatened retribution against both CBO and O'Neill, whose term as director was to expire in January 1999.[108] In fact, Speaker Gingrich threatened CBO's funding openly, in a letter to House appropriations subcommittee chair James Walsh (R-NY), by pointing out that CBO's budget estimates "have been consistently wrong—and wrong by a country mile."[109] House Majority Whip Tom Delay (R-TX) was even more direct: "When a team bats zero, you get new players. We cannot run this House unless CBO makes more accurate projections."[110] But O'Neill wondered later how serious the concerns about CBO estimates really were:

> At our appropriations hearing, this one member came in and made a speech— "We always fire the CEO when they can't balance the books." And then he went into this tirade about dynamic scoring and "CBO is too dumb headed to recognize dynamic scoring," although I hadn't presented anything that was to be dynamically scored. Afterwards I said, "if you're so unhappy, I would really be happy to come and talk to you, because you seem to have a lot of problems with CBO and with this dynamic scoring." And he said, "I don't even know what dynamic scoring is. I have no beef against CBO. Somebody handed me this thing to read". . . . So a lot of that goes on.[111]

CBO director O'Neill did not budge in response to these criticisms. She was clear that she would take recommendations from anyone about CBO's methods, but equally direct in saying that "the final judgment of what we do has to be independently arrived at or it's worthless. If CBO is perceived as playing favorites, it can't function."[112] Undoubtedly, the fights with the House Republican leadership, who had championed her appointment four years earlier, contributed to O'Neill's decision to return to academia when her term expired.[113] Although she stood her ground on the importance of CBO's independence, news reports suggested that she was unlikely to be reappointed.[114] These disagreements certainly got attention in the press, but O'Neill's view of her meetings with Speaker Gingrich, particularly over macro budgetary issues (as opposed to cost estimates, for example) were actually quite cordial. Further, by her report she was not afraid of being fired.

> The two or three times that I went with Bob Dennis [the head of the Macroeconomic Analysis Division] to talk about how we did the estimates, there was always a bunch of reporters saying "Did he fire you? Did he fire you?" but actually, one of the things that is beneficial about being an academic in that job is that you have a place to go to. There really isn't much that they can threaten you with. And I had basically exhausted all the [academic] leaves I could exhaust, so I really had no intention of staying on. . . . It wasn't a personal concern of mine.[115]

CBO and the Surplus and Return to Deficits

Fiscal year 1998, the last full year of the O'Neill tenure, was the first year since 1969 in which the federal government had run a budget surplus. The macrobudgetary questions that dominated the initial period of O'Neill's successor, Dan Crippen, centered on disposing of the surplus, rather than what to do about the deficit—which had dominated at least the previous fifteen years. By the end of Crippen's tenure, however, owing in part to the Bush tax cuts and also to the budgetary and economic effect of September 11, the large forecasted deficits had returned.

The selection of Crippen as CBO director rekindled the ongoing debate about dynamic scoring. Many believed that Crippen, who had been a White House aide under President Reagan, would bring supply-side methodology to CBO analyses. This view may have always been a bit ill placed. Crippen had worked for Senator Howard Baker and his chief congressional sponsor for the CBO job was Senator Domenici. Neither Baker nor Domenici could have been described as avid supply-siders.

CBO found it necessary during the Crippen era to serve as the arbiter of the parties' pledge to save the Social Security surplus. By early 2000, once it was clear that the goal of budgetary balance had been achieved, both parties agreed that, going forward, the budgetary norm should be to balance the budget, excluding the Social Security surpluses. This issue surfaced at the end of the Clinton presidency, when Democrats used CBO analyses of appropriation bills to charge that the Republicans were raiding Social Security. This forced the Democrats, at least temporarily, to rethink their notion that Crippen was the darling of the Republican right.[116]

This issue, of course, was of little economic significance. It was important because any party charged with failing to protect Social Security ran the risk of having the other party use that charge to "bludgeon their opponents in next year's elections. Of all the parties in the budget process, only Crippen and the nonpartisan CBO have the credibility to say who is right."[117] The agreement to save the Social Security surpluses held until the tragic events of September 11, when the needs (real and perceived) to spend funds on homeland security and then fighting wars in Afghanistan and Iraq took precedence over the Social Security issue.[118]

The surplus dominated the macrobudgetary picture during Crippen's tenure. The 1997 balanced budget plan had predicted that surpluses would first show up in fiscal year 2002. They arrived much earlier than that; the federal government had surpluses not only in 1998 (the last year O'Neill was director) but in fiscal years 1999 and 2000. Then, in probably the key forecast of the Crippen era, CBO in January 2001 projected in its annual report that baseline surpluses would total $5.6 trillion between fiscal year 2002 and 2011.[119] They were careful to note that, as always, this projection represented the midpoint of what was a substantial possible range of outcomes, especially in the out years. This baseline estimate was fully consistent (in fact almost identical), however, to the OMB estimate included in the baseline budget submitted by President Bush two months later, and paved the way for the Bush tax cuts of both 2001 and 2003.[120] In fact, immediately on receiving word of the forecast, White House spokesman Ari Fleischer seized on it by declaring that the "government is awash in surplus money. There's plenty of room for cutting taxes."[121]

A significant decision had paved the way for the role these estimates ultimately played. Through 1995, CBO baseline projections had covered five years. Starting in 1996, however, the budget committees began to insist that CBO do ten-year baselines and cost estimates. This was done when the budget was still in deficit, to gain better information on longer-term effects of legislative changes. This was in turn done in large part to combat the tendency of some in Congress to push the costs of new legislation outside of the five-year estimating window, thus hiding the ultimate cost. By 2001, however, the ten-year estimates had a different effect. They showed substantial future surpluses, thus making for a smoother path for tax cuts and spending increases. However, the basic analytic problem is that ten-year numbers tend not to be very reliable, and therefore are not a very good basis for long-term policy. As Douglas Holtz-Eakin argued, "if I had my druthers I wouldn't do ten-year estimates. I'd do one, five and fifty. The ten-year window is something that Congress wanted. We delivered it. You try to educate people on the point estimate versus the trajectory. How much it's induced policy, I don't know. It's certainly induced legislation to be written in a certain way. Think of tax policy in the current context. The administration's policy hasn't been altered a bit. The laws that they pass to support it have sunsets, and phase-ins."[122]

In any event, once again in 2001, as was true in 1990, in 1993, and in 1997, a CBO analysis was used in determining the path for broad budget policy. The difference was that the 2001 policy was not deficit reduction, but instead surplus reduction. There is little doubt that the CBO estimates made it much easier to enact the Bush tax cuts. In fact, Federal Reserve Board chairman Alan Greenspan, who had been a deficit hawk through the 1990s, declared in early 2001 that he thought the time was right to cut taxes.[123] Never mind that the CBO analyses in the past had often proven wrong, particularly for the out years. Never mind that CBO itself admonished Congress not to pay too much attention to its point estimates because they occupied the middle ground of a rather substantial range. The Bush tax cuts went forward. The combination of those cuts, the war on terrorism, and the weakening economy led to a staggering revision of the CBO forecast by January 2002. In their annual report issued that year, CBO forecast a $4 trillion drop in ten-year surpluses from the $5.6 trillion forecast only one year earlier.[124]

In addition, an internal controversy developed over what might seem a minor symbolic issue. Crippen and Anderson sought to change the nature of the covers of CBO reports to communicate more clearly the main messages contained within the reports. Previously these covers had been somewhat bland and uninteresting, if not outright obscure. (An infamous cover of a report from the early 1990s pictured men in top hats peering at columns of numbers.) Crippen and Anderson thought that the cover of the reports should communicate the main idea or ideas of the report. The practical effect of this was to take a graph that represented a highlighted trend in a given report and putting that graph on the cover. Some longtime staff balked at this change, feeling that the practice encouraged the message to be taken out of context. In their view, the report should speak for itself, and should offer only analysis, rather than implicit "sound bites."[125] The practice, however, continues to this day, with little apparent residual controversy or damage to CBO's credibility.

By the time that Crippen's successor, Douglas Holtz-Eakin, was selected as CBO director in February 2003, the budget outlook had changed so dramatically that all of the forecast surpluses had been wiped out. The dynamic scoring debate remained. Crippen had made several statements that were skeptical, if not outright critical, of dynamic scoring in the six months prior to his departure. Len Burman, who had been at CBO and had worked in the Clinton Treasury Department, recalled that Crippen told Congress, "you want us to tell you that when you cut taxes it is going to make the economy grow [but] . . . the answers are all clustered around zero."[126] Because Holtz-Eakin had worked in the Bush

White House, however, it was expected that he might be more sympathetic to the growth effects of the Bush proposals than his predecessors had been.[127]

Holtz-Eakin did decide very early in his term that the agency would provide a dynamic score of President Bush's fiscal year 2004 budget, which the president would present in early 2003. He reported that he got some pushback from career staff when he proposed this, but ultimately insisted that the agency would provide such scoring of the president's budget.[128] In their annual analysis of the president's budget, issued on March 25, 2003, Holtz-Eakin surprised both skeptical Democrats and expectant Republicans by finding very little economic feedback effects from the president's policies. The agency found that though tax cuts in the budget would increase economic growth, the positive effects associated with tax changes would be almost entirely offset by the negative effects of cutting spending. CBO used nine dynamic models to evaluate the Bush budget, and the vast majority indicated that the dynamic effects did not markedly lessen future deficits.[129] This openly challenged the Bush administration assumption that the tax reductions in the president's budget would generate enough positive feedback to pay for 40 percent of them.[130]

Holtz-Eakin recalled that he did not view dynamic scoring to be that big a deal, and that it was not much of a departure from what CBO had been doing. He explained in an interview not long after being appointed that he believed that dynamic analysis was "scientifically correct," but that he was unwilling to take a dynamic look at some of the president's policies and not others; in particular, to look at taxes but not spending.[131] In 2004 he explained it this way:

> It's one of the great ironies of the whole thing that somehow I became the poster boy for dynamic scoring. We don't [estimate] the tax legislation, which is where all the heat is. So the only vehicle we had was the president's budget, because that's the only place where things are spelled out enough. . . . So all it really amounted to was taking what CBO usually does, which are baseline budget projections where policy affects the economy, and then imagining you snapped your fingers and put in place an entirely new budgetary policy as presented by the president and seeing what you would do for your baseline, and then comparing the difference.[132]

In addition to dynamic scoring, the other notable development in macrobudgetary forecasting during the early 2000s was the decline of the baseline, as defined by law and custom, as a useful measure of the budgetary future. The CBO baseline had always been somewhat limited in its forecasting utility because CBO is required, by law, to assume the continuation of current law in its baseline. For revenues and mandatory spending this means that CBO estimates the budgetary effects of continuing current law into the future. For discretionary spending, this typically means assuming that discretionary appropriations grow with inflation.

The problem in the early part of the twenty-first century was that both of these assumptions seemed particularly distant from reality. In the case of revenues, because the Bush tax cut had a number of sunset provisions designed to lower its reported cost, the baseline was only an accurate forecast assuming that these provisions were actually allowed to expire. Further, the baseline assumed the continuation of the alternative minimum tax (AMT), because current law stipulated that it would continue, in spite of increasing pressure to modify it in a way to affect fewer taxpayers.[133] In addition to these issues on the tax side, the CBO role during this period was related to estimating the uncertain costs associated with several expensive spending issues that dominated:

- The Medicare prescription drug bill, which was enacted in 2003, had a $400 billion cap under the budget resolution, and was estimated by CBO to cost $395 billion. Later estimates by CBO and the Bush administration indicated that these early cost estimates were understated. Even later, CBO suggested that the rate of enrollment in the prescription drug plan was lower than expected, so that the initial estimate might have actually been too high (for more detail on the prescription drug bill, see chapter 4).
- The costs of military actions in Iraq and Afghanistan were highly uncertain, particularly given the difficulty of predicting the length of time that continued deployment would be necessary.
- A tragic and very expensive 2005 hurricane season created huge demands on the budget, both for initial response to Hurricanes Katrina and Rita and for reconstruction after the fact.
- In 2008, a major disruption of the global financial system, driven by the collapse of the US mortgage market and the banking sector's investment in risky mortgage-backed securities, led to a number of costly interventions by the government into the private sector, and decisions to provide costly infusions of capital into banks and other private institutions.

CBO responded to this uncertainty by informing Congress not only about what would happen under current law and current policy, but also about the cost of making changes to the status quo. In its January 2009 report, for example, CBO noted that if all of the tax provisions scheduled to expire were continued, if the Congress fixed the alternative minimum tax so that it affected fewer taxpayers, and if discretionary spending continued to grow at its recent annual rate, these changes would add $6.2 trillion to the ten-year baseline deficit figures.[134] Uncertainty of the cost associated with these events made the CBO projections perhaps less reliable—and possibly least helpful of any projections made over the agency's history—because the projections were forced to assume events that seemed increasingly unlikely to materialize.

In addition to the sheer costs of these new policies, the budget process itself was under significant pressure during the early 2000s. Something that had been unheard of in the first twenty-two years—the failure to adopt a budget resolution—became routine after 1998. In fact, for four of the next nine fiscal years—1999, 2003, 2005, and 2007—there was no budget resolution. Over this period, the Republican congressional majority argued that, to the extent that the PAYGO process was reinstituted, it should apply to spending increases and not tax cuts. At the conclusion of his term, Crippen angered some in the Congress by arguing in blunt (perhaps too blunt) terms that the budget process was dead.[135]

The bottom line is that CBO after 2002 was operating in an environment in which all consensus on the proper target for fiscal discipline had broken down. In such an environment, CBO continued to provide information on the ever-increasing deficit three times per year, and very little attention was paid to that information.[136] By January 2009, given the alarming scope of actions that had been taken to rescue the economy, the budget deficit finally was projected to exceed $1 trillion per year. In fact, the CBO report issued during that month pro-jected a baseline deficit of $1.2 trillion in fiscal year 2009, without accounting for the cost of an economic stimulus.[137] The actual fiscal year 2009 deficit exceeded $1.4 trillion.[138] Not only would a deficit of this size exceed the 2008 deficit of $455 bil-lion (a record in nominal dollars) by almost $1 trillion, but it would represent almost 10 percent of GDP, significantly higher than the previous post–World War II deficit of 6.0 percent of GDP in fiscal year 1983. It would also mean that the deficit in-creased by more than 6 percent of GDP in a single year (2008 to 2009); a one-year increase this large has occurred only once in the United States, between fiscal years 1942 and 1943, directly after Pearl Harbor.[139] By January 2010, CBO informed Congress that the actual deficit for 2009 was $1.4 trillion, and estimated that the fiscal year 2010 deficit would decline only slightly, to $1.35 trillion (9.2 percent of GDP).[140]

By mid-2010 it was unclear how the federal government was going to extricate itself from these long-term structural deficits. A baseline that included policy changes in the fiscal year 2010 budget projected that more than $10 trillion would be added to deficits between fiscal years 2011 and 2020, in other words, that the average deficit would be more than $1 trillion annually.[141] CBO's analysis of the Obama fiscal year 2011 budget indicated that the president's policies, if enacted, would reduce those average annual deficits by only $100 million (10 percent) per year.[142] The continued imbalance caused the president to appoint a commission, the majority of which was made up of Republican and Democratic members of Congress, to make recommendations on how to reduce federal deficits, but only after the 2010 midterm congressional elections.[143]

CBO and Long-Term Forecasting

The late-Crippen and early–Holtz-Eakin-period also marked the ascendancy of long-term forecasting (that is, fifty to seventy-five years) at CBO. Beginning in the early 1980s, concerns began to arise that the federal government would be unable to sustain funding for the major programs—Medicare and Social Security—that provided funds for senior citizens. Although both programs had become more generous over time, a major culprit was demographics. The retirement of the Baby Boomers would create a bubble of beneficiaries and (most important) drive down the ratio of current workers, whose payroll taxes are used to finance benefits and current beneficiaries.

CBO's role in this debate had been to periodically make note of the problem when advising members of Congress on the desirability of reducing federal budget deficits. The arrival of the surplus, and the political imperative to save Social Security, led CBO to conclude that expanding its long-term forecasting capability would enable it to better contribute to the important future policy debates surrounding Social Security and Medicare. Accordingly, CBO issued periodic reports on long-term budget pressures beginning in 1997.

It is worth noting, however, that Dan Crippen in particular started CBO on the path of identifying it as central to CBO's mission to illuminate these longer-term fiscal policy debates. Accordingly, in May 2000 he did something unusual, at least for a CBO director—he wrote an op-ed piece for the *Washington Post*.[144] In this article he identified the Social Security problem as not about trust fund insolvency, but instead the economic sustainability of Social Security and other programs. This decision was not without some controversy. Crippen was criticized by some people who believed that he had stepped over the bounds of what a CBO director should say by some explicit comments concerning Social Security. There is, further, every reason to believe that both Crippen and Anderson wanted to illuminate the Social Security debate, and particularly the debate, early in the Bush administration, about private accounts.[145]

A long-term forecast required a long-term model, which in effect created a competitor for the Social Security Administration's (SSA) Office of the Chief Actuary, which had historically been viewed as the estimator of record concerning the program's long-term health. CBO forecast in 2004, for example, that the Social Security trust fund would run out of money in approximately 2052, about ten years later than SSA had projected.[146] This was, notably, not the first time an alternative long-term forecast had been produced. In fact, the GAO had used long-term budget forecasts since the early 1990s, and assumptions about Social Security and Medicare were critical to those models. But they had not purported to explicitly forecast the fiscal health of Social Security, as the CBO analysis did.

Orszag expanded the capacity of CBO to deal with the analytical problems associated with these long-term budget challenges, especially as they related to the increasing costs of the health care programs. In that sense, there was some movement away from focusing on the demographic causes of the longer-term fiscal problems, and much more focus on health care generally, and controlling health care costs specifically.[147]

The emphasis on health reform continued under Elmendorf, particularly in light of President Obama's commitment to health care reform. The president (and Orszag, who became his new budget director) argued that health reform was necessary, not only to reduce costs in the short term and provide benefits to the uninsured, but also to bend the curve over the long term by reducing long-term health care costs. These costs, according to virtually all projections in 2009, would create unsustainable costs going forward, not only for the federal government, but also for the economy.

In this context, Congress during 2009 and 2010 was debating a number of health reform proposals. Although President Obama clearly had particular goals in mind, he eschewed the Clinton-era approach of dropping a fully-formed legislative proposal into the collective lap of Congress in favor of working with congressional committees of jurisdiction to craft a bill that would meet the president's objectives. As in 1993, CBO was charged with estimating the cost of these proposals. And as in that earlier period, this effort made Elmendorf the center of attention in congressional deliberations on health care reform. The CBO role in the 2009–10 health care reform debate is considered in detail in chapter 7.

Conclusion

The CBO has played a central role in the development of budget policy since it was created in 1974, one that can be divided into four related roles.

Focusing the agenda. CBO baseline forecasts have frequently served as the starting point for major changes in budget policy. This was certainly true in 1990, 1993, and 1997 (major deficit reduction efforts), but was also true in 2001, when forecasted large surpluses set the stage for the Bush tax cut.

Estimating the aggregate effects of major budget policies. When Congress or the president decides on overall budget policy, CBO is frequently required to certify that proposed changes in law actually have the budgetary effects required by appropriation legislation. For example, reconciliation bills, as enacted many times since 1981, rely on CBO to estimate compliance with reconciliation targets.

Helping reform the budget process. As a participant in the process, as well as an agency with expertise in budgetary matters, CBO has helped draft many of the rules that have made the process work. For example, CBO assistance was indispensible when it came to converting the Gramm-Rudman-Hollings idea into a workable set of procedures. Additionally, the Federal Credit Reform Act of 1990 was driven in large part by analyses of the failures of existing budgetary accounting to send appropriate signals concerning credit programs.

Strengthening the legislative branch in debates with the White House. If one of the purposes of creating CBO was to enhance the ability of Congress to challenge presidential budget proposals, it has been a rousing success, starting with challenges to the Ford and Carter budgets, becoming more prominent with its analyses of the Reagan economic program, and peaking in the confrontation between Congress and President Clinton in 1995 and 1996.

In light of the federal government's failure to come to grips with both the short- and long-term macro budgetary challenges during the first decade of the twenty-first century, it needs to be said that history also demonstrates the limitations of budget and policy information to influence budget outcomes. Neutrally analyzed and presented information cannot substitute for—or compensate for absence of—political will. Certainly it appears that the existence of CBO may have promoted more realistic budgetary information, and it has certainly made the Congress a stronger player in the budget process. It is hard to imagine that the budget committee, the budget resolution and reconciliation—all institutions and processes that have made the Congress a much more equal player in the budget process and which have decreased the influence of the president—could have been as successful without CBO.[148] Whether that is a credit to CBO or simply makes CBO part of the problem is a matter of some debate.

Notes

1. The best books are Allen Schick, *Congress and Money* (Washington, DC: Urban Institute Press, 1980); Rudolph Penner and Alan Abramson, *Broken Purse Strings* (Washington, DC: Urban Institute Press, 1988); Allen Schick, *The Capacity to Budget* (Washington, DC: Urban Institute Press, 1990); and, most recently, Irene Rubin, *Balancing the Federal Budget: Trimming the Herds or Eating the Seed Corn?* (Boston, MA: Chatham House, 2003).

2. Alice Rivlin, interview with the author, October 23, 2003.

3. Robert Reischauer, interview with the author, March 23, 2004.

4. "The Economy: Greenspan versus Rivlin," *The Economist,* January 31, 1976: 37.

5. Ibid.

6. Hobart Rowan, "Hill Budget Chief Blast Spending Cuts," *Washington Post,* October 22, 1975, A23.

7. Brock Adams (D-WA), Letter to Alice Rivlin, October 28, 1975, National Archives, File 52–98–0003, Box 1.

8. "The $30 Billion Misunderstanding," *National Journal* 9, no. 2 (1977): 62.

9. James L. Rowe Jr., "Doubt Is Cast on Balanced Budget and Jobs Goals," *Washington Post,* December 6, 1977, A1.

10. "Stimulus from Carter Plan Seen Possibly Falling Short," *Washington Post,* February 2, 1978, F1.

11. "Budget Assumptions: A $13 Billion Spending Gap," *National Journal* 11, no. 12 (1979): 468.

12. Art Pine, "Hill Office Estimates '81 Budget Deficit at $24 Billion or More," *Washington Post*, March 6, 1980, A8.

13. Rivlin, interview, 2003.

14. "Two Computers Are Better than One," *Washington Post*, December 12, 1977, A22.

15. Rivlin, interview, 2003.

16. Helen Dewar, "CBO Analysis to Show Administration Falling Short of Budget Goals," *Washington Post*, March 24, 1981, A4.

17. "Counting Up the Costs," *Washington Post*, April 17, 1981, A12.

18. "Don't Punish the Economic Messenger," *New York Times*, April 7, 1981, A18.

19. Ibid.

20. Rivlin, interview, 2003.

21. Martin Tolchin, "The Bearer of Bad News Has Fewer Friends," *New York Times*, July 4, 1982, Section 3, 5.

22. John M. Berry and Helen Dewar, "Deficit of $80 Billion Looms for '82, Hill Told," *Washington Post*, September 11, 1981, A1.

23. "The Auditors and the Budget," *Washington Post*, February 6, 1982, A16.

24. John M. Berry and Helen Dewar, "CBO Sees Far Higher Deficits," *Washington Post*, July 28, 1982, A1.

25. Harold Jackson, "Sum Lady," *The Guardian*, April 3, 1982, 13.

26. Roy Meyers, "Congressional Budget Office," in *Encyclopedia of Public Policy and Administration*, edited by Jay Shafritz (Boulder, CO: Westview Press, 1998): 491.

27. Richard Kogan, interview with the author, June 28, 2004.

28. Van Ooms, interview with the author, January 29, 2004.

29. Everett Ehrlich, interview with the author, June 23, 2004.

30. Alice Rivlin, interview with the author, January 8, 2010.

31. Walter Williams, *Honest Numbers and Democracy: Social Policy Analysis in the White House, Congress and in Federal Agencies* (Washington, DC: Georgetown University Press, 1998), 222.

32. Rivlin, interview, 2010.

33. James L. Blum, "The Congressional Budget Office: On the One Hand, On the Other," in *Organizations for Policy Analysis: Helping Government Think*, edited by Carol Weiss (Newbury Park, CA: Sage Publications, 1992), 218–35.

34. Hobart Rowan, "Penner Warns of Debt Buildup," *Washington Post*, December 6, 1983, E1.

35. Congressional Budget Office, *The Economic and Budget Outlook: Fiscal Years 1985–1989* (Washington, DC: GPO, January 1984); see also Hobart Rowan, "Reagan Waits, Red Ink Flows," *Washington Post*, March 4, 1984, H1.

36. Penner, interview.

37. Lance LeLoup and Linda Kowalcky, "The Politics of Statutory Debt Limitation," *Public Administration Review* 53, no. 1 (1993): 14–27.

38. Senator Warren Rudman, as quoted in Elizabeth Wehr, "Congress Enacts Far-Reaching Budget Measure," *Congressional Quarterly Weekly* (December 14, 1985): 2604.

39. Penner, interview.

40. Paul Van de Water, interview with author, February 10, 2004.

41. *Balanced Budget and Emergency Deficit Control Act of 1985*, P.L. 99–177, 99th Cong., 1st sess., December 12, 1985.

42. Robert Pear, "President Is Told How He Must Cut Federal Spending," *Washington Post*, January 21, 1986, A1.

43. *Bowsher v. Synar*, 478 U.S. 714 (1986).

44. Anne Swardson, "CBO Says $45 Billion in Cuts Needed to Meet Deficit Goal," *Washington Post*, August 20, 1987, B1.

45. "Budget Skunk," *The Washington Post*, July 23, 1989, D6.

46. Kogan, interview.

47. Joan Pryde, "Congressional Budget Office Pans FSLIC Aid Plan," *The American Banker* 151, no. 117 (1986): 3.

48. Ibid.

49. "FSLIC Markup Delayed," *Congressional Quarterly Weekly* (June 28, 1986): 1478.

50. Penner, interview.

51. Steve Blakely, "Beefing Up Insurance Fund: Panel Approves S&L Bailout That Meets CBO Objections," *Congressional Quarterly Weekly* (July 19, 1986): 1612.

52. Ibid.

53. Kogan, interview.

54. Paul Blustein, "Hill, OMB Estimates $38 Billion Apart," *Washington Post*, January 21, 1990, A10.

55. Congressional Budget Office, *The Economic and Budget Outlook: Fiscal Years 1992–1996* (Washington, DC: GPO, January 1990).

56. Susan Rasky, "Substantial Power on Spending Is Shifted from Congress to Bush; Procedure Intended to Guarantee Cuts Are Made," *New York Times*, October 30, 1990, A1.

57. Wendell Primus, interview with the author, June 29, 2004.

58. Jacob "Jack" Lew, interview with the author, January 15, 2004.

59. Jason DeParle, "The Budget Battle; Crux of Tax Debate: Who Pays More?" *New York Times*, October 15, 1990, 9.

60. Primus, interview.

61. Roy Meyers, interview with the author, July 12, 2004.

62. Ann Devroy, "Bush Threatens Veto If Congress Tries to Regain Power to Estimate Budget Cuts," *Washington Post*, December 22, 1990, A4.

63. Hobart Rowen and Steven Mufson, "Recession May Scuttle Budget Pact," *Washington Post*, January 12, 1991, C1.

64. Lawrence J. Haas, "Deficit Doldrums," *National Journal* 23, no. 36 (1991): 2149–53.

65. "Clinton Now Focusing on Deficit: Spending Plans May be Cut Back, Aides Acknowledge," *Minneapolis Star-Tribune*, December 20, 1992, 1A.

66. Robert Pear, "Clinton Backs Off His Pledge to Cut the Deficit in Half," *New York Times*, January 7, 1993, A1.

67. Eric Pianin and David S. Hilzenrath, "Clinton to Press Major Deficit Cut," *Washington Post*, January 12, 1993, A1.

68. Lucinda Harper and Michael K. Frisby, "Top Democrats Say Tax Cut Seems Doubtful," *Wall Street Journal*, January 11, 1993, A1.

69. "Key Democrats Want Jobs Plan to be Early Priority," *Congressional Quarterly Weekly* (January 30, 1993): 212–13.

70. Bob Woodward, *The Agenda: Inside the Clinton White House* (New York: Simon and Schuster, 1994), 166.

71. Richard Berke, "Clinton's Economic Plan," *New York Times*, February 17, 1993, A16.

72. Leon Panetta, interview with the author, March 22, 2004.

73. House Committee on the Budget, *The Administration's Budget Proposals*, 104th Cong., 1st sess., August 3, 1995, 28.

74. Alice Rivlin, "More than Enough," *Washington Post*, July 27, 1993, A10.

75. Eric Pianin, "'93 Deficit Outlook Has Improved, CBO Says: But Budget Act's 5-Year Savings Would Fall $63 Billion Short of $496 Billion Goal," *Washington Post*, September 9, 1993, A8.

76. Alissa J. Rubin, "'Dynamic Scoring' Plan Exposes Deep Divisions within GOP," *Congressional Quarterly Weekly* (December 10, 1994): 3500–3503.

77. Ann Devroy and Eric Pianin, "President to Counter Hill Budgets," *Washington Post*, May 23, 1995, A1.

78. George Hager, "Clinton Shifts Tactics, Proposes Erasing Deficit in 10 Years," *Congressional Quarterly Weekly* (June 17, 1995): 1715.

79. Rivlin, interview, 2010.

80. Hager, "Clinton Switches Tactics."

81. George Hager and Alissa J. Rubin, "Last-Minute Maneuvers Forge a Conference Agreement," *Congressional Quarterly Weekly* (June 24, 1995): 1814–19.

82. George Hager and Eric Pianin, *Mirage: Why Neither Democrats Nor Republicans Can Balance the Budget, End the Deficit, or Satisfy the Public* (New York: Random House, 1997), 66.

83. "The Good-Behavior Bonus," *Washington Post*, July 10, 1995, A16.

84. Eric Black, "By the Numbers: Clinton Once Railed against His Current Stance," *Minneapolis Star-Tribune*, November 17, 1995, 21A.

85. Panetta, interview.

86. House Committee on the Budget, *The Administration's Budget Proposals*, 104th Cong., 1st sess., August 3, 1995, 28.

87. Ibid.

88. Alissa J. Rubin, "Reality of Tough Job Ahead Dampens Joy over Deal," *Congressional Quarterly Weekly* (November 25, 1995): 3597–99.

89. Ibid.

90. George Hager, "Problems in Opening Round Could Signal Bigger Woes," *Congressional Quarterly Weekly* (December 2, 1995): 3635–40.

91. Eric Pianin and Clay Chandler, "CBO Warns of Pitfalls in New Forecast; Slower Growth Seen as Balanced Budget Goal Draws Closer," *Washington Post*, December 12, 1995, A1.

92. Carolyn Lochhead, "Clinton Giving a Bit on Budget: He'll Use CBO Figures, Won't Accept Tax Cut," *San Francisco Chronicle*, December 19, 1995, A1.

93. "Clinton Submits Balanced Budget; 7-Year Plan a Nod to GOP," *Minneapolis Star-Tribune*, January 7, 1996, 1A.

94. June O'Neill, interview with the author, September 29, 2004. Stiglitz was the head of the President's Council on Economic Advisors, Summers was the deputy treasury secretary, and Minarik was the chief economist at OMB. Other interviewees recalled the meeting and its purpose. They reported Summers and Minarik being present, but could not confirm whether Stiglitz was in attendance.

95. Robert Dennis, interview with the author, November 4, 2004.

96. Clay Chandler, "Revised CBO Estimates May Smooth Budget Talks," *Washington Post*, November 23, 1996, D1.

97. Clay Chandler, "Budget Bonus Presents Clinton with Choices," *Washington Post*, December 25, 1996, D1.

98. Clay Chandler, "Hitting the Jackpot on Capitol Hill; CBO Gives Negotiators a Windfall of $225 Billion in Tax Revenue," *Washington Post*, May 3, 1997, A15.

99. James Blum, interview with the author, November 4, 2004.

100. Irene S. Rubin, *Balancing the Federal Budget*, 107.

101. Blum, interview, November 2004.

102. O'Neill, interview.

103. Blum, interview, November 2004.

104. Thomas Kahn, interview with the author, October 27, 2004.

105. Congressional Budget Office, *The Budget and Economic Outlook: Fiscal Years: An Update* (Washington, DC: GPO, September 1997).

106. William M. Welch, "Clinton Lays Claim to Title of Deficit Eliminator," *USA Today*, January 6, 1998, 6A.

107. House Policy Committee, *Congressional Budget Office Continues Its Bipartisan Tradition of Big Mistakes*, 105th Cong., 2nd sess., May 5, 1998.

108. See Eric Pianin, "Forecast to Dampen GOP Tax Cut Hopes," *Washington Post*, June 23, 1998, A4; and "Bullying the Referee," *Washington Post*, June 12, 1998, A26.

109. "Gingrich Steps Up Attack on CBO," *Washington Post*, June 11, 1998, A5.

110. Eric Pianin, "Hungry for Tax Cut, House Leaders Are Pressuring CBO," *Washington Post*, June 12, 1998, A6.

111. O'Neill, interview.

112. Ibid.

113. Eric Pianin, "June O'Neill to Depart CBO Early," *Washington Post*, October 29, 1998, A25.

114. Andrew Taylor, "Reappointment Unlikely, CBO Chief Bows Out," *Congressional Quarterly Weekly* (October 31, 1998): 2952.

115. O'Neill, interview.

116. Eric Pianin, "In Session: Congress; Climate Is Cooler for Kasich's Budget Scolding," *Washington Post*, October 11, 1999, A23.

117. George Hager, "Brunt of Budget Battle Falls on CBO Chief's Findings," *Washington Post*, October 23, 1999, A2.

118. See Philip Joyce, "Federal Budgeting after September 11th: A Whole New Ballgame, or Is It Déjà Vu All Over Again?' *Public Budgeting & Finance* 25, no. 1 (2005): 15–31.

119. Congressional Budget Office, *The Budget and Economic Outlook: Fiscal Years 2002–2011* (Washington DC: GPO, January 2001).

120. Office of Management and Budget, *Budget of the United States Government: Fiscal Year 2002* (Washington DC: GPO, April 2001), 224.

121. Janet Hook and Alissa J. Rubin, "Budget Surplus Estimate Jumps by $1 Trillion, Aiding Bush's Tax Cut," *Los Angeles Times*, January 31, 2001, A12.

122. Holtz-Eakin, interview, 2004.

123. "Greenspan Eyes Tax Cuts," *CNN Money*, January 25, 2001, www.money.cnn.com /2001/01/25/economy/greenspan.

124. Congressional Budget Office, *The Budget and Economic Outlook: Fiscal Years 2003–2012* (Washington, DC: GPO, January 2002).

125. The practice continues to this day (2010), and no one seems very excited about it any more.

126. Leonard Burman, interview with the author, June 29, 2004.

127. Edmund L. Andrews, "New Chief for Budget Office," *New York Times*, January 10, 2003, A18.

128. Holtz-Eakin, interview, 2004.

129. Jeff Madrick, "The Congressional Budget Office's Updated Forecasting Methods Don't Help the White House's Argument for Tax Cuts," *New York Times*, April 17, 2003, C2.

130. Edmund L. Andrews, "Study Says Tax Cuts Will Make Deficit Soar," *New York Times*, March 26, 2003, A12.

131. John Maggs, "Accountable to No One?" *National Journal* 35, no. 19 (2003): 1467.

132. Holtz-Eakin, interview.

133. The AMT was put in place in 1969 as a shadow income tax that would prevent wealthy taxpayers from avoiding tax through sheltering income. AMT income thresholds were not indexed for inflation, however, which resulted in many people paying the AMT who were not—or at least did not consider themselves to be—wealthy.

134. Congressional Budget Office, *The Budget and Economic Outlook Fiscal Years 2010–2019* (Washington, DC: GPO, January 2009).

135. John Maggs and David Baumann, "Speaking His Mind," *National Journal* 34, no. 27 (2002): 2002.

136. Edmund L. Andrews, "Who's Afraid of the Deficit?: Cassandras Are Out of Style," *New York Times*, November 19, 2002, C1.

137. Congressional Budget Office, *The Budget and Economic Outlook: Fiscal Years 2010–2019*.

138. Congressional Budget Office, *The Budget and Economic Outlook: Fiscal Years 2011–2020* (Washington, DC: GPO, January 2010).

139. Office of Management Budget, *The Budget of the United States Government: Fiscal Year 2009, Historical Tables* (Washington, DC: GPO, 2008), 24–25.

140. Congressional Budget Office, *The Budget and Economic Outlook: Fiscal Years 2011–2020*.

141. Office of Management and Budget, *Budget of the United States Government: Fiscal Year 2011* (Washington, DC: GPO, February 2010).

142. Congressional Budget Office, *An Analysis of the President's Budgetary Proposals for Fiscal Year 2011* (March 2010).

143. Office of Management and Budget, *Budget of the United States Government: Fiscal Year 2011*.

144. Daniel Crippen, "Social Security Mirage," *Washington Post*, May 18, 2000, A27.

145. Barry Anderson, interview with the author, March 10, 2005.

146. Avrum D. Lank, "Social Security May Outlive Expectations: Report Disputes When Fund Will Run Out," *Milwaukee Journal-Sentinel*, June 15, 2004, 1D.

147. Marilyn Werber Serafini, "The CBO Chief's Diagnosis," *National Journal* 40, no. 1 (2008): 32–33.

148. Louis Fisher, perhaps the leading scholar on the budgetary separation of powers in the United States, argues that the existence of the congressional budget process has encouraged fiscal irresponsibility on the part of the president, because it created a task

for the Congress—to act comprehensively on the budget—that is largely inconsistent with the incentives facing Congress. See in particular Louis Fisher, "Federal Budget Doldrums: The Vacuum in Presidential Leadership," *Public Administration Review* 40, no. 6 (1990): 693–700. Also see Philip Joyce, "Does More (or Even Better) Information Lead to Better Budgeting?: A New Perspective," *Journal of Policy Analysis and Management* 27, no. 4 (2008): 945–59.

Chapter 4

Microbudgeting

THE SECOND MAJOR responsibility given to CBO was estimating the cost of legislative proposals Congress considered. This function, equivalent to the fiscal note requirements of many state and local governments, was considered critical because it would help Congress understand more fully the fiscal effects of proposed legislation. Before CBO was created, these cost estimates, as likely as not, would come from either advocates of the proposal (who would have an incentive to downplay the cost) or opponents (who would have an incentive to overstate it). Related to cost estimating is scorekeeping, which involves determining whether legislation considered by Congress meets fiscal targets, such as those included in the budget resolution.

This responsibility—cost estimating and scorekeeping—is not well understood outside the small number of budget technicians, congressional staff, agency officials, and interest groups most directly affected. This chapter outlines that process, including the challenges in establishing it, the necessary data and decision processes that support it, and the issues for policymaking that are raised by the resulting estimates.

How Did CBO Organize?

The Congressional Budget Act requires that bills reported out of authorizing committees (those that establish new programs or change existing ones) include a cost estimate outlining the five-year cost of the proposed legislation.[1] Early on, CBO director Rivlin (see chapter 2) made the decision that cost estimating would be the province of the BAD, which would be responsible for nuts and bolts budget analyses, as opposed to the broader policy analyses that would be done by CBO's program divisions.

The challenge for the CBO founders in setting up a cost estimating and scorekeeping function was made complex by the twin challenges of establishing a process that had heretofore not existed and establishing that process within an organization (Congress) that was not used to having its estimates challenged, least of all by its own employees. It is hard to overstate what a sea change this would be for congressional committee chairs used to coming up with their own numbers. As longtime House Budget Committee aide Shirley Ruhe said, this was really about "the importance of having an institution that would give us cost estimates that were based on a uniform set of economic assumptions that were an analytical set of numbers for five years, as opposed to what Sonny Montgomery [then chairman of the House Veterans Affairs Committee] used to do when he would get up on the House floor and say, in his Southern drawl, 'I have this new kind of bill he-ah, and it only costs $5 million,' and [then it turns out that] the next year it cost $1 billion."[2]

As important as cost estimating was, it was not going to happen by itself. Establishing the capacity to conduct credible policy analyses within CBO was a daunting task, one that fell to Jim Blum to implement. Blum was one of the handful of people that Rivlin had assembled in late 1974 to discuss how to organize CBO, and he was chosen to head BAD, which was going to do all the budget numbers—the baseline, the cost estimates, and scorekeeping. Blum was enthusiastic about heading BAD because he was sure that this was where the action would be.[3]

With a leader in place, the task remained for CBO to hire staff for the division and to establish procedures for cost estimating and scorekeeping. The first task was made easier by the transfer to CBO of the staff of the Joint Commission on the Reduction of Federal Expenditures, which had been established independently by the appropriations committee to perform a scorekeeping function a number of years earlier.[4] Many other staff, though, needed to be hired to carry out tasks with no clear federal precedent. Among the key staff hired in the first year were Dick Emery, who had worked at OMB, and C. G. Nuckols, who had headed up the cost estimating unit within the Department of Defense. Nuckols was ideally suited for this new role. Jim Blum discussed his approach to hiring:

> Essentially we were looking for people to head up those cost estimating units who had some strong background, primarily economics, for doing cost estimating work. I considered this work to be quite analytical. . . . it was something different than what the OMB budget examiners are doing. You are actually analyzing what the potential . . . effects are of all of these pieces of legislation coming around. And it was probably more akin to the kind of work that C. G. was doing in the Defense Department doing cost analysis of defense programs, which is why we were so happy to get someone with that background to come to the division.[5]

Still, this was a brand-new function. Initially, CBO had few staff used to doing this type of work, and the work was being done in the context of a Congress that was either not used to anyone second-guessing its cost estimates, openly hostile to the new budget process, or both. CBO was assisted by the fact that they were not required to begin producing estimates right away but were instead given the first year as a sort of dry run. The agency quickly found that one of the biggest challenges was simply being aware of the bills for which estimates would be required. One of the key factors in contributing to the success of cost estimating was the development of effective communication between CBO staff and committees in Congress. Alice Rivlin noted that "it was to the credit of the staff. We were all encouraging them from the top, but the staff was building relationships with staff."[6] That is, committees needed to be educated as to the existence and responsibilities of CBO that they might notify CBO in a timely fashion that a bill was going to be reported out of committee. As Jim Blum added, "the management problem was really one of getting [the cost estimate] included in committee reports."[7] To assist in this process, the agency established a Budget Estimates Tracking System (BETS), which monitored bills as they moved through Congress. BETS was designed to determine the percentage of the CBO cost estimates that made it into committee reports. CBO continues to keep track of the extent to which committee reports included CBO cost estimates (this number is typically in the 90 percent to 95 percent range), and now also keeps track of the percentage of committee-reported bills for which a CBO cost estimate was completed prior to floor action (this number has been approximately 99 percent).[8]

Building the Baseline

The starting point for estimating each account and program is the baseline, which, as discussed in chapter 3, represents the activity of the program or account that is projected under current law. For mandatory spending programs, this means that the spending for the program or account would be driven by what the law currently says in terms of who is eligible and how much they receive. An analyst for Social Security, therefore, would start by asking what recipients would receive if no changes were made in either eligibility or the generosity of the monthly payment. Deriving the baseline thus involves estimating both the eligible population and the level of benefits they would receive. Similarly, for the food stamp program, renamed the Supplemental Nutrition Assistance Program (SNAP), spending in the baseline is determined based on how many individuals are eligible to receive the benefit, how much that benefit would be, and how many people would actually receive the benefit. For discretionary programs, the baseline is determined by adjusting current spending for inflation to determine how a given agency or program could deliver the same real level of services in future years.

The baseline is important for cost estimating because the costs identified in these fiscal notes must be compared with some presumed current level. The cost for a bill that would reduce the age at which Social Security benefits could be paid would be marginal against the baseline. Conversely, the savings associated with a bill that would increase the age would also be compared with current law. For discretionary programs, an authorization that would expand a program beyond the level provided for in current law would be counted as a cost. For example, if a bill passes that would create a new requirement that the Transportation Security Administration (TSA) inspect all luggage, the cost associated with that bill would be that to comply with that requirement, over and above current legal requirements. (If, under current law, the TSA was already inspecting one-half of all luggage, only the cost of inspecting the marginal additional half would be identified as the cost of the bill.) This concept of current law is informed by the baseline, but is not necessarily the same as the baseline. Constructing this baseline is important, of course, not only for cost estimating, but also for forecasting the implications of current policies for the future fiscal path of the country (see chapter 3), and supporting the development and enforcement of the annual budget resolution.

Federal Cost Estimating

Section 403 of the Budget Act requires that each bill ordered reported (eligible to be considered on the floor) by a congressional committee (excluding appropriation bills) to the floor of the House or Senate include a CBO cost estimate. The preparation of a cost estimate involves three steps beyond the construction of the baseline. First, discovering that a bill has, in fact, been ordered reported—that is, that a cost estimate will be necessary. Second, determining what that bill actually does. Third, estimating how much the bill would cost (or save) relative to current law (the baseline).

When Is an Estimate Required?

Congressional committees consider hundreds of pieces of legislation each year. For CBO to know that a cost estimate is required, the agency needs to know which bills are ordered reported by a committee in a timely way. If not, the agency has little chance of doing a credible cost estimate before the bill is considered on the floor of the House or the Senate. Some committees work closely with CBO, keeping it informed as they work on legislation. In other cases, CBO staff need to take the lead in identifying bills that will require an estimate. In most cases, they are advised to contact committees in their respective substantive areas to determine what, if any, legislation may be on the agenda for that committee for that year. Knowing what legislation might be considered can help CBO staff to determine what issues might be on the agenda for a given Congress. Particularly when cost estimates will involve substantial research, understanding what is on the agenda is important to getting a head start on the estimate.

Of course, that a committee or committee staffer intends to report a bill is not the same thing as the bill actually being reported. Thousands of bills are introduced in each year in each Congress; only an average of six hundred to eight hundred actually result in a CBO cost estimate being prepared. It is important, therefore, for cost analysts to monitor not only which bills might affect their accounts, but also the status of those bills. In some cases congressional committees will assist in this process; in other cases it is prudent for CBO analysts to monitor bill status on their own. Apparently a major initial impediment to CBO cost analysis was the failure of CBO to get analyses into committee reports, largely because the agency was unaware of the status of the bill.[9] Over time this problem has almost completely disappeared as relationships between CBO and congressional committees have become more routinized.

Organization for Cost Estimating

BAD has always organized itself for cost estimating in a functional manner. Five units currently produce these federal estimates:

- National and Physical Resources;
- Health Systems and Medicare;
- Low-Income Health Programs and Prescription Drugs;
- Income Security and Health; and
- Defense, International Affairs, and Veterans Affairs.

This current organization reflects the substantial additional emphasis placed on health care over the past ten years. Until the mid-1990s, health cost estimating was part of a larger human resources unit; it was broken out separately in 1995, and again more recently into the two units that exist today.

In each of these units, cost analysts are assigned responsibility for various budget functions and accounts (there are more than fifteen hundred expenditure accounts in the federal budget). Depending on the size and complexity of the account, a single analyst may have responsibility for multiple accounts, or in rare cases (such as Social Security or Medicare) multiple analysts may be assigned to a single account. The responsibility for a cost estimate generally accompanies the account-by-account responsibilities for the baseline. Each unit is headed by a unit chief, whose responsibility it is to be the first line of review for each cost estimate, as well as coordinating the development of the baseline for each cost unit.

The Nature of Costs: Collecting Data for a Cost Estimate

The nature of costs differs by the type of spending. For mandatory spending, estimating the effect of new legislation involves understanding how this new legislation would change baseline spending, and the estimate is largely driven by adjustments to existing models. The baseline estimate for food stamp spending, for example, will have made certain assumptions concerning the number of beneficiaries and the level of payments received. For new legislation, answering the cost question would then involve knowing exactly how the bill would affect one or both of these variables. This task may be analytically difficult, but it is conceptually straightforward. Armed with the knowledge concerning the effects of new legislation in beneficiaries or payment levels, it is relatively simple for the analyst to adjust existing models to account for these effects. Even in this case, however, the analyst often needs to make behavioral assumptions.

For a complex, caseload-driven program, the CBO cost analyst typically forecasts future costs relying on computer models. And the adjustments to costs would be driven by changes in assumptions in those models that are themselves driven, in part, by behavioral changes. Former unit chief Paul Cullinan described a typical approach to an estimate of a proposed change to raise the age at which an individual could receive Social Security benefits.

> First, in all likelihood . . . we would go in and do it without any behavioral response just to see . . . what type of impact people are going to be responding to. And, then we come in and try to decide based upon [the] literature, based upon our own analyses, what the potential behavioral response to those changes would be. For instance, you wouldn't expect people who . . . retire at age sixty-two to change their behavior very much by extending the retirement age to age seventy. . . . But, you know [that] as those reductions became larger, maybe some of them would move. We'd also have to figure out how many people might be responding by applying for disability benefits. Both because there's a longer period in which you can receive, or become eligible for disability benefits with a higher normal retirement age but also because you protect the full benefit as opposed to having an actuarial reduced benefit for the rest of your life.[10]

For discretionary spending, a bill may authorize a particular dollar amount of spending, or create a new program or a demand for new service under an existing program without specifying a particular dollar amount. Here it is less clear that the bill will lead to additional federal spending, because a decision may be made later to substitute the new activity for an existing one. The analyst, therefore, can state what the cost of the new discretionary authorization would be if it were funded, but the analyst cannot know whether the bill will lead to that marginal increase in spending.

The job of cost estimating is made even more difficult because a bill can create federal spending without specifically saying that it does. For example, a bill may establish a federal guarantee of a loan made by the private sector. This does not represent immediate cash outlays by the federal government, but can result in future outlays when recipients default on these loans.[11] Another bill may create a federal entitlement to health care benefits, or may sell assets of the government, which can have a positive (one-time) effect on revenues while potentially depriving the government of a future stream of revenues.

The cost analyst is not only concerned about what the bill does. The analyst is also concerned about when it does it, because the cost estimate typically requires information concerning both the budget authority and outlay effects of legislation at least five years into the future. A particular piece of legislation, for example, may provide budget authority of $5 billion in fiscal year 2011, but the outlays could be spread out over five years from 2011 through 2015.

Sources of Data

Of course, knowing what information is needed to do a cost estimate is not the same thing as having that information. Collecting such data requires the estimator to access many sources of data, including academics, representatives of interest groups, and agency officials. Cost estimates for existing mandatory spending programs typically involve determining how changes in eligibility requirements or payments will affect the program's cost. There may be many individuals, inside and outside the government, who are experts in a particular substantive area and can be relied on for advice that can be used to construct the estimate.

For discretionary programs, the analyst may have a relatively easy time of it, particularly in those cases where a specific dollar level of authorization has been specified. If the bill creates a new work requirement for an agency or creates a new federal grant or loan program, however, the analyst needs to estimate the level of work generated or funds that will be awarded, even if the amount is not specified in the legislation. In this case, the analyst must estimate how much additional work will be generated, or how much will be necessary in loan or grant funds to fulfill the requirement. This does not mean that the amount would actually be added to the agency's appropriation. An agency may not receive funding to implement a new program or function, but the requirement may partially or wholly displace an activity already being carried out. The CBO cost analysis is attempting to quantify the cost of the bill assuming that the activity is subsequently funded, not to predict whether appropriations will actually be provided.

There are a number of challenges in obtaining information from external sources. Perhaps the most significant is determining whether there is any bias in the information. That is, if a CBO analyst asked the National Rifle Association (NRA) for input on a cost estimate for new gun control legislation, it might reasonably assume that the NRA has every incentive to overstate the cost of the legislation. On the other hand, a gun control advocacy group such as Handgun Control, Inc. might have the opposite incentive. This can be particularly tricky when analyzing administration proposals, such as those included in a president's budget. Assuming that agencies are obliged to support these proposals, it is reasonable to suspect the numbers produced. CBO usually deals with such potential bias by collecting information from multiple sources. Former CBO cost analyst Jim Hearn noted, when he did the cost estimate on the so-called Motor-Voter legislation, which required state and local governments to permit voter registration at the same time that driver's licenses were renewed, that he needed to factor in the reluctance of state and local governments to implement the legislation. He did eventually find knowledgeable people who "were just being totally honest because they didn't know they had an axe to grind" and once there were a few such estimates to put together he began to be able to develop useable numbers.[12]

The cost analyst can sometimes turn to experts within CBO's program divisions for assistance in producing cost estimates. As discussed in chapters 6 and 7, CBO simply could not have developed the cost estimates necessary for analyzing the various changes to health programs proposed since the early 1990s without collaboration between the program divisions and BAD. Similarly, estimates of the cost of various financial market interventions have relied heavily on input from MAD and CBO's newest division, the Financial Analysis Division, since 2008.

CBO cost estimates are also enhanced by open lines of communication between OMB and CBO, which were enhanced substantially at the CBO analyst to OMB examiner level after the passage of GRH (see chapter 3), which forced each agency to understand how it differed from the other in its baseline estimates. Rudy Penner, who was director of CBO at the time, said that he thought the state of communication between CBO and the executive branch prior to this point was "very bad, and beyond my capability to improve it: but Gramm-Rudman really did. It really forced everybody to work intimately together . . . at both the macro and micro levels."[13] Barry Anderson, who was at OMB at the time, agreed: "from a technical perspective, from a technician's perspective, which is virtually all of CBO and the vast majority of OMB, it brought us a lot closer together."[14]

The quality and consistency of CBO cost estimates seems to be enhanced by the process, established early in CBO history, of multiple layers of review. Each estimate goes out of CBO under the director's signature, is reviewed by the relevant unit chief, by the assistant director for budget analysis and one of his deputies, and by the director or designee (normally the deputy director). Given the time pressures under which these estimates are produced, it is no small feat to be able to keep the estimates moving while providing for many layers of substantive review. Out of necessity, the most thorough and detailed substantive reviews have always occurred within BAD. Although CBO directors have been interested in cost estimating to varying degrees, none has played a consistent, hands-on role, choosing (rationally) to get more involved in high profile or costly bills. Former director Rudy Penner indicated that he thought he was more interested in the individual cost estimates than Alice Rivlin had been and "I think that came as a bit of a shock to the cost estimators."[15] In fact, Paul Cullinan recalled Penner telling the story of an early cost estimate that reached his office regarding whether burial plots would be counted as assets for computing some government benefit: "he raised the question (to the analyst), how did you actually do this? And you know they came in and they brought him information they had gotten from X, Y, and Z on the average cost of the plots, and data. They said X number people had them . . . and I think after that, Rudy sort of said, gee these people do their work, so why should I repeat what they are doing?"[16]

How Are CBO Cost Estimates Communicated?

Once the cost estimate has been signed by the CBO director, it is transmitted to the relevant committee to be included in the committee report accompanying the legislation and simultaneously posted on the CBO website. Committees thus cannot control access to CBO cost estimates. This differentiates CBO from, for example, GAO, because at GAO committees or individual members frequently release the results of GAO reports. In practice, however, these GAO reports are issued within thirty days of their receipt by the requester. This CBO work for committees also contrasts with the work of the Congressional Research Service (CRS), almost all of which is done for individual members on a confidential basis.

Since early in its history, CBO has disclosed the methods and assumptions underlying its estimates. A cost estimate, therefore, does much more than provide the numbers. It also discusses the approach taken in deriving the estimate, and the sensitivity of the estimate to particular variables or methods chosen. Although many CBO cost estimates are only a page or two long, the necessity to disclose the methodology results in cases where cost estimates can be much longer. For example, the estimate for the House- and Senate-passed versions of the Medicare prescription drug bill in 2003 was sixty-seven pages, mostly because of the need to disclose the basis for the estimate.[17] That of the House-passed stimulus bill in 2009 was twenty-three pages.[18] That for the final version of the Obama health reform bill was thirty-five pages, roughly evenly divided between text and tables.[19] The CBO cost estimate on the climate change legislation considered by the House in 2009 is another notable example of a detailed cost estimate that disclosed detailed methodology and the basis of the estimate.[20] The importance of disclosing the assumptions is magnified by the necessity that CBO choose a point estimate, when in fact any number of costs from a range is possible. CBO generally receives high praise from outsiders for the transparency of its estimates.[21]

How Many Cost Estimates Each Year?

As noted, thousands of bills are introduced in Congress in a given year. Because CBO is required to produce cost estimates only for legislation actually reported by a congressional committee, only a fraction of these bills result in an estimate. CBO did more than 9,000 formal estimates in the fifteen years between 1995 and 2009, an average of 622 per year (see table 4.1). Of these, 7,970, an average of 531 per year, were of costs associated with reported bills. The remainder were for direct spending and revenue estimates (early in this period, the PAYGO process required that mandatory spending or revenue legislation, in aggregate, not have a negative budget impact in any year), enacted bills for which estimates had not been done earlier, and other estimates (many of which resulted from requests, largely from committees, for estimates associated with introduced bills).[22]

Although variation is certainly substantial at times from year to year (the highest total is almost double the lowest number), what is perhaps most remarkable about these numbers is how stable the estimate requirements are over time. With the exception of 2000 and 2001, no year either exceeds or falls short of the average by more than 16 percent; in six years, the number of estimates remains within about 5 percent of the average. An apparent trend of increasing workload is worth noting, however. CBO prepared more than 1,500 cost estimates during the 110th Congress (2007–8), which was a jump of more than 350 from the 109th (2005–6). There was, however, a drop for the first session of the 111th Congress to only 485 estimates, down almost 300 from the first session of the 110th. This may have to do with the dominance of health care reform on the congressional agenda, which may have forced out other legislation. Whether the workload will hold steady, or change up or down, is not predictable.

In a sense, however, these formal estimates represent just the tip of the iceberg. For many pieces of legislation, the process is an iterative one, with CBO responding to many drafts and estimating the effects of bills at various stages of the legislative process. Far from a process where a bill is dropped in CBO's lap as a one-time event, CBO actually works very closely with congressional staff—generally committee staff—in providing a lot of informal or "preliminary" estimates for legislative proposals *before* those proposals are finalized and made public. CBO quite frequently works with committee staff in reviewing their draft proposals (often even before legislative language is written) and providing such staff with preliminary numbers for those proposals.

The main reason, then, that a lot of significant legislative proposals come in with a cost at or just under a given target (such as the prescription drug estimate, which is discussed in box 4.1, or the Obama health reform legislation, described in chapter 7) is that the congressional staff and members continue to refine their proposals in response to preliminary estimates so that they can craft a proposal that will meet their budgetary target. Thus it should not be a surprise when a given proposal comes in at or just below its targeted level. Rather, this results from a significant amount of back-and-forth between CBO and the committees in question.[23]

There is nothing nefarious about this process. It is CBO's normal way of doing business, and CBO provides such assistance to both the majority and the minority using the same ground rules about confidentiality. CBO discusses its approach to cost estimating—and transparency—on its website:

CBO seeks to ensure that key parties in the Congress who are involved in any particular issue have equal access to its analytic work. Insofar as possible, CBO delivers its cost estimates and analyses to all interested parties simultaneously. Requests for confidentiality are honored only for cost estimates for legislative proposals that have not been made public.

The Director of the Congressional Budget Office transmits by letter all formal budget and mandate cost estimates of legislative proposals and all requested analyses. CBO sends its formal cost estimates for reported bills and estimates prepared at committee request to the Chairman and Ranking Minority Member of the reporting or requesting committee. When the requester is a budget committee or individual Member, CBO also sends a copy of its cost estimate simultaneously to the Chairman and Ranking Minority Member

Table 4.1 Number of CBO Cost Estimates Produced

Year	Bills	Reported[a]	Passed[b]	Direct Spending and Revenues[c]	Other[d]	Total	Average %
1995	4,354	519	21	4	55	599	96
1996	2,191	471	97	6	60	634	102
1997	4,656	457	51	16	107	631	101
1998	2,876	522	96	12	49	679	109
1999	5,514	548	54	8	65	675	109
2000	3,454	655	150	33	58	896	144
2001	5,501	360	35	14	35	444	71
2002	3,455	619	44	19	67	749	120
2003	5,704	574	23	21	64	682	110
2004	2,762	540	41	23	48	652	105
2005	6,829	498	24	11	65	598	96
2006	3,729	462	39	10	57	568	91
2007	7,461	681	10	28	52	771	124
2008	3,620	652	29	28	43	752	121
2009	7,433	412	11	11	51	485	78
Total	69,539	7,970	725	244	876	9,330	
Average	4,636	531	48	16	58	622	

Source: CBO internal estimates, provided February 2010.

[a] Cost estimates completed for bills approved by an authorizing committee. Most of these estimates are completed when a bill is "ordered reported."

[b] Estimates completed at this stage used to be called PAYGO letters. They focus on a bill's impact on direct spending and revenue. Although PAYGO expired in 2002, CBO continues to prepare such estimates for the two Budget Committees.

[c] Generally prepared for quickly-moving legislation for which there is insufficient time to complete estimates earlier. Some of these estimates are for bills that never make it through committee markup.

[d] CBO also sometimes completes estimates at other stages in the legislative process: when bills are introduced, for amendments, follow-up letters on prior estimates, and for conference reports.

of the committee of jurisdiction; for an introduced bill or amendment, CBO sends a copy of the estimate to the sponsor and the Chairman and Ranking Minority Member of the committee of jurisdiction, as well to as the requester.

In contrast, CBO staff may provide informal cost estimates at various stages of the legislative process as Members or committees evaluate proposals. Informal estimates are preliminary because they do not undergo the same review procedures required for formal estimates.[24]

Impact of Cost Estimates

Much of the CBO cost estimating function operates somewhat under the radar of public attention. It is relatively rare for CBO estimates to take on a high external profile. When they do, it often involves the analysis of some major proposal coming from the executive branch. Clearly the CBO cost estimates of the Obama health reform bills (see chapter 7) had a major impact on the eventual outlines of that legislation. Part of the controversy surrounding the CBO analysis of the Clinton health reform (see chapter 6) concerned the approximately $130 billion difference between the administration and CBO concerning the five-year costs to the federal government. Another high-profile example from the same era came when CBO analyzed the potential savings from Vice President Al Gore's National Performance Review (the so-called reinventing government initiatives) and estimated that they would save $305 million over five years, compared to the vice president's estimate of $5.9 billion over the same period.[25] This was seen as a significant blow to the credibility of the administration's reform initiative, which had been touted as not only good management, but also a tool for deficit

---

■ **Box 4.1** The Medicare Prescription Drug Bill

The proposal by President George W. Bush to provide for a prescription drug benefit for Medicare, and the subsequent passage of this Medicare prescription drug bill, led to the most controversial cost estimating issue since the Clinton health care reform proposal of 1994. In part the controversy was driven by the sheer cost of providing such a substantial new benefit to so many beneficiaries. Moreover, this issue involved the fact that the estimate Congress used when deciding on the bill was almost immediately called into question. There were extraordinary charges after the fact that the Bush administration had willfully withheld information on real costs from the Congress in an effort to smooth the way for passage of the prescription drug legislation.

Since its creation in 1965, Medicare had not covered the cost of prescription drugs for senior citizens. As the cost of these drugs rose, numerous proposals had been made to expand benefits by reversing this exclusion. President Bush promised, in the 2000 presidential campaign, to propose the addition of this benefit if he were elected president. Although the president's first two years were largely dominated by his income tax proposals, and then responding to the September 11 terrorist attacks, he made the pursuit of Medicare prescription drug legislation a priority of his third year in office (2003). His January 2003 State of the Union Address established a price ceiling of $400 billion for Medicare prescription drug

reduction. This was reminiscent of an earlier period when both CBO and GAO reviewed the estimates of the Grace Commission, which had been appointed by President Reagan to root out "waste, fraud, and abuse" in government. CBO determined that the policy proposals would save less than $100 million, far less than the $424 million estimated by the commission.[26]

A more recent, but lower profile, example of the effect that a CBO cost estimate can have came in 2004, and concerned a gap between the Bush administration and CBO over a federally insured mortgage program. The administration had estimated that the legislative changes that they were proposing would generate $200 million in revenues over five years. Although this estimate assumed that the fees charged to borrowers would more than offset any subsidy costs resulting from defaults or foreclosures, CBO estimated that the net subsidy cost would be positive rather than negative.[27] The main reason for that was CBO's assumption that the default rate would be "much higher" (1 percent in the first year, and 30 percent over thirty years) than that estimated by the administration.[28] In this case, the CBO cost estimate appears to have stopped the bill dead in its tracks. In addition, given developments in the housing market, in retrospect it seems undoubtedly true that even CBO's numbers were wildly optimistic.

Before the health care reform debate of 2009 and 2010, perhaps the two highest profile recent CBO cost estimates involved the Medicare prescription drug bill in 2004 and the economic stimulus bill in 2009. In the first case, CBO found itself embroiled in a controversy that centered around the head of the Center for Medicare and Medicaid Services (CMS) instructing the Medicare chief actuary to withhold information from the Congress on the expected cost of the legislation (see box 4.1 for a thorough discussion of the issues surrounding this estimate).

costs over ten years, and this $400 billion ceiling was included in the fiscal year 2004 budget resolution.[1] Although cost was generally agreed to, details of the plan were much less clear: What kind of benefits would be provided? To whom would these benefits be provided? Initially the administration had supported providing a relatively high level of benefits to those who left Medicare for private plans, but by June 2003 they indicated that they would "accept equal prescription drug benefits for people in the traditional Medicare program as those who join private health plans."[2]

In a situation when Congress was considering a costly new entitlement, the price tag of the bill had been agreed to in advance, and the legislative proposals were somewhat of a moving target, it was not surprising that CBO would find itself in the middle of controversy. As was the case with the Clinton health care reform almost a decade earlier, substantial uncertainty existed over how to reliably estimate the costs. This is particularly true because CBO was not attempting to gauge the marginal cost increase associated with increasing an existing benefit; there was instead no benchmark.

Among the many uncertain factors that CBO and other cost analysts needed to confront was the estimate of precisely how many seniors would enroll in the new program. In addition, since the value of the benefit depends largely on the cost of drugs, the estimate was sensitive to assumptions concerning the future price of medications.[3] This uncertainty caused some expectation that, regardless of CBO's cost estimate, and regardless of how

(continued on next page)

sincerely CBO attempted to come up with a correct and credible estimate, the actual cost would almost surely be greater than CBO's estimates. Former top Medicare official Gail Wilensky was typical of this group when she argued that "if history is any guide it will cost more than we think. Not because people are deliberately low-balling the estimates, but because we have never been able to correctly estimate the cost of a new benefit."[4]

As is typically true with these kinds of legislative proposals, the continuous changes and back-and-forth in the conference led to CBO being in almost constant contact with the conferees, who needed to understand the cost implications of the numerous changes that they were considering. The House- and Senate-passed bills had been scored by CBO at $425 billion (House) and $430 billion (Senate). The conferees, therefore, needed to make changes that would make the bill less costly than what came out of either house.[5] Doing that involved getting informal CBO estimates of various Medicare changes as they were proposed.

Ultimately, the conference agreement passed both the House and the Senate in November 2003, and the president signed the Medicare Modernization Act (MMA—Public Law 108-173) into law in December 2003. CBO's analysis of the conference agreement put the final cost at $395 billion. According to a CBO report,

> estimating the costs of providing that basic benefit involved three main steps: determining the number of beneficiaries who would decide to enroll in a Medicare drug plan, estimating the average and total costs of providing those enrollees with covered benefits, and using the resulting estimate of gross costs to calculate offsetting premium receipts on the basis of the law's subsidy formulas. In addition, CBO had to calculate whether and to what extent employers that currently provide drug coverage to their retirees on Medicare would continue to do so once the new drug benefit was in place, and whether they would take advantage of an alternative mechanism in the MMA to receive direct payments from Medicare for continuing to provide qualified drug coverage to those retirees.[6]

For a normal CBO cost estimate, that would be the end of the story. Remarkably, very rarely does anyone ask CBO to reflect on the accuracy of its estimates after the fact. The story of the Medicare estimate took on a new twist just before the release of the president's fiscal year 2005 budget in early 2004, though, when OMB director Joshua Bolten disclosed that the administration believed that the estimate of the ten-year cost of the bill was not $395 billion as CBO had said—but $534 billion. This led to immediate speculation that these estimates were not new at all, but were rather cost data from 2003 that had been intentionally withheld from Congress because they might have affected the prospects for or the specific contents of the legislation.[7] By 2004 the administration would not have been concerned about high actual cost data being in the public space, as the administration was taking a different overall approach to the budget, arguing that domestic programs needed to be reduced in order to hold the line in response to newly forecast increases in the budget deficit.

Suspicions of intentional withholding of cost estimates were given greater credibility when Richard Foster, the chief Medicare actuary, revealed that he had been ordered, when the legislation was being debated, not to provide information to Congress that would have placed the cost of what was being debated above the $400 billion agreed price tag.[8] Evidence to substantiate this claim existed in the form of a June 2003 email exchange between Foster and an aide to Centers for Medicare and Medicaid Services (CMS) head Thomas Scully, in which Foster was warned that if he provided requested estimates to Democratic staff without Scully's authorization "the consequences for insubordination are extremely severe."[9]

Ultimately a House Ways and Means hearing held on March 24, 2004, at which both Foster and CBO director Douglas Holtz-Eakin testified on their various cost estimates, centered around the accuracy of the estimates and the alleged withholding of the numbers from the Congress. Both Foster and Holtz-Eakin stressed the uncertainty of any projection about the cost of a future change of this magnitude. To underscore the technical basis for significant deviation between estimates, they noted major differences between the estimates had to do with the takeup rates, or the number of eligible beneficiaries who would sign up for the benefits.[10] In a subsequent interview, Holtz-Eakin argued that "for us to be different by $140 billion is nothing," given the $1.6 trillion in projected drug spending by seniors over the period.[11] But while acknowledging that both estimates were within the margin for error, Foster also repeated his assertion that he had been ordered not to release information suggesting higher costs to Congress, and testified that he had released information to the White House in June of 2003 putting the estimate of an early version of the bill at $500 to $600 billion.[12]

CBO stuck with its original estimate of $395 billion, despite the administration's revision of their estimate, until early 2005, when the ten-year (2004–13) estimate was revised upward to $436 billion.[13] CBO seems largely to have stuck to its earlier estimate because of the uncertainty associated with the estimate. Until the drug benefit took effect, and given that there is no track record for CBO to review that would provide any evidence of the accuracy or inaccuracy of the estimate, CBO simply held firm to its estimate pending further information. By 2010, CBO acknowledged that its earlier 2003 estimate, at least of the portion of the bill that involved the provision of prescription drug benefits (there were other provisions of the MMA that involved attempts to enact offsetting savings), was actually too high, based on the spending effects through 2009.[14]

This case illustrates several key factors that are important to understanding CBO cost estimates. First, cost estimates matter. If no cost constraint had existed—and CBO had not been required to produce an estimate—a different bill would have emerged from conference. Second, because the cost estimate matters, CBO is an important shadow player at the conference table when conferees are resolving differences: it also played a key role in the development of the outlines of the legislation before the conference. Third, estimating costs—particularly over ten years for a new program—is a dicey proposition. For all of the controversy over the difference between CBO and the administration cost estimates, both of them were likely well within the margin of error. In fact, CBO now believes that its estimate—which was lower than the administration's—was too high.

Notes

1. Andrew Taylor, "Medicare: Bill's True Cost a Study in Guesswork," *Congressional Quarterly Weekly Report* (October 25, 2003): 2616.

2. Robert Pear, "Bush Will Accept Identical Benefits on Medicare Drugs," *New York Times*, June 9, 2003, A1.

3. Andrew Taylor, "Medicare: Bill's True Cost," 2616.

4. Ibid.

5. Ibid.

6. Congressional Budget Office, *A Detailed Desctiption of CBO's Cost Estimate for the Medicare Prescription Drug Benefit* (July 2004), vii.

7. Amy Goldstein, "Higher Medicare Costs Suspected for Months," *Washington Post*, January 31, 2004, A1.

8. "The Actuary and the Actor," *New York Times*, March 16, 2004, A26.

9. Kate Schuler and Mary Agnes Carey, "Estimates, Ethics and Ads Tarnish Medicare Overhaul," *Congressional Quarterly Weekly Report* (March 20, 2004): 699.

10. Goldstein, "Higher Medicare Costs."

11. "For Us, $140 Billion Is Nothing," *The Hill*, July 13, 2004, 1.

12. Kate Schuler, "Challenged Estimates of Benefit's Costs Worry Medicare Drug Law Backers," *Congressional Quarterly Weekly Report* (March 27, 2004): 750.

13. Robert Pear, "Drug Cost Estimate Is Raised," *New York Times*, March 5, 2005, A14.

14. Douglas Elmendorf, Letter to Representative Maurice Hinchey, "Budgetary Impact of Specified Tax and Spending Actions," May 11, 2010, www.cbo.gov/search/pub_sitesearch.cfm?criteria=Hinchey&filt_subject=any&filt_doctype=7&filt_datespec=All&filt_datetype=range&filt_datestart=01/03/2010&filt_dateend=06/10/2010.

In the second case, the controversy largely revolved around estimates of how fast funds provided under the American Recovery and Reinvestment Act would spend out. In other words, the administration and key congressional committees wanted CBO to estimate that much of the spending would occur in the first two years, to more strongly argue that the effects would be stimulative. In fact, CBO's more conservative estimates concerning how much of the ARRA money would be spent in 2009 turned out to be a little higher than actual fiscal year 2009 stimulus spending.[29]

Scorekeeping

The scorekeeping function—that is, tracking the cost of legislation against the constraints imposed by the law or the budget resolution—was the one function of CBO that predated the agency. The individual staff of the scorekeeping unit within BAD existed before CBO as part of the Joint Committee on the Reduction of Federal Expenditures, which in 1968 began publishing a scorekeeping report, which was designed to track congressional budget actions relative to the president's budget.[30] Therefore, the four employees who made up the scorekeeping unit within the Joint Committee were simply transferred to CBO under the Budget Act. As Jim Blum noted in an interview, "they were actually the first CBO employees, right after Alice once she was sworn in. It was an easy matter to say we'll keep that unit intact because they clearly already have a relationship with the appropriation committees, they were essentially already doing that sort of thing."[31]

Scorekeeping, in a nutshell, involves tracking costs against some budget constraint. These constraints can have their foundation either in law or in the congressional budget resolution. The main initial focus, however, was on scoring relative to the resolution. CBO's job is to inform the budget committees in each house concerning how legislation stacks up relative to these constraints. Cost estimates feed into the scorekeeping process. The majority of the scorekeeping process involves the regular appropriation bills.[32] These bills, which must pass each year, need to live within the overall limits, both the so-called 302(a) limits established in the budget resolution for committees, as well as the 302(b) allocations, which subdivide the committee allocation among the appropriation subcommittees.

Scorekeeping relates to both appropriations and other legislation. It was particularly important during the period that the federal budget process was governed by the BEA, when scorekeeping took on added significance because of the enforcement procedures established by the BEA. For discretionary spending, the budget authority and outlay limits both needed to be adhered to at both the appropriations committee and subcommittee levels. Because outlays were limited in addition to budget authority, the spend out rate became a critical element in these scorekeeping estimates.[33] In addition, during these years legislation could trigger across-the-board cuts under either the discretionary spending caps or the PAYGO process. A new Pay-As-You-Go Act of 2010 is also creating substantial work for BAD analysts.

For scorekeeping purposes, it was particularly important during this BEA period not only that costs be estimated, but that they be assigned to the proper category (discretionary versus mandatory). The importance of this categorization stems from the existence of the separate enforcement processes created by the BEA for mandatory and discretionary programs. In the former case, the requirement was that overall effect of changes in mandatory spending and revenues was deficit neutral over the course of a given congressional session; if not, a sequestration of selected mandatory programs was triggered. Discretionary spending is enforced in a different way. Between 1991 and 2002, a sequestration could be triggered through enacting appropriations in excess of the BEA's budget authority or outlay limits. Even without these limits, however (they did not exist between 1977 and 1990, and have not since 2002), scorekeeping must determine whether appropriation bills adhere to the limits established by the budget resolution and the subcommittee allocations that are under the jurisdiction of the House and Senate budget committees.[34]

Because of the importance of scorekeeping after passage of the BEA, budget controllers (OMB, CBO, and budget committees) have codified a set of scorekeeping guidelines in an attempt to establish clear and consistent rules for the scoring of legislative proposals. The complexity of the federal budget and the lengths to which advocates of budgetary benefits are willing to go to enact their budgetary proposals convinced these controllers that it was essential for the rules to be consistently applied. These rules are too lengthy to be reproduced here, but box 4.2 presents a summary.

Without a scorekeeping system, it would be impossible to enforce the annual budget resolution, because the aggregate limits in the budget resolution are meaningless unless they can be translated into (relatively) binding constraints. The scorekeeping system tracks the progress of approximately twelve hundred spending accounts from the time bills are reported out of committee until the bills they contain are enacted. And, though it is the budget committees that must advise the parliamentarians in each house as to whether a point of order can be raised against a particular piece of legislation or an amendment to legislation, it is the CBO analysis that provides the technical basis for those judgments. Keeping the scorekeeping database up to date involves substantial interaction between CBO cost analysts and their counterparts in CBO's scorekeeping unit. Keeping Congress informed involves almost constant communication between CBO, the appropriations committees and subcommittees, and the budget committees.

Box 4.3 recounts a case from the early 1990s where adherence to scorekeeping rules forced a powerful senator to back off of a proposal to use funds provided in a highway bill to finance construction of a federal courthouse in his state.

■ **Box 4.2** Scorekeeping Guidelines

The budget scorekeeping guidelines established most recently under the Balanced Budget Act of 1997 "are to be used by the House and Senate Budget Committees, the Congressional Budget Office, and the Office of Management and Budget (the scorekeepers) in measuring compliance with the Congressional Budget Act of 1974 (CBA), as amended, and the Balanced Budget and Emergency Deficit Control Act, as amended. The purpose of the guidelines is to ensure that the scorekeepers measure the effects of legislation on the deficit consistent with established scorekeeping conventions and with the specific requirements in those Acts regarding discretionary spending, direct spending, and receipts."[1]

There are sixteen scorekeeping rules in all, some quite lengthy. A summary of the major thrust of each follows:

a. List the appropriations normally enacted in appropriation bills.
b. Prior outlays are to be classified according to the split between mandatory and discretionary spending of the account from which the outlays occur.
c. If the appropriations committee enacts legislation affecting direct (mandatory) spending, these effects will be scored against the appropriation committees' 302(b) allocation. Conversely, direct spending savings included in both an appropriation bill and a reconciliation bill will be credited to the reconciliation bill. This requirement is known euphemistically—or perhaps just mystically—among scorekeepers as the "score the do-er" rule.
d. The transfer of budget authority to a discretionary account will be scored as an increase in discretionary budget authority and outlays in the account to which the transfer is made.
e. Governs the scoring of permissive transfers, assuming that they occur (in full or in part) unless sufficient evidence exists to the contrary. Outlays from such transfers will be estimated based on the best information available, primarily historical experience and, where applicable, indications of executive or congressional intent.
f. Reappropriations of expiring balances of budget authority are scored as new budget authority in the fiscal year in which the balances become newly available.
g. Advance appropriations of budget authority are scored as new budget authority in the fiscal year in which the funds become newly available for obligation, not when the appropriations are enacted.
h. Governs the scoring treatment of rescissions of unobligated balances (balances that exist in accounts that have not yet been obligated for expenditure), and transfers of unobligated balances, covering both the timing of the scoring and how each account (the donating and the receiving account) will be treated.

Unfunded Mandates Reform Act of 1995

CBO's original requirement, as discussed, was to estimate the costs to the federal government stemming from legislation passed by Congress. From relatively early in CBO's history, however, concerns began to surface that bills that imposed costs on state and local governments got much less attention than those that had impact on the federal budget. This was part of a general worry among states and localities that the federal government did not appropriately account for the costs that federal law passed on to these subnational jurisdictions; the particular

i. The date that an appropriation bill specifies determines the year for which new budget authority is scored, except for advance appropriations.
j. Specifies when budget authority and outlays will be scored in cases where the authority to obligate funds is contingent upon the enactment of an appropriation, an authorization, or an action by the Executive branch.
k. Establishes rules for scoring lease-purchases, capital leases, and operating leases.[2]
l. Provides instructions on how (and when) to score write-offs of uncashed checks, unredeemed food stamps, and similar instruments.
m. Prohibits the reclassification of spending and revenues (for example, from discretionary to mandatory, special fund to revolving fund, on-budget to off-budget, revenue to offsetting receipt), for the purpose of enforcing a budget agreement.
n. Prohibits an increase in receipts or decrease in direct spending as a result of provisions of a law that provides direct spending for administration or program management activities.[3]
o. Establishes rules governing the sale of assets, providing in particular that asset sales that are costly to the government must be scored on a new present value basis.
p. Establishes rules for the scoring of legislative changes in limits on outstanding debt where an account is financed by indefinite borrowing authority (added in 1997).

The application of these rules is complex, arcane, and not well understood outside of the small priesthood of budget technicians. Their effects, however, are very real. They can be keenly felt, as they were especially during the twelve fiscal years governed by the constraints established by the BEA. They also represent an extraordinary example of cooperation between budget controllers, and between the branches (primarily OMB and CBO). This testament to professional cooperation is particularly noteworthy considering that ten of the twenty fiscal years these guidelines have been in effect (1991 through 2010) have been characterized by divided government.

Notes

1. These scorekeeping guidelines were published most recently in the *Conference Report to Accompany H.R. 2015, The Balanced Budget Act of 1997,* Public Law 105-33, 105th Cong., 1st sess., (July 20, 1997), 1007–14.

2. The complexity of the lease-purchase scoring rule is indicated by the fact that it by itself consumes two pages in the scorekeeping guidelines. See box 4.3 for further elaboration.

3. Congress could not, for example, provide direct spending for increased IRS enforcement activities and plan to pay for it through increased revenues from that enforcement.

concern surrounded what are called unfunded mandates, or costs passed on without the resources to pay for them. The first legislative response that affected CBO surfaced in 1981, when Congress passed the State and Local Cost Estimate Act (SLCEA). This bill required CBO to specifically notify Congress if any bill imposed an aggregate cost on states and localities in excess of $200 million, or if the cost had an extraordinary regional impact.[35]

CBO was provided with additional resources to implement this law, but these additional staff were spread throughout the existing federal cost units, and each federal analyst was given responsibility to include (as appropriate) a state and

■ **Box 4.3** The Brooklyn Courthouse

In 1992 Senator Daniel Patrick Moynihan's (D-NY) effort to finance the construction of a new courthouse for the Federal District Court of the Eastern District of New York provided an illustration of the significance of a CBO cost estimate and the accompanying application of scorekeeping rules. This estimate involved the application of complex scorekeeping rules concerning federal lease-purchase agreements.

Before the details of this controversy are outlined, some background on the lease-purchase rules is in order. In the late 1980s Congress and the president began to enact laws authorizing agencies to enter into lease-purchase agreements as a preferred way of financing capital projects. For example, in 1988, Public Law 100-480 authorized the architect of the Capitol to "enter into . . . an agreement for the development of" an office building and required that the agreement provide that all "costs incurred with respect to the building to be constructed under the agreement will be at no cost to the United States." But the law also specified that before the architect can enter into that agreement, the architect first "shall enter into an agreement for the lease of such a building by the Architect" and that the terms of that lease agreement require that the "obligation of funds for lease payments . . . may only be made on an annual basis" from an account that may have funds appropriated to it in the future.[1] While the legislation was being considered, it seemed clear from the language of the bill that the entire development of the building was contingent on the future appropriation of funds for lease payments. Once the bill was enacted, the architect of the Capitol did in fact sign a contract with a developer for the construction and lease of a building that is now the Thurgood Marshall Judiciary Building, even though no appropriations had been provided in advance as the law seemed to require. Only after the building was completed did the architect request that Congress provide appropriations to cover the lease payments that he had already obligated the federal government to pay.

Using this Judiciary building legislation as a model, Congress and federal agencies seemed to have found a way to avoid being charged the entire amount associated with the acquisition of a building or other capital asset up front, as would occur if the federal government was going to construct or buy a building outright. Instead, costs would be charged to their budgets in much smaller installments over time, even though the sum of those costs represents a higher overall cost to the government than would have occurred if the government had purchased the asset outright.

Concerned that this practice represented a more expensive and less-than-transparent way of committing the government to a (usually substantial) future expenditure of resources, the budget scorekeepers (OMB, CBO, and the budget committees) adopted in 1990 a set of scorekeeping guidelines, including one that specified how lease-purchases would be scored in the future (and retroactively change the scoring of some lease-purchases that had already been enacted; see box 4.2). The scorekeeping guidelines state that "budget authority will be scored against the legislation in the year in which the budget authority is first made available in the amount of the estimated net present value of the government's total estimated legal obligations over the life of the contract."[2] In other words, for a lease purchase, the full amount of the estimated cost to the government over the life of the contract would be scored in the first year. The 1990 scorekeeping guidelines noted one exception to this rule, which turned out to be crucial in the case of the Brooklyn Courthouse. The exception reads as follows: "Unless language that authorizes a project clearly states that no obligations are allowed unless budget authority is provided specifically for that project in an appropriations bill in advance of the obligation, the legislation will be interpreted as providing obligation authority, in an amount to be estimated by the scorekeepers."[3]

What does this mean in terms of the example at hand? The Intermodal Surface Transportation Efficiency Act (ISTEA) of 1991 includes a provision, inserted by Moynihan, to authorize the administrator of the General Services Administration (GSA) to lease a building from the United States Postal Service (USPS) to house the federal courts in the Brooklyn Courthouse. Because this provision met the definition of a lease-purchase, and because it omits the necessary language stating that "no obligations are allowed [i.e., GSA cannot sign a lease with USPS] unless budget authority is provided specifically for that project in an appropriations bill in advance of the obligation," the CBO cost estimate for the bill scored the entire amount for the acquisition of the courthouse space as direct (mandatory) spending, resulting in additional outlays of $457 million over the 1993–96 period.

Section 1004 of the ISTEA also includes a provision—inserted at the insistence of the House Ways and Means Committee—that requires the secretary of transportation to execute an across-the-board reduction in all obligations authorized by ISTEA to the extent that the rest of the provisions in the bill result in a net increase in outlays over the 1992–95 period. The Ways and Means Committee felt compelled to do this in order to protect mandatory spending for programs under their jurisdiction from a pay-as-you-go sequestration (under the Budget Enforcement Act of 1990) that might have been caused by enactment of the highway bill. Implementing section 1004 of ISTEA would have required "the outlays over the 1992–95 period [to] be offset by a reduction in 1992 obligations for highway programs sufficient to prevent net pay-as-you-go spending from exceeding zero in each year.... OMB, which was responsible for implementing this provision, estimated that the reduction in highway obligations necessary to produce pay-as-you-go cost no greater than zero in any year would be $1 billion."[4]

The bottom line, of course, is that Senator Moynihan's Courthouse provision would have ultimately cost a whole lot of members of Congress a combined $1 billion in terms of transportation projects for their states or districts. But after ISTEA was enacted (December 19, 1991), Senator Moynihan felt compelled to introduce a subsequent bill (S. 2641. P.L. 102-334, enacted August 6, 1992) that made the GSEA lease of the Brooklyn Courthouse contingent on future congressional enactment of appropriations for the cost of the lease payments and that restored some of the cuts that had been implemented on the transportation projects in ISTEA.

In an April 9, 1992, letter to CBO director Robert Reischauer, Senator Moynihan appeared to try and lay part of the blame for this debacle on CBO by informing Reischauer that CBO cost analyst Jim Hearn had been given a copy of the relevant provision in advance, and asking "didn't Mr. (Jim) Hearn advise Mr. (Mark) Kadesh (Senator Moynihan's staffer) that some changes were necessary to endure that the Brooklyn Courthouse provision would have no cost?"[5] This seems an odd question, since according to the response sent by Reischauer to Moynihan, Hearn did inform Mr. Kadesh that changes would be necessary to the courthouse language to prevent that language from being scored with direct spending outlays for a lease-purchase. The problem was that Moynihan did not make the required changes—i.e., insertion of the words "subject to appropriations action" into the language—prior to inserting the courthouse provision into the conference report on ISTEA.[6] So, the bill was enacted that includes language authorizing the GSA acquisition of the Brooklyn Courthouse through a lease-purchase—at great cost in lost transportation funds to others around the country.

This story is a good illustration of (a) just how arcane the cost estimating/scoring rules can be, (b) the risk to members of Congress (and their staffs) of ignoring or not understanding them, and (c) how strong the temptation can be to blame CBO—or the scorekeeping rules themselves—for undesirable outcomes, regardless of evidence substantiating that blame may lie somewhere else.

(continued on next page)

Beyond the controversy surrounding securing the money, the courthouse hit other speed bumps along the way, mostly related to its architectural design and opposition from community groups.[7] Ultimately, the Brooklyn Courthouse was constructed, but groundbreaking did not occur until 2000. The official dedication ceremony was held in June 2006, although the courthouse had already been in use for some time (and Senator Moynihan himself had died) by the time it was dedicated.[8]

Notes

1. Public Law 100-480, the Judiciary Building Development Act, the text of which can be found in the *Congressional Record*, September 23, 1988, 25217–19.
2. This language is found in scorekeeping rule 11 (see box 4.2).
3. Ibid.
4. Letter from Robert D. Reischauer to Daniel Patrick Moynihan, April 14, 1992. From National Archives, accession no. 520-04-1010, Box 1.
5. Letter from Daniel P. Moynihan to Robert D. Reischauer, April 9, 1992, National Archives, Accession Number 520-04-1010, Box 1.
6. Letter from Robert Reischauer to Moynihan.
7. Joseph Fried, "Courthouse Proposal Leaves Brooklyn Post Office Unscathed," *New York Times*, May 17, 1994, B3.
8. Dennis Holt, "Brooklyn Broadside: Courthouse Ceremony Evokes Thoughts of Moynihan, Dearie," *Brooklyn Daily Eagle*, June 20, 2006.

local cost estimate as part of the cost estimate for each bill. Increasingly, as mandates continued to be enacted, the state and local constituency in Congress became convinced that the law was doing nothing to curb the congressional appetite for unfunded mandates, and that CBO staff gave much more attention to the federal costs of legislation than the state and local effects.

When the Republicans took over both houses of Congress in 1994, unfunded mandates again became an important issue, but for a new reason. The House Republicans, who had included a constitutional amendment to required an annually balanced federal budget as part of its Contract with America, found it difficult to gain the support of some state governors for the amendment unless legislation reducing the possibility of unfunded mandates was also passed. State governors were critical to Senate passage; the amendment was thought to face an easier route to passage in the House.

Against this backdrop the first bill (S. 1) of the new Congress was an attempted prohibition against unfunded mandates. The bill eventually became law as the Unfunded Mandates Reform Act (UMRA) of 1995, and created a new requirement for CBO to analyze bills and estimate the costs of any mandates in the bill. As it relates to intergovernmental mandates that fall on states and localities, the bill both defines mandates and establishes a threshold for associated costs. In this law, a mandate is defined to include legislative actions or regulations that impose an "enforceable duty" on state, local, or tribal governments, or the private sector. The law did not generally include as mandates conditions of assistance,[36] nor did they include a number of other actions that concern, for example, the protection of constitutional rights or national security. CBO is required, under UMRA, to provide an estimate of mandate costs if the total cost to states and localities exceeds $50 million in any of the first five fiscal years after the mandate takes effect ($100 million for private sector mandates).[37] These figures are adjusted annually for inflation; in 2010 the figures were $70 million and $139 million.

This unfunded mandate requirement differs from the previous state and local cost estimate statute in three respects. The first has to do with its enforcement. The law creates a point of order against Congress considering a bill on the floor of the House or Senate unless the committee report accompanying that bill includes a CBO mandate statement. In cases when intergovernmental mandates have direct costs above the annual threshold, Congress may not act on the legislation if it does not also include either an authorization of appropriations or direct spending authority sufficient to offset the mandate's cost.[38]

The second way in which UMRA differs from SLCEA is in CBO's organizational response. CBO made a specific decision in 1995 to respond to UMRA by creating a separate unit within BAD, the sole responsibility of which was to take charge of implementing the state and local mandate requirements of the statute. In doing so, CBO rejected the approach that had been taken when the SLCEA was passed, signaling that it intended to make UMRA a much higher priority. This may seem like a subtle difference, but it has been critical to the law's implementation. The unit has actively reached out to interest groups representing the state and local government constituency, having frequent meetings with the major intergovernmental lobbying organizations.[39] In addition, the state and local estimates are the priority for the analysts in CBO's state and local cost estimating unit. They do not—either in reality or perception—play second fiddle to the federal cost estimates.

A third difference, of course, between the SLCEA and UMRA is that the latter explicitly requires not only intergovernmental mandate statements, but statements concerning the impact of legislation on the private sector as well. Although these private sector mandate statements are included in the cost estimates of legislation, they are not prepared by BAD staff. Rather, the program divisions are responsible for the analysis of private sector mandates. In fiscal year 2009 sixty private sector mandates were enacted into law, in twenty-six pieces of legislation. Of these mandates, seventeen exceeded the threshold of $139 million.[40]

Although the unfunded mandate legislation has unquestionably increased CBO's attention to mandates, it is difficult to determine the extent to which this attention has actually affected the imposition of mandates. First, it must be said that most of the bills considered by Congress since the passage of UMRA do not include mandates. In fact, CBO transmitted more than eight thousand mandate statements between 1996 and 2009. Of these, just over one thousand (1,026, or 13 percent) identified intergovernmental mandates, but only ninety-one had costs that exceeded the threshold identified by the law.[41] Through 2009 only eleven laws containing mandates with costs over the mandated threshold were enacted. Those include the following:

- increases in the minimum wage, enacted in 1996 and 2007;
- a reduction in federal funds for the food stamp program in 1998;
- a preemption of state taxes on prescription drug plans in 2003;
- a temporary preemption of state taxes on internet services in 2004 and a subsequent extension of that preemption in 2007;
- a requirement that states and localities meet certain federal standards in the issuance of driver's licenses in 2004;
- the elimination of matching federal payments for some child support spending in 2006;
- a requirement that state and local governments withhold taxes on certain payments for property and services in 2006; and
- requirements that public transit carriers train workers, and that commuter railroads install train control technology, enacted in 2007 and 2008.[42]

In other cases, legislative proposals have been altered in response to the costs of mandates. For example, several bills that had costs above the threshold when CBO analyzed them initially were amended to bring those costs below the threshold. These included, for example, requirements that driver's licenses show Social Security numbers and a moratorium on the taxation of certain internet transactions.[43]

It is clear that CBO has taken the implementation of the act seriously, and that in some cases providing information on the effects of mandates has made Congress less likely to impose them. It is possible that the existence of UMRA has itself discouraged the imposition of mandates, and that this is part of the explanation for the small number of mandates imposed. However, Gullo noted that critics of UMRA identify three reasons to be somewhat hesitant in touting success of the legislation.

- Conditions of assistance, as are commonly used to encourage state and local governments to take actions that they might not choose to take (such as raising the drinking age in order to receive federal highway funds or meeting test requirements for receiving education funds), are not considered mandates under UMRA's definitions.
- Certain types of costly mandates are specifically omitted from UMRA's requirements, including, most significantly, the election reform legislation of 2001 (deemed to concern the constitutional right of citizens to vote) and

the Americans with Disabilities Act (which, among other things, creates accessibility requirements for public buildings), each of which imposed substantial costs on state and local governments.

- Federal preemptions of state law generally do not fall above the threshold, but still can impose substantial limitations on state and local governments.[44]

Interviews with individuals outside of CBO confirmed the impression that CBO is taking these estimates much more seriously than was true under the old state and local cost estimates legislation. Ray Scheppach, the head of the National Governor's Association and a former high-level CBO administrator in the early years, said that he believes that the estimates under UMRA have made a difference because "they worried the members so that they found another way to do it, rather than a mandate," adding that "I think they [CBO] do a good job on that piece."[45] Paul Posner added that "as someone who looked at that in the 1980s and saw CBO really ignore this issue . . . they made a major investment of analysts. . . . I think they deserve tremendous credit for having made the investment and they're widely respected."[46]

Conclusion: Overarching Issues Related to Microbudgeting

A number of lessons and conclusions can be taken from this discussion of CBO's role as it relates to staffing the day-to-day information needs of Congress.

1. Forming and maintaining relationships with committees and committee staff is critical to CBO's ability to produce credible cost estimates and to perform its scorekeeping work in a timely fashion. Many estimates involve complex analyses conducted in a compressed time frame. For that reason, the sooner that CBO knows that a committee is planning to report out a piece of legislation, the greater the chance that CBO will be able to conduct its cost estimate in a timely and accurate manner. Committees do not, however, always have an incentive to keep CBO informed, particularly when more analysis is likely to lead to higher assumed costs.

2. The challenge of providing numbers to Congress is made more complicated by the necessity for internal consistency. That is, given CBO's desire to be not only accurate, but also fair across all advocates and opponents of particular provisions, CBO's estimates must use methodologies that accurately reflect the relative cost of all similar pieces of legislation as well as the costs of an individual piece of legislation. Thus when the agency was providing estimates of prescription drug proposals, it was as important to maintain a consistent set of standards as it was to get initial estimates correct. Moreover, legislative proposals must be scored consistently over time.

CBO relies on past precedents in scoring these proposals, in much the same way that the judicial system relies on legal precedents in seeking a consistent application of the law. In fact, much of the reason for the development of the complex scorekeeping rules has to do with the need to maintain consistency across different proposals and committees. This is not only fair, but it protects CBO, the budget committees, and OMB against charges that they determine costs in an arbitrary fashion, depending on their own desires to make it easier or more difficult for legislation to be enacted.

3. An organization such as CBO faces substantial human resources challenges. It is not easy to locate individuals with the appropriate skill set and then train those individuals to perform effectively as a CBO cost analyst. The Budget Analysis Division, for this reason, has over time developed its own subculture within CBO (even having its own softball team, the BAD Assets). Turnover among staff is relatively low and continuity is remarkable—particularly at the higher levels. As of 2010, both the assistant director for budget analysis and one of the two deputy assistant directors in the unit had been with the agency for twenty-five or more years. There is also a very strong tendency to promote from within. It is rare for a supervisor within BAD (unit chief, deputy assistant director, or assistant director) to be hired from outside the agency.

4. Cost estimates matter. They affect how legislation is drafted, and they affect its prospects for approval. Much of this effort actually occurs during the informal communication between CBO and congressional committees during the bill-drafting process. For example, the specifics of the prescription drug bill would have been different had there been no $400 billion targeted price tag and no CBO estimate. Congress would have changed the legislation had CBO estimated that the bill would cost more. Estimates of federal costs, or unfunded mandates, result in legislation being changed or scuttled entirely. Also, as James Blum noted in 1992, the cost estimates "often have an impact on legislation because they are used to determine whether the committees are in compliance with the annual budget resolutions and reconciliation instructions."[47] This is what the drafters of the Budget Act wanted. They wanted to create a situation where how much something cost would affect its prospects for becoming law. It would be hard to argue with the success of CBO on these terms.

There is a flip side to this success. That is, CBO cost estimates have made costs more important, but perhaps at times this goes too far. That is, in many cases costs trump all other considerations, and legislation is drafted or changed for the sole purpose of affecting scoring, with little regard for whether the resulting legislation is sound public policy.

In terms of the function of CBO cost estimates anticipated by the 1974 Budget Act, however, there is little doubt that they have provided credible information that did not exist before and that they have an effect on legislation. Overall evidence appears to suggest that CBO cost estimates are, by and large, viewed as credible and nonpartisan. CBO directors appointed by both Republicans and Democrats have come under fire for CBO cost estimates from both Republicans and Democrats. In fact, CBO director Reischauer had some of his more uncomfortable moments when Democratic members were on the other end of the phone, and both O'Neill and Holtz-Eakin were on the receiving end of criticism from House Republican leaders or committee chairs. O'Neill noted, for example, that though it was the popular perception that former House Speaker Newt Gingrich took her to task for macrobudgetary estimates, most of the discussions that they had were over his dissatisfaction with cost estimates, specifically for Medicare. "He had a whole bunch of diabetes add-ons one year and was trying to convince me through emissaries . . . that these bills would save money," recalled O'Neill. "And . . . we painstakingly showed that . . . saving lives wasn't the same thing as saving money. There must have been something like seven bills like that, and I think he was madder about them than any other thing."[48]

In the end, CBO's microbudgeting work is quite influential, but in a way that normally has a much lower profile than its macrobudgetary work. Although certainly there were a great many people who became aware of CBO cost estimating during the health reform debate of 2009 and 2010, these kinds of effects had been felt behind the scenes over CBO's entire history. In many cases, however, the effects of these cost estimates and of scorekeeping can be evaluated mostly in terms of what did not happen. That is, the existence of CBO cost estimates causes legislation to be revised in a way that affects the cost. It is difficult to imagine that this attention would be paid to the costs of legislation were there not a Congressional Budget Office, and indeed a congressional budget process. In the end, of course, it is impossible to prove the counterfactual—that is, what the costs of legislation would be without a process, or without a CBO.

Notes

1. Roy Meyers, "Congressional Budget Office," in *Encyclopedia of Public Policy and Administration*, edited by Jay Shafritz (Boulder, CO: Westview Press, 1998), 486–92.

2. Shirley Ruhe, interview with the author, October 14, 2003.

3. Nancy D. Kates, *Starting from Scratch: Alice Rivlin and the Congressional Budget Office*, Part B (Cambridge, MA: Harvard University, 1989). This was confirmed in interviews for this book, by both James L. Blum on February 8, 2004, and Richard Emery on July 8, 2004.

4. Blum, interview, February 2004.

5. Ibid.

6. Rivlin, interview, 2003.

7. Blum, interview, February 2004.

8. Peter Fontaine, written communication, August 3, 2010.

9. Ibid.

10. Paul Cullinan, interview with the author, November 4, 2004.

11. This is less true since the passage of the Federal Credit Reform Act of 1990, which charges budget authority and outlays in the current year based on the present value of the long-term costs to the federal government associated with the loan guarantees. Estimating these future costs, and converting them to present values—as the Credit Reform Act requires—is its own daunting task.

12. James Hearn, interview with the author, October 27, 2004.

13. Penner, interview.

14. Anderson, interview.

15. Penner, interview.

16. Cullinan, interview.

17. Congressional Budget Office, Cost Estimate, H.R. 1, *Medicare Prescription Drug and Modernization Act of 2003,* and S. 1, *Prescription Drug and Medicare Improvement Act of 2003,* 108th Cong., 1st sess., July 22, 2003.

18. Congressional Budget Office, Cost Estimate, H.R. 1, *American Recovery and Reinvestment Act of 2009,* 111th Cong., 1st sess., January 26, 2009.

19. Douglas Elmendorf, Letter to the Honorable Nancy Pelosi, *Concerning the Amendment in the Nature of a Substitute to H.R. 4872, the Reconciliation Act of 2010,* March 20, 2010.

20. Congressional Budget Office, *Cost Estimate on H.R. 2454, the American Clean Energy and Security Act of 2009,* June 5, 2009.

21. Paul Posner, interview with the author, July 15, 2004.

22. These data on cost estimates by year come from an internal CBO analysis prepared by CBO in March 2010. Used with permission.

23. This discussion was informed by a written communication with Peter Fontaine, August 3, 2010.

24. See statement on CBO website, www.cbo.gov/aboutcbo/policies.cfm.

25. "Reinventing Arithmetic," *Washington Post,* November 19, 1993, A28.

26. Spencer Rich, "Experts Cite Flaws in Grace Panel's Claims for Savings," *Washington Post,* February 29, 1984, A13; Robert Rothman, "Few Grace Commission Suggestions Adopted," *Congressional Quarterly Weekly* (November 24, 1984): 2990.

27. Brian Collins, "Downpayment Bill Hurt by Estimate," *National Mortgage News* 28, no. 41 (2004): 14. Under the Federal Credit Reform Act of 1990, direct loan and loan guarantee costs are computed on a subsidy basis, representing the present value of the cost to the government over the life of the loan. For a guarantee program, costs are frequently driven by default rates.

28. Michael S. Gerber, "CBO, OMB Analyses of Mortgage Bill Arrive at Very Different Conclusions," *The Hill,* June 30, 2004, 11.

29. See Congressional Budget Office, *The Budget and Economic Outlook; Fiscal Years 2010 to 2020,* appendix A, 95–98.

30. Priscilla Aycock, interview with the author, November 10, 2004.

31. Blum, interview, February 2004.

32. Until 2005, there were thirteen subcommittees (and therefore thirteen bills) in each house. A change in committee jurisdictions in 2005 resulted in only ten subcommittees in the House and twelve in the Senate. When the Democrats regained control

of the Congress in 2007, they established twelve subcommittees, with matching jurisdictions, in each house.

33. Because budget authority can frequently lead to outlays in multiple years, programs with slow spend out rates (such as many defense procurement activities) normally have an easier time fitting within outlay caps than programs with faster spend out rates. See Allen Schick, *The Federal Budget: Process, Politics, Policy*, 3rd ed. (Washington, DC: Brookings, 2007).

34. Under the Congressional Budget Act, allocations are made to each Congressional committee of spending amounts that may not be exceeded by that committee. In the case of the Appropriations Committee, these committee limits are further translated into limits for each of the appropriations subcommittees.

35. Congressional Budget Office, "The Feasibility of Preparing State and Local Cost Estimates," November 1981, www.cbo.gov/ftpdocs/113xx/doc11315/1981_11_feasibility .pdf.

36. These are requirements that state and local governments must meet in order to receive federal money. For example, the requirement to meet particular testing standards under the No Child Left Behind Act is a condition of receiving federal education money.

37. Theresa Gullo, "History and Evaluation of the Unfunded Mandates Reform Act," *National Tax Journal* 57, no. 3 (2004): 559–70.

38. Ibid., 562.

39. Theresa Gullo, interview with the author, October 28, 2004.

40. Congressional Budget Office, *A Review of CBO's Activities in 2009 under the Unfunded Mandates Reform Act* (March 2010), 4.

41. Data on total bills reviewed and mandates statements issued from Leo Lex, chief, State and Local Government Cost Estimates Unit, Congressional Budget Office. Listing of intergovernmental mandates enacted taken from Congressional Budget Office, *A Review of CBO's Activities in 2009*, 68–69.

42. Ibid., 6.

43. Gullo, interview.

44. Gullo, "History and Evaluation of the Unfunded Mandates Reform Act," 568–69.

45. Ray Scheppach, interview with the author, October 3, 2003.

46. Posner, interview.

47. James L. Blum, "The Congressional Budget Office: On the One Hand, on the Other," in *Organizations for Policy Analysis: Helping Government Think*, edited by Carol Weiss (Newbury Park, CA: Sage Publications, 1992), 221.

48. O'Neill, interview.

Chapter 5

Policy Analysis

AS DISCUSSED IN chapter 2, Alice Rivlin's early decision to separate policy analysis from budget analysis was a controversial and risky choice. By all accounts, she envisioned a Brookings-like role for the policy divisions, and wanted them to do comprehensive analyses of issues facing Congress that affected the economy and the budget. It is worth restating at this point that Rivlin's selection as CBO director represented the ascendancy of legislators in the policy analysis camp over those who envisioned a more limited number-crunching role for CBO. Creating program divisions for performing policy analysis, however, guaranteed neither that anyone would listen to them, nor that they would survive. Rivlin never got the level of resources she had originally hoped for the program divisions, and ended up having to divert dollars from these divisions to BAD (see chapter 2).

By 2009 the policy analysis divisions in CBO consumed about 45 percent of the staffing capacity of CBO: 109 of 242 authorized positions.[1] Policy analysis at CBO covers analytical issues as broad as the federal budget itself—from national security, to health policy, to various schemes in which microeconomic or financial analysis is most useful to determining the appropriateness of policies chosen. It also touches larger macroeconomic issues, those associated with the choice of revenue sources, and the distribution of the revenue burden across different income classes.

CBO's policy analysis work touches every aspect of the federal budget. This chapter focuses in-depth attention on only two cases—the Carter energy policy and government-sponsored enterprises (GSEs)—and by no means is intended to communicate that CBO has not had impacts in other areas, or that these represent the most important analytical work it has done. They are chosen to illustrate two points—first, how CBO established itself and how it surprised some in the Congress, and, second, the limitations of CBO analysis in affecting policy in a political environment, even though the potential effects of CBO's work can sometimes be seen in retrospect.

Creating a Demand for Policy Analysis: The Carter Energy Plan

Congress, as of 1977 when President Carter took office, was unaccustomed to having the kind of detailed information on the economic and budgetary effects of policies that Rivlin anticipated the program divisions creating. In reality, members were not really sure they wanted such analyses, and to the extent that the Congress saw the CBO as filling that void, they tended toward ambivalence. According to Rudy Penner, even by the time of his appointment "the appropriators were always complaining that we didn't serve their cost estimating needs . . . and so they saw—and to some extent the budget committees as well—saw all the policy analysis work of CBO as detracting resources away from what they really wanted, which was the scorekeeping, and that was a constant battle. . . . The policy analysis units had to be defended."[2]

The first hurdle for Rivlin was to develop the analytical and organizational capacity to produce policy analyses. It was not necessarily easy to find the type of people who had the academic training and skills to both analyze proposed legislation (Rivlin wanted to hire PhD economists) and write clear, accessible documents for a congressional audience. This challenge was made a bit easier by the fact that CBO was new and this made it an attractive placement, as did the reputation of Rivlin herself. Hiring assistant directors for the program divisions was only the second priority, preceded by hiring the deputy director and the heads of BAD and the Macroeconomic Analysis Division (MAD).

Having a group of people able to do policy analysis did not guarantee that anyone wanted their analysis. Here was a new institution, with a very uncertain mandate, that needed to develop a constituency in Congress for policy analysis work. Initially, this had to involve a certain amount of selling products to Congress, and a certain amount of judgment on the part of CBO on which topics to address. In contrast, the work of BAD, which was more immediate and more central to the day-to-day work of Congress, had a much higher profile. Further, to the extent that BAD could keep Congress happy, it would buy time for CBO to develop both the supply of and demand for policy analysis.

The Carter Energy Policy

By all accounts, the event that put CBO policy analysis on the map was its analysis of President's Carter's energy policy. The energy plan was the centerpiece of Carter's domestic agenda, developing a comprehensive energy policy for the nation in response to the energy supply crunch of the late 1970s, which itself was caused by the Arab oil embargo. This policy was a significant event in the history of CBO for several reasons. First, it helped establish CBO as a credible voice for economic policy analysis. Second, the report and its aftermath created substantial controversy, particularly related to a press conference Rivlin held after the release of the report. Third, it helped establish the credibility of CBO as an independent voice, particularly because it had criticized a major policy initiative of a Democratic president when the Democrats were in control of the Congress.

Jimmy Carter was elected president in November 1976, a time when energy was at the center of the national policy agenda. The increase in oil prices that had accompanied the Arab oil embargo of the mid-1970s had substantial effects on the US oil supply, resulting in gasoline shortages and steep increases in gasoline prices: between 1973 and 1974 nominal average price per gallon rose 37 percent— the prior year-on-year increase had been only 7 percent.[3] Against this backdrop, Carter promised that the major domestic priority of his administration would be to come up with a comprehensive plan that would reduce the dependence of the United States on foreign oil. He unveiled his plan on April 20, 1977, describing the energy crisis as "the greatest domestic challenge that our nation will face in our lifetime."[4] The plan included the following components:

- retaining price controls on oil and natural gas that had been implemented during the Ford administration;
- ending price controls on gasoline after the summer of 1977;
- imposing a tax of five cents per gallon on gasoline starting in 1979, and increasing by five cents per gallon in each year that the nation used more gasoline than it produced;
- imposing a tax on manufacturers of so-called gas guzzlers that failed to meet national fuel economy standards; and
- establishing various conservation standards and incentives for coal, for buildings, for businesses, for major appliances, and for the use of solar energy.[5]

President Carter introduced this draft legislation to a Congress in which both parties were controlled by the Democrats, which suggested at least the possibility that the bill might have an easy time in passage. In reality, the bills that emerged included some of the provisions of Carter's plan as introduced, but not all of them.

The CBO had no clearly defined role to play in analyzing the Carter plan, at least when the bills to enact it were introduced. CBO had, up to that point, confined its analytical work to bread and butter issues central to its mission—largely, baseline budget projections (and underlying economic forecasts) and cost estimates of proposed legislation. The new policy analysis capacity, however, seemed ideally suited to evaluating the Carter energy proposal, given that it was the centerpiece of the entire Carter economic agenda. If CBO did not do an analysis of the proposal, it would certainly call into question whether CBO was going to be a player in the policy debate or simply crunch numbers.

Still, for political reasons if nothing else, CBO needed to obtain sponsorship for its analysis. Ray Scheppach, who ended up supervising the CBO report, recalled that he made contact with the various committees of jurisdiction almost immediately after the president made the proposal. He spoke, in particular, to staffers for Senator Henry Jackson (D-WA) and Representative John Dingell (D-MI), who were chairs of the major committees of jurisdiction in the Senate and House, respectively: "I figured if we were going to get into this, two things were very important. One was that we had to do it quickly, and second of all I needed political protection. . . . we basically generated the request from Scoop Jackson's people and I think from Dingell's people. . . . I spent a fair amount of time trying to get myself a certain amount of political protection."[6]

Scheppach was a key player, in that he had come from the Budget Analysis Division and both Rivlin and Bob Levine trusted him.[7] In addition, the existence of the Ad Hoc Committee on Energy, chaired by Representative Lud Ashley (D-OH), was a unique opportunity for a foray into the authorizing committee market. According to Everett Ehrlich, who arrived just as work on the report was finishing up, "here was a special entity, it [the committee] was ad hoc, it was going to come and go, it dematerialized back into the political ether, so it was a perfect target for the authorizing [committee] market to be developed. . . . It was a unique place to take this to."[8]

Having gotten the request, CBO had only a month to six weeks to prepare the report, and key staff spent a lot of nights and weekends working on the analysis.[9] Nine staff were identified as major contributors to the report, more than 5 percent of CBO's professional staff at that point.[10] The effort itself was relatively low profile within Congress. Ray Scheppach recalled later that the fact that CBO was working on the report was not well known outside of the "ten or twelve" staff on the Hill who were most directly involved in energy policy.[11]

The CBO Report and Its Aftermath

The CBO report analyzed the major elements of the Carter plan, focusing in particular on the extent to which the policies the president proposed was likely to actually lead to the level of energy conservation envisioned. The report focused on five aspects of the plan: pricing crude oil, pricing natural gas, conversion to coal, automobile-related proposals, and tax credits for home insulation and solar energy.[12] The report estimated that, taken together, the president's plan would achieve a significantly smaller reduction in oil imports than the administration's plan. Whereas the administration had projected that these aspects of its plan would result in a reduction of 3.2 million barrels a day by 1985, the CBO report referred to the president's figures as "overoptimistic," estimating savings at only 2.3 million barrels per day.[13]

The difference with the administration turned out to be controversial. CBO agreed that the level of utility conversion of oil to coal would be consistent with administration estimates, but disagreed with the amount of oil that would be saved from industrial conversion. Further, it questioned whether the president's proposals would mean savings from reducing gasoline consumption, particularly consumption by the trucking industry. Finally, it estimated that the majority of the estimated savings associated with increased insulation would have been saved with or without the president's proposed insulation tax credit.[14]

CBO released the results of its analysis somewhat unconventionally: by having a press conference to release the study. This was not the first time it had held one.[15] Ray Scheppach recalled having mixed feelings about the press conference, because it might provide a high profile for the report, but at the same time was politically risky: "I remember Carter . . . used the title 'the moral equivalent of war' and the first thing out of Alice's mouth was 'this is obviously no moral equivalent of war'. . . . Alice liked the press, which was good and bad. . . . It really did something for our ability to establish our independence, which I think was very important. . . . In her comments, she ratcheted it up as quite confrontational."[16]

Almost immediately, the press began to report the findings of the study and quote Rivlin directly as challenging the credibility of the president's plan. The major immediate concern was not the analysis itself. It was that influential members of Congress, including those who had requested the report, were first hearing about the results not from CBO itself, but from the press (as discussed in chapter 2).

CBO as an Independent Voice

Whatever the immediate controversy resulting from the report and its release, CBO clearly established itself during this period as having a role to play not only in terms of the short-term budget impacts of legislation and the longer baseline budget projections, but also on in the arena of broader policy analysis. There was an audience for CBO's analyses on the policy front. Rivlin or her surrogates testified seven times during May and June 1977 before the various committees with jurisdiction over the pieces of the energy policy.[17]

Despite the stated concerns about CBO's role, Rivlin noted almost thirty years later that there were no efforts to put pressure on CBO to reach a different conclusion, or to punish CBO after the fact. She found it significant that no one ever called her to complain or to threaten her or the agency. "And that's why I thought that somehow they weren't really serious," she said. "They were annoyed, but they weren't going to throw their weight around."[18]

In the end, the Carter energy policy became law. It is difficult to establish the causal linkage between the CBO analysis and the eventual policy. Clearly, CBO staff made the agency a player—by virtue of having produced a widely read report—in a way that would not otherwise have happened. The sheer amount of CBO testimony is one indicator of that outcome. In addition, CBO staff were very involved in the drafting of the policy. If they had not done the report, and if the quality of the report had not developed their credibility, they would not have been involved.[19]

Ray Scheppach recalled later that, although the specific impacts of the CBO report were hard to characterize, the report clearly made the CBO staff that worked on it players as the policy was being drafted. Because President Carter had staked so much on the policy, and because Congress was controlled by the Democrats, the CBO analysis had the effect of slowing down the decision making and creating more deliberation. "I think by us being out fast with a relatively decent study it slowed that process down and I think created a lot more vetting of the pieces of it. So I think in that sense it had an impact, within the individual components."[20]

In a foreword to a book on the congressional response to the Carter energy policy, then US Senator Bill Bradley (D-NJ) made special note of the CBO's analyses, calling them "particularly helpful in correctly defining the energy problem and evaluating alternative federal policies to attain the appropriate energy-policy goals."[21] In discussing these analyses, Senator Bradley used adjectives that should have reinforced the decision to develop a policy-analytic capability at CBO: timely, objective, respected, influential, and careful.[22] Although the foreword to any book might be forgiven for a little hyperbole, when one considers that CBO, as a policy analysis organization, was not on the radar screen for Congress before the Carter energy report, this sort of testimonial is noteworthy.

The CBO report had other effects as well. First, as Everett Ehrlich explained, in a theme that has been repeated countless times over CBO's history, it "injected a note of sobriety about what the results would be. I think that was helpful. Where else would that have come from?" Second, it had a demonstration effect. CBO "showed Congress, meaning committee staffs in large part, how such an analysis would be done. . . . Policy analysis was not the fully blown industry that it is today. It was new on the Hill, so showing people how you break a problem down, had value." In the end, the impact of the impact of the CBO report can only be looked at in comparison to other analytical products. Although there were other broader conceptual discussions of energy issues, "this sort of nuts and bolts piece about this is what you might get, was really unique to us. So as analysis went, it really did all right."[23]

The report may have had effects on the plan, but it unquestionably had consequences for the institution, particularly on the recognition of CBO's capacity to do policy analysis. CBO established a precedent that major initiatives affecting the economy, whether they came out of the administration or Congress, were likely to be subject to CBO analysis.

Rivlin noted that the energy report gave CBO credibility with the Republicans that they previously did not have. There had been several times during the Ford administration when CBO analyses had undermined the president's position. Rivlin claimed that, at those times, CBO had been dismissed as a "tool of the Democrats."[24] The Carter energy study changed that, because "we did an objective analysis and we undermined some of the hype, in the sense that our analysis suggested that the president's proposals saved less oil than the administration was alleging. And that was somewhat embarrassing to some of the Democrats. The Republicans loved it, and it established our nonpartisan credibility as nothing else could have. . . . This was the first time that I remember that I was making the Democrats mad and the Republicans happy and they just loved it."[25]

Everett Ehrlich, who later supervised CBO's energy policy analysis work, agreed that the Carter energy report did a lot to put the CBO program divisions on the map. The important point, he noted, was that Scheppach and his colleagues "produced what was a credible product and suddenly we were there. So I think that sooner or later all of that would have happened. But it happened then because all of the planets came into line in a unique kind of way."[26]

Organizing for and Delivering Policy Analysis

It should be clear that Rivlin's dream of having Brookings-type analytical work as a significant part of CBO's portfolio got a substantial boost from the kind of high-profile analysis CBO did on Carter's energy policy. This was, however, only one issue of hundreds of potential policy initiatives affecting the federal budget. Rivlin, in response to these potential targets for analytical work, began to focus on organizing CBO to do policy analysis in a number of areas:

- macroeconomics
- natural resource and commerce issues
- tax policy
- health and human resource issues
- national security
- budget reform, budget concepts, and government management issues

Although the names of some CBO divisions and the specific means of organizing to deliver products have changed in some cases over time, these still represent the issues that CBO is involved in, and CBO policy analysis reaches every area of the federal budget.

Macroeconomic Studies

What is now MAD, which started out as the Fiscal Analysis Division and changed its name in the 1990s, is responsible first and foremost for developing CBO's economic model and forecast, which underlie the baseline estimates that CBO produces twice a year. In addition to that, however, the division prepares studies that relate to the broader economic effects of fiscal or social events. For example, in the past several years the division has published studies concerning the broader economic effects of both chronically large budget deficits and a flu pandemic.[27] Most recently, it has been heavily involved in informing Congress concerning the possible effects of actions taken to address the global economic meltdown.[28]

The main impact of this macroeconomic work historically has been to support CBO's periodic baseline budget forecasts. It was initially a rather surprising notion (see chapter 4) to some that CBO would have its own forecast, but that forecast is now an institutional part of federal budgeting. To maintain credibility, these forecasts must have two characteristics. First, they must be accurate. Second, they must be viewed as mainstream—that is, not leaning two far in one economic direction or another. On the first point, CBO periodically publishes evaluations of its forecasting track record, and these analyses suggest that CBO has historically been within the mainstream in terms of its economic forecasts.

The main way that CBO has attempted to maintain the credibility of its economic forecasts is by having them reviewed by a panel of economic advisors. This panel was an early innovation, and attempts to subject CBO's twice-yearly economic forecasts to review by a group of economists from across the academic and political spectrum. Currently, the CBO Panel of Economic Advisors includes twenty prominent economists, including the first two directors of CBO. Although the panel has always played a more or less quality control role, its role has changed over time. Early on, it was very focused on reacting to CBO's short-term forecast and the details that went into that forecast. More recently, since about the mid-1990s, the focus has been more on the larger economic picture, and the panel has been asked to react to the story that the agency is currently telling about the economy—in other words, whether the story that CBO is telling about the economy makes economic sense.[29] The most important aspect of this panel, however, is that it is constructed explicitly to represent different professional viewpoints on the economy, so that the arguments CBO advances can be debated to anticipate any places the forecast deviates from the mainstream. The point is to have as much information as possible before finalizing both the forecast and the story behind it.[30]

One important aspect about CBO's macroeconomic work is that, to the extent that CBO was intended to support congressional independence in the budget process, CBO was supposed to help to keep the executive branch honest. In fact, one of the positive effects of CBO is what often comes with having more than one estimator. In this case, the knowledge by OMB and the Treasury that CBO will have its own independent forecast tends to moderate their own work. One long-time congressional staffer put it this way: "I think CBO really gave the Congress independence from OMB and I think in the process, although I think this might be a little hard to prove . . . they put limits on how far OMB could be different in terms of macroeconomic projections and then that has in turn lots of implications on budget projections."[31] One longtime observer noted that "just having in the Congress an independent source of numbers and analysis . . . strengthens the balance of power."[32]

Tax Policy

CBO's role in tax policy was a bit ambiguous—and precarious—from the outset. In fact, in the March 1975 meeting at which Rivlin had to identify the issues that would face the new organization (see chapter 2), it was not a foregone conclusion that CBO would even have a role in tax policy. This uncertainty probably stemmed primarily from the fact that the Congressional Budget Act did not give CBO the authority to do cost estimates on the tax side. Rather, the powers that be on the tax writing committees ensured that this power would remain with the JCT, which works for these tax committees. Over time, CBO developed two roles for itself in tax policy. The first was the development of the baseline. The second was the writing of studies on tax policy issues. The necessity of doing the baseline provided CBO with the opportunity to understand many aspects of tax policy and how they affect the level of projected receipts to the government. Thus studies on issues such as capital gains taxation, the AMT, and the estate tax are fair game for CBO analyses.[33]

CBO had perhaps a bigger challenge in establishing its bona fides in tax policy than in any other substantive area, for two reasons. First, of all of the committees in Congress, the tax writing committees (and the appropriations committees) were the most skeptical and threatened by the new budget process. They therefore viewed CBO with a somewhat jaundiced eye. Second, because the JCT already existed and worked for the tax writing committees, the prospect of CBO stepping on the analytical toes of the JCT was sensitive. Rosemary Marcuss, the assistant director for tax analysis for fifteen years (1983–98), said that it was very difficult to attempt to navigate in the world in which the tax committees and the JCT were already the important players. Like the other program divisions, the tax division had to sell its work, but it needed to do so in a more competitive environment. The member who probably did more than anyone else to give CBO a mandate to do tax policy studies (as opposed to simply preparing the annual revenue baseline) was House Ways and Means Committee chairman Dan Rostenkowski (D-IL), working mainly through his long-time aide Wendell Primus. Rostenkowski and Primus became the earliest, and most frequent, requestors of CBO tax policy work.[34]

A specific manifestation of this Ways and Means–driven work had to do with the evaluation of the effects of tax policies, by income groups. CBO had begun by the mid-1980s to do analyses on the distributional effects of taxes, a practice that continues to this day. This developed out of a view on the part of Congress that it needed to know more than just how much revenue legislation cost—it needed to know who bore the burden of the tax. In fact, this came out of work that had begun in the early 1980s on the spending side of the budget, where "how you structured a benefit increase or decrease often had very substantial distributional consequences."[35] This was extended to the tax side of the budget certainly by the time the Reagan administration was pursuing the Tax Reform Act of 1986, if not before. That is, it was intended to be revenue neutral, but questions about whether it was also income neutral were also on the agenda.[36] By the time Congress was considering a plan to balance the budget in 1990, "the CBO distributional analyses were the driver of much of the final shape of what was and wasn't acceptable."[37] That some of the tax effects were not as progressive as some Democrats wanted almost caused the 1990 deal to be scuttled at particular points, as Wendell Primus recalled:

> There was one meeting that I will never forget, . . . we had reached agreement from Saturday night and there was a Rose Garden ceremony Sunday afternoon announcing this deal that had been negotiated between George Bush Senior and the Democratic leadership . . . there were two political figures that were not at the summit, at least for most of it, one was Tom Foley, the speaker, and one was the president, but [Majority Leader Richard] Gephardt (D-MO) had said that we are going to make sure that the burden is progressively borne . . . well, then we went to this Sunday caucus where Gephardt had to explain what the deal was that they had blessed at the Rose Garden ceremony. And the very first question was what had happened to the distribution table. Who was bearing the burden of the deficit reduction package, at least as best we could estimate it, or as best CBO could estimate it, in reality? And, you know he admitted it didn't turn out the way he wanted it to, it was pretty proportional and at that point he began losing control of the caucus, you could just tell and Foley took the mike away from him and basically went into a harangue about we have become slaves to these distribution tables, you know now is the best time to cook a deal. . . . And he was not a great fan of those distribution tables, I learned.[38]

This attention to distributional analyses continues today. CBO was asked on numerous occasions, for example, to analyze the before-and-after distributional effects of the Bush tax cuts, and now routinely publishes reports on how the distribution of the tax burden has evolved over time.[39]

Health and Human Resources

More than half of the federal budget involves providing direct benefits to individuals. It was thus inevitable that CBO would focus a significant amount of attention on programs such as Social Security, Medicare, and Medicaid. Some of its main clients here, moreover, are the tax writing committees (House Ways and Means and Senate Finance), which have jurisdiction over the first two of these large spending programs. As with CBO's tax work, much of the agency's analysis here focuses on the effects of particular policies on income and poverty. In the past, CBO's work focused on analyzing policy options concerning issues that Congress is focusing legislative attention on. For example, CBO did a lot of analytical work in support of welfare reform before Congress passed that legislation in 1996. The division has also focused attention on programs such as student loans and income security programs, such as food stamps.[40]

In addition, given the magnitude of these programs and the long-term challenges facing the federal budget, CBO health and human resource work focuses on the future cost implications of changes in policy. For example, how can future health care costs be reduced as a share in the overall economy, which has clear implications for federal costs in this area? Peter Orszag, director of CBO in 2007 and 2008, increased the number of staff devoted to analyzing health care options specifically to better inform Congress when and if it gets around to enacting comprehensive health care reform, regardless of whether the focus of that reform is lowering costs, reducing the number of uninsured Americans, or both.[41] In addition, CBO has reviewed options for making Social Security financially viable in the long run. Chapters 6 and 7, which are case studies of CBO's role in analyzing the 1994 Clinton health care reform and the 2009–10 Obama health care reform, provide specific examples of how CBO's analytical work was used to inform the policy debate concerning that issue.

This division has a very broad portfolio, but its emphasis has changed over time, in particular to emphasize health over other parts of its portfolio. As CBO assistant director Bruce Vavrichek explained, health used to be just one of four areas covered by the division, with housing and community development, education, and welfare also claiming almost equal shares of attention and staff. It was far different by the mid-2000s: "health had less than a quarter of the staff, and now it has 75 percent . . . when you have as many problems and people actually don't have the answers to them that's when you do more and more work."[42]

The recent dominance of health sector analysis in the work of the division was evidenced by three events that are covered in other sections of this book—the Obama health care reform plan (chapter 7), the Clinton health care reform plan (chapter 6), and the Medicare prescription drug bill (chapter 4). All these cases are notable for the extent to which the program divisions and BAD worked together to bring the analytical issues and the estimates of cost together. In fact, CBO health analysts had been working with Hill staff for more than three years before the drug benefit bill passed in Congress. Much of this contact was staff to staff rather than issuing formal studies. Part of the reason this policy discussion was so protracted is that markets for Medicare prescription drugs were wholly new, and little was known about how they would develop.[43]

National Security

Sticking with the theme of big money, CBO has also historically put substantial resources into analyzing national security issues. These analyses focus on issues related to the current and future costs of the defense program. For example, in 2008 CBO analyzed the future cost implications of the navy's shipbuilding program, as well as the future costs associated with the wars in Iraq and

Afghanistan.[44] It also routinely does analyses of the long-term budgetary effects of current defense plans. At least recently, these have been updated at least annually, if not more frequently.[45]

Changes in the trajectory of the defense budget have changed the portfolio of CBO. For example, a significant effort went into attempting to project the cost of the Reagan defense buildup in the early 1980s.[46] Similarly, the cost of the wars in Iraq and Afghanistan was a significant emphasis during the first decade of the 2000s. This includes not only the direct costs of these wars but also their effects on costs and capacities for DOD elsewhere. As with the other program divisions, the National Security Division (NSD) initially had to sell its products to Hill staff, mainly the House and Senate armed services committees, but that process became more of a product of the give and take between CBO and these committees over time.[47] In fact, one former CBO staffer said that the studies tended to sort themselves as follows: "Occasionally (a study request) was out of the blue from the Hill to us with no prior consultation. That maybe would be 20 percent. Maybe 5 or 10 percent where we did a really hard sell job to get permission to do something that we wanted to do anyway. And the other 70 percent was more of an interactive process where . . . the personal relationships mattered and having ongoing conversations mattered, and out of those back and forth conversations came the ideas for the study."[48]

Bob Hale, a longtime NSD staffer who was assistant director from 1981 to 1994, observed that Congress was not usually interested in having the CBO do broad defense policy pieces. Rather, the niche of the division was in doing what he called quantitative analysis—in this context, this meant providing estimates of the long-term costs of various defense policy options.[49] Sometimes that meant analyzing the cost of a proposed plane or weapons system. Other times, it may focus on the cost of an entire policy initiative, such as missile defense.[50] In still others, it might involve looking at the cost of various personnel or benefit options.[51] There is a particular, and somewhat unique, role that CBO can play in this regard, in that permitting the Pentagon to corner the market on cost analysis of future defense plan can create "a big problem . . . because they're acting as both the principal advocate for this weapon and the only place capable of generating cost information—you really need a neutral body, even if the neutral body is limited in its resources analytically and technically."[52]

As in other sectors, a key question is what determines when CBO products have relevance in the arena of national security—and when they do not. Bob Hale, who had a long career at the Pentagon after leaving CBO (most recently when President Obama named him to be DOD comptroller), did not find during his tenure at CBO that the Pentagon paid much attention to CBO unless a member forced that attention. His perception was that, more broadly, the question of influence came down to whether you are "both clever enough and lucky enough to have an analysis that comes out that's relevant to an issue that's on the minds of a member or a defense committee."[53]

If one can generalize, however, about the conditions that make CBO national security analyses more likely to get attention, a couple of points appear relevant. The first is that budget offices, in general, tend to be more influential during times of budget contraction than of budget increases. Hale observed that, during his tenure at CBO, the Pentagon tended to be good at figuring out how to spend more, but it was more reluctant to provide Congress with information about how to spend less. This was in large part because it was not in DOD's interest to spend less.[54] Moreover, often CBO is playing the role of the skeptic or the fiscal conservative, and this puts it on the losing side of the debate in the early years of an expansion. But eventually there is a slowing in growth (and then perhaps even a decline, as in the early 1990s) and people pay more attention to arguments that essentially state that there are trade-offs, and that you can't have everything.[55] If there is a single theme to CBO's defense work, which is common to both times of budget increases and retrenchment, it is just that—that investment in costly defense and weapons systems has opportunity costs, and that what may be "only" billions of costs in the short run can lead to tens or hundreds of billions in the long-run.

Energy, Natural Resources, and Commerce (Microeconomic Studies, as of 2000)

As noted, CBO's first high-profile policy analysis work was on the energy sector. They expanded this work in the late 1970s to focus on environmental policy as well. These two areas continue to be a key focus of their work. Starting in the early 1980s, though, the agency expanded analytical efforts. Everett Ehrlich, who was an assistant director at the time, told this story:

> In '81 I had my pivotal meeting with Rivlin in which I told her that my staff could not get by doing energy and environment forever . . . that we would get bored, we would lose our best people, and that we should be doing trade, technology, commerce. . . . As I remember, it was at the end of the day and I had reserved a half hour. . . . 'Alice, we simply cannot use all those people on energy . . . and we simply need to be doing this because that's what's coming next.' And she looked at me and said, 'All right then. Go do that.' And I remember looking up and saying 'Well, I have 28 minutes left. How are you?'[56]

The breadth of CBO's work in this area is clear. A sampling of CBO work since 2006 includes the following titles:

- "Federal Climate Change Programs: Funding History and Policy Options" (March 2010),
- "The National Flood Insurance Program: Factors Affecting Actuarial Soundness" (November 2009),
- "Alternative for Future U.S. Space-Launch Capabilities" (October 2006), and

- "Factors That May Affect Future Spending from the Universal Service Fund" (June 2006).[57]

Relationships between the program divisions and BAD have historically been particularly strong in the Natural Resources and Commerce area, for several reasons. First, Roger Hitchner, who was an analyst and eventually assistant director, got his start in BAD. Second, the periodic reauthorization of various programs (such as would be reflected in the highway bill) presents a natural opportunity that exists to a greater extent in this area than any other (except for defense, which has an annual authorization).[58] Further, the leadership has always emphasized to their staff the importance of keeping in touch with BAD counterparts and assisting them with the time-sensitive work of cost estimating in addition to the production of longer-term studies.[59]

Hitchner, who when interviewed was about to retire from CBO as assistant director, reflected on the impact of his division on policy. First, he acknowledged that it is inherently difficult to get the timing right. That is, many of the studies take so long to do that it is hard for them to be influential at the precise moment that Congress is ready to do something. In the end, he said this: "we have a very impressive set of publications out there but you can point to very few that . . . changed a law in this area, or this really pissed somebody off. . . . they're really adding to the policy mix. And analysts here have to have faith that they're making a difference. People love it when something gets picked up by some trade publication. But sometimes it's for a misquote. . . . It's nice to be mentioned on the floor, but it's not very often that it happens."[60]

Budget Process and Concepts and Government Management

CBO's views have always been solicited on the inner workings of the budget process itself. This can include the analysis of changes to the budget process (there are a great many of these proposals), such as amending the constitution to require a balanced budget or a line-item veto for the president, or creating a biennial budget process. CBO has also done a limited amount of work concerning government management issues, primarily federal pay and benefits.[61]

Perhaps more important are the number of conceptual issues that concern the ways in which particular transactions are recorded in the federal budget. These issues are important because they affect the manner in which signals about the budgetary effects of particular policies are sent to policymakers. For example, the Federal Credit Reform Act of 1990, which began the practice of calculating the cost of credit programs on an accrual basis, came about because the prior cash basis of calculating credit costs was thought to disadvantage direct loans (which looked like grants) compared to guaranteed loans (which had no apparent cost, at least in the short run). CBO has done substantial budget concepts work on issues as varied as deposit insurance, pension guarantees, flood insurance, and the budgetary implications of government-sponsored enterprises.[62] This last is highlighted in the next section.

The issue of the operation of the budget process itself was established implicitly as an exception to the CBO prohibition against taking positions on issues. As Dick Emery recalled,

> CBO directors have always testified on budget process and have always taken an active interest in making recommendations for strengthening budget process and for having a view on appropriate budget concepts and procedures. And so the initial function of that group (the Budget Process Unit) was to deal with helping to figure out how to make the budget process work. There was a fair amount of initial work on S. 2, which was Senator Muskie's sunset legislation (to sunset federal programs). There was also a fair amount of work on the concept behind 302 allocation; how the money should be allocated among committees of jurisdiction. . . . We also did a lot of work on credit and the various studies of credit budgeting. . . . We also did something that CBO still is required to do which I believe is a total waste of time, which is looking at expiring authorizations and unauthorized programs.[63]

Over time, the organizational locus of these studies has changed several times. In large part, this is because these budget concepts issues are not single policy issues, but instead cross policy lines. The logical place, perhaps, for this function, was within BAD. The tension between the responsibility for the operation of the budget process and the desire to adopt reforms to that process was palpable in some cases, and resulted in tension, at times, between the rest of BAD and the budget process unit.[64] When Reischauer named Jim Blum as deputy director in 1991, he also created the Special Studies Division (SSD), to be headed by Bob Hartman, who had been functioning as a kind of special assistant and de facto deputy director to Reischauer. Under Hartman, the SSD had freer rein to pursue budget concepts and budget reform issues. Eventually the analysts from this division were merged into the Microeconomic Studies Division, and after that into the Macroeconomic Studies Division, where they were as of 2009. The major remaining function of this group was the analysis of the effect of financial markets on the federal budget. In 2010, in the wake of the near collapse of the U.S. financial sector, CBO established a new division, called the Financial Analysis Division (FAD), to carry out the agency's analysis of financial markets.

CBO Productivity: Studies by Period

Finally, it is useful to review the productivity of CBO over time, in terms of the number of studies produced—more than eleven hundred studies from when it first opened its doors in 1975 through 2009. Understandably, CBO did not, at first,

Table 5.1 CBO Studies by Period

Period	Studies
1975–79	36
1980–84	166
1985–89	226
1990–94	202
1995–99	177
2000–2004	165
2005–9	167
Total	1,139

produce many reports. In fact, as noted, very little CBO policy analysis work was done before its analysis of the Carter energy plan. By the end of 1976, CBO had produced only one report other than the ones statutorily required. Part of this was simply lack of awareness on the part of Hill staff about what CBO could do. Another part, of course, is the nature of the production of such studies. If a study takes six to nine months to complete, it is reasonable to expect that the production of reports would lag when work was actually done. At any rate, there were five studies (including the Carter energy study) published in 1977. This ballooned to twenty-nine in 1978, and to thirty-six in the 1975 to 1979 period.

Table 5.1 shows the number of studies published, by five-year period, over CBO's history. After the 36 produced between 1975 and 1979, 166 studies were produced from 1980 to 1984, 226 between 1985 and 1989, 202 between 1990 and 1994, and 177 between 1995 and 1999. More than 300 have been published since 2000.

Potential Benefits and Limitations— Analyzing the Risks Posed by GSEs

On September 7, 2008, the Treasury Department announced, in an extraordinary move, that it was taking over the two largest housing government-sponsored enterprises (GSE)—the Federal National Mortgage Association (Fannie Mae) and the Federal Home Loan Mortgage Corporation (Freddie Mac). CBO later estimated the cost to American taxpayers of this takeover at $389 billion.[65] Most Americans had barely heard of these behemoths, and fewer still were aware that the takeover represented the culmination of decades of concern about the financial safety of the GSEs and the potential financial exposure of the federal government created by their activity. To those who had followed this story, the event hardly came as a surprise. CBO had been at the center of these warnings and this analytical work for at least twenty years.

GSEs—Fannie and Freddie

GSEs are so-called because they are chartered by Congress. They exist somewhere between public and private institutions, with strong federal support but
private ownership. Fannie Mae traces its lineage to 1938, after Congress created
the Federal Housing Administration (FHA) in 1934 to insure lenders against default by borrowers. Private firms, it was thought, would invest in these mortgages, but the demand did not materialize. This led to the creation of the Federal
National Mortgage Association (later Fannie Mae), as part of the Reconstruction
Finance Corporation, largely to fill the role of purchasing these FHA mortgages,
along with federally guaranteed loans to World War II veterans. The federal government thus had not only assumed the credit risk on these loans, but was funding them as well. In 1970 Congress created the Federal Home Loan Mortgage
Corporation (or, as it came to be called, Freddie Mac).[66]

Fannie Mae and Freddie Mac do not do any direct lending, but they do purchase loans from private lenders. The payments made by borrowers are sometimes bundled and repackaged as mortgage-backed securities (MBSs). Significantly, even if home buyers default on their loans, it is not the ultimate owners of
these MBSs who lose money. Fannie and Freddie make good on these defaulted
loans, meaning that they (i.e., to date, US taxpayers) are ultimately on the hook
for this risk.[67]

The advantage of GSE status is not that these institutions carry with them
a broad, explicit federal guarantee. In fact, the GSEs are required to disclose to
investors that no federal guarantee exists for their obligations. The advantage
comes from the fact that investors believe that the guarantee exists, in large part
because of other provisions of law such as their line of credit to Treasury and
their exemption from investor protection laws.[68] Consequently, the GSEs bor-
row at interest rates below rates paid by even AAA-rated private firms because
their debt is considered less risky than the debt of these (the safest) private institutions.[69] As history has confirmed, "evidence suggests that financial markets
believe that the federal government would come to the rescue of Fannie Mae and
Freddie Mac (and hence their creditors) in the event of financial difficulties."[70] In
other words, investors believe, at some level, that their rich Uncle (Sam) will bail
them out if they get in trouble.

CBO's Analysis of GSEs, Profitability, and Risk

The first CBO analysis of the risk and profitability of a GSE came with the issuance of a study of the Student Loan Marketing Association (Sallie Mae) in 1985.
Although it did not deal with the housing GSEs, the conclusion—that Sallie
Mae received a financial benefit because of its implicit federal guarantee—foreshadowed the debate that would follow in the next quarter century. This argument—that there was a benefit being transferred to Sallie Mae as a result of the

appearance of a federal guarantee, and that this benefit could be valued—was as novel as it was controversial. Many would have argued and indeed continued to argue that a subsidy that had never required any cash outlay by the federal government was not a subsidy at all. The argument made in the study was that the implicit guarantee carried with it an opportunity cost. That is, by giving away the implied guarantee, government was providing something of value free that could be sold to others by the GSEs. The gift was imposing a cost on taxpayers and other stakeholders equivalent to one in which the federal government gives away land or other valuable assets. If guarantees don't have a cost, why not have the federal government guarantee debt by all private entities?[71]

The most comprehensive analysis of the risks posed by the GSEs, however, was issued in 1991, when CBO, the GAO, and the Treasury Department each—at the request of Congress—issued reports concerning the risks posed by each GSE. CBO's report was issued in May 1991, and looked at the potential risks associated with each of the five GSEs—Sallie Mae, Fannie Mae, Freddie Mac, the Farm Credit System, and the Federal Home Loan Banks (FHLBs). This study was issued during the Reischauer era, and Reischauer later recounted that Fannie Mae head Jim Johnson "came to see me with twenty pages of comments" to the effect that the study was wrong and that "CBO would embarrass itself" if it was released.[72] Reischauer had the authors respond to the comments, and then sent the comments and responses "to some academics, who said we had it right. So we went ahead and released it."[73]

CBO testified multiple times during 1991 on the conclusions of this report:

- The GSEs achieve their public purpose by borrowing on the strength of an implicit federal guarantee, which transferred to the government "a large portion of the risk that creditors normally bear."[74]
- The GSEs pose a varying level of risk to the federal government, and Fannie Mae and Freddie Mac pose a "low level or risk of loss to the government from their exposure to credit risk and interest rate risk."[75]
- "Federal supervision is inadequate to ensure that Fannie Mae, Freddie Mac, and Sallie Mae will not increase their exposure to risks or lower their capitalization in the future."[76]

The conclusion of other reporting agencies—at least in terms of the risk to the government—was similar to CBO's conclusions. In fact, Comptroller General Charles Bowsher was quoted as saying, "Congress and the regulators just aren't watching the situation closely enough. Problems can develop."[77] In response, the Congress—in the Federal Housing Enterprise Safety and Soundness Act of 1992—established a new regulator for the housing GSEs, called the Office of Federal Housing Enterprise Oversight (OFHEO). If the creation of this new regulator was not caused by the reports of CBO and these other agencies, it certainly directly followed the issuance of these reports. Unfortunately, OFHEO turned out to be a weak regulator, weak in the sense that it did not, for example, have the power to adjust the required capital requirements for Fannie and Freddie. These were set in statute.

The Safety and Soundness Act also required reports on Fannie Mae and Freddie Mac to be completed by CBO, GAO, the Department of Housing and Urban Development (HUD), and Treasury. These reports were to "study the desirability and feasibility of repealing the charters of the GSEs, eliminating federal sponsorships of the enterprises, and permitting them to operate as fully private entities."[78]

In 1996 CBO issued its report, and for the first time attempted to quantify the value of the subsidy provided to the GSEs. The GSEs, of course, had continued to dispute that there was any subsidy at all, arguing that the cost of the GSEs to the government was zero, because there had (as yet) been no direct appropriations. According to CBO, however, the value of that subsidy was $6.5 billion in 1995. Perhaps most controversially, CBO claimed that only $4.4 billion of that subsidy was passed on in the form of lower borrowing costs to homeowners, which meant that $2.1 billion was retained—that is, earned as profit—by the GSEs. In unusually colorful language, CBO argued that "the GSEs are a spongy conduit— soaking up nearly $1 for every $2 delivered."[79] Perhaps even more colorful was CBO's argument that the GSEs were unlikely to lose their federal subsidy without their agreement, because "once one agrees to share a canoe with a bear, it is hard to get him out without obtaining his agreement or getting wet."[80]

The GSEs disagreed vehemently with the CBO conclusions, and used their own rather intemperate language in response. A Fannie Mae spokesman said that the report was "a case of policy wonks piling their own prejudices on top of faulty analysis, and if these digit-heads could figure out a better way of delivering credit to millions of families with the use of private capital while paying the government billions of dollars in federal taxes, then they can get a real job in Washington."[81]

Starting on April 17, 1996, and continuing through August 1 of that year, a House Banking Committee subcommittee, chaired by Richard Baker (R-LA), held four days of oversight hearings on Fannie Mae and Freddie Mac. During these hearings, the subcommittee received testimony from the four agencies that had conducted the mandated studies, and heard from top officials of the two GSEs. Although the general conclusions of the four requested reports were similar in that all of them concluded that there was still risk to the federal government from the GSEs, the GSEs and their supporters on the committee reserved their harshest criticism for the CBO study, and in particular the notion of the retained benefit. Freddie Mac CEO Leland Brendsel dismissed the "spongy conduit sound bite" as based on "academic estimates of our phantom cost to the government."[82] Fannie Mae executive vice president Robert Zoellick agreed, stating that "CBO produces figures that convey a very false image of precision."[83] June

O'Neill, who was CBO director at the time, later recalled, "I never felt so much like Joan of Arc as when I was dealing with Fannie Mae and Freddie Mac."[84]

Over four days of hearings, committee members and various witnesses discussed issues related primarily to whether the specific approach (that is, conferring GSE status) in the case of Fannie and Freddie was the most cost-effective means possible, with the lowest risk to the taxpayer. Chairman Baker, in particular, defended the CBO study, saying that "CBO was one of the first organizations to make a critical comment concerning potential difficulties with the S&L industry in the 1980s, and I feel that your perspectives should not be considered lightly."[85]

CBO was not alone in its concern that GSE status could carry with it some future risk to the taxpayer. OFHEO director Aida Alvarez reported the results of a credit risk study that OFHEO had done assuming varying levels of credit losses for the GSEs. This analysis showed that there was no risk to the federal government under most scenarios except in a scenario where there were "high or severe credit losses as might be the case if the higher interest rates did not reflect higher inflation rates or if house prices were depressed for an unrelated reason."[86] Alvarez considered this a "very unlikely scenario," but, in a prescient comment, said also that "recent history is full of examples that were judged extremely unlikely before they occurred."[87]

Attempts to Regulate Fannie and Freddie

In the aftermath of these 1996 reports, discussion about the GSEs and the risk they might pose to the government was extensive. CBO itself updated its subsidy estimates (reflecting the growth of the enterprises) in 2001, calculating that the implicit subsidy to all the housing GSEs (including Fannie, Freddie, and the FHLBs) by 2000 was $13.6 billion, and that $3.9 billion of that was retained by Fannie and Freddie, and that another $2.7 billion was retained by the FHLBs.[88]

The GSEs themselves disagreed strongly with this analysis, as they had the previous one. They sent letters to both CBO director Dan Crippen and Congressman Baker, outlining their objections to the report. In addition, high-level Fannie Mae officials met with CBO officials in an effort to change CBO's mind concerning its analysis. The arguments that Fannie Mae made were similar to its earlier arguments. They disagreed with the notion that the GSEs receive any subsidy, and they certainly disagreed with the argument that a portion of the subsidy was retained. In response to these letters, Crippen used unusually pointed language, arguing that some of the arguments of the GSEs "strain[ed] credulity."[89] Crippen also pointed out the inconsistency of, on the one hand, arguing that the GSEs have no funding advantage, and on the other hand, resisting privatization. In a letter to Baker, Crippen asked, "if the federal imprimatur were not valuable, why all the effort to maintain it?"[90]

Fannie and Freddie turned up the heat on their critics. For years, press accounts had suggested that the GSEs operated very sophisticated lobbying efforts, designed to protect them against further regulation and preserve their GSE status. Jim Leach (R-IA), who was chair of the House Banking Committee when the Republicans held the Congress, claimed that "no institution in America has as sophisticated tentacles into the legislature and the executive branch as Fannie Mae."[91]

Now members of Congress, including Baker and Representative Christopher Shays (R-CT), saw firsthand the ability of the GSEs to flex their political muscle in response to any criticism or attempt to rein them in. They used grassroots lobbying efforts from constituents to members, hired consultants to refute analyses they opposed, and generally made life difficult for their critics. According to Baker, "when their interests are threatened, the response is almost army-like. They're tactical, and they're everywhere."[92] In 2003 Fannie threatened to sue Baker if he released information that he had received from OFHEO on the salaries paid executives at both companies; he kept this information secret for a year.[93] More broadly, in the 2000 election, "Freddie Mac was the biggest corporate soft money donor, and Fannie Mae was number five."[94]

During this time, the GSEs continued to not only put pressure on Congress, but also attempt to both influence and discredit their critics. Former CBO director Douglas Holtz-Eakin recalled, "There [were] the visible efforts by Fannie and Freddie to stroke me when I showed up at CBO. . . . Obviously, they were sick of seeing these studies and they wanted to make a friend in me . . . and I unfortunately was immediately suspicious and it didn't work. My reaction was to go to [a Fannie Mae event] and just whack them as hard as I could, which I will never forget—the deathly silence as I walked out. . . . they left me permanently jaundiced about them."[95]

The reputation, as well as the bottom lines, of the two GSEs, took a substantial hit in 2003 when major accounting irregularities were uncovered at both firms, leading to the resignations of top officials at both Fannie and Freddie, including both Brendsel and Raines. In addition, the Bush administration began to pursue a greater regulatory role for the federal government more aggressively. A top administration official argued in late 2003 that "even a small mistake" in managing their risk could have large effects on the overall economy, particularly since securities issued by the GSEs are owned by many other institutions.[96]

In early 2004 Federal Reserve chairman Alan Greenspan formally joined the chorus of people cautioning Congress about the risks associated with Fannie and Freddie. He cited a Federal Reserve study by Fed economist Wayne Passmore, whose findings were largely in line with those of the CBO studies of 1996 and 2001.[97] It said that substantial benefits accrued to the GSEs from their status, and, as Greenspan reported in his testimony, "Congressional Budget Office and other estimates differ, but they come to the essentially same conclusion: A substantial portion of these GSEs' implicit subsidy accrues to GSE shareholders in the form of increased dividend and stock market value."[98] He argued for preventive action "sooner, rather than later."[99] Further, he said that the Fed was "concerned about the growth and scale" of the GSEs' debt and acquisition activities, and advocated that these activities be capped "to prevent a financial crisis in the future."[100] On April 7, 2005, this warning was reiterated by Treasury Secretary John Snow. In advocating the administration's proposal for a new regulatory system for the GSE's, Snow argued that reforms were necessary to "lessen the potential for systemic risk."[101]

In response to the concerns raised by these various reports, Congress did nothing. In fact, it took no legislative action after OFHEO was created in 1992. The Baker hearings did not result in any legislation to further regulate the GSEs, nor did the efforts of the Bush administration. Numerous warnings, not only by CBO, but also by Treasury, HUD, GAO, and the Fed, fell on largely deaf ears. A May 2006 letter to majority leader Bill Frist and Senate Banking Committee chair Richard Shelby (R-AL), signed by twenty Republican senators (including soon-to-be 2008 presidential candidate John McCain [R-AZ]), urged a Senate floor vote on the Federal Housing Regulatory Reform Act.[102] It seems reasonable to assume that the notable absence of response can be attributed to the sheer scope and depth of opposition mounted by the GSEs.

The Resulting Government Takeover

Although originally there had been a question of privatization of the GSEs, events made it moot. The federal guarantee transformed in short order from an implicit to explicit: the federal government now owns the GSEs. Could this have been prevented? From one perspective, it appears that given the magnitude and reach of the financial crisis that began cascading in 2008, and given that the federal government has been forced to bail out banks and other private financial institutions, the GSEs might have needed a federal bailout regardless of what they and the government had done to manage their risk exposure. This interpretation, however, may well paint an inappropriate picture of the GSEs as victims. There is an alternate view, best argued by Peter Wallison and Charles Calomiris, which contends that "the GSEs sold out the taxpayers by taking huge risks on substandard mortgages, primarily to retain congressional support for the weak regulation and special benefits that fueled their high profits and profligate executive compensation. As if that were not enough, in the process, the GSEs' operations promoted a risky subprime mortgage binge in the United States that has caused a worldwide financial crisis."[103]

Wallison and Calomiris's point was simply that the GSEs had through their own investment practices substantially increased the risk exposure of the federal taxpayer, not only to losses by Fannie and Freddie, but to the kind of systemic meltdown that ultimately occurred. The powerful political pressure the GSEs wielded effectively discouraged Congress from enacting needed reforms. To quote an observer, the bailout "was programmed from the day Congress wrote a blank check for the implicit guarantee of the government-sponsored enterprises and then proceeded to ignore the unconscionable buildup of risk in these thinly capitalized institutions."[104] The response of politicians, who should know better, has been surprise; for example, House Speaker Nancy Pelosi (D-CA) railed about "the privatization of profits and the socialization of costs" in the two failed GSEs.[105] Even if they had only looked at CBO analyses and warnings covered in this discussion, and none of the many available from other sources, leaders in Congress certainly had ample opportunity to know that substantial potential existed for the kinds of problems that ultimately developed.

Holtz-Eakin echoed the view of Wallison and Calomiris that had the GSEs been better regulated by Congress it could have made a big difference in the magnitude of the financial crisis, and in the extent of obligations the federal government had to absorb.

> If they had listened, there would not have been continued pressure for Fannie Mae and Freddie Mac to lower their standards for purchasing mortgages to be bundled and guaranteed and that would have meant there was no demand for bad mortgages being written which means that even guys who want bad mortgages—in the end the whole game was unloading them. They created the market for unloading them and they didn't cause the whole thing but that really could have mattered. And the signal it sent that the Congress and administration's progressively pushing them to be more aggressive told the internal guys . . . let's go in and make a lot of money (and if) things go bad they got us into it, they'll get us out. And that moral hazard showed up in enormous ways. It also showed I think really how poorly the Congress runs things. Remember there was a big accounting scandal and that didn't slow any of this down one bit. Even though they couldn't understand the books and arguably the management couldn't understand the books they never thought twice. I find that astounding.[106]

So what to make of CBO's role in all of this? It is hard to imagine what more CBO, as a nonpartisan arm of the Congress, could have done to reduce the potential risk and prevent this costly taxpayer bailout. However, this episode highlights the substantial limits to the influence of information, if policymakers do not want to be informed. In this case, even with sustained analysis, significant attention to the communication of the results of this analysis—and at least one receptive ear in the person of Congressman Baker—there was no way to overcome the political pressure that Fannie and Freddie had at their disposal and were willing to apply to guard themselves against increased regulation and to protect their profits. In the end, it is hard to argue with Harvard economist Kenneth Rogoff that "there was tremendous coddling of Fannie and Freddie in the face of a lot of evidence that they really weren't helping homeowners all that much. I think it was very, very clear what was coming, and that they were a huge, huge, risk to the American financial system. . . . It really was criminal neglect."[107]

Conclusions: Policy Analysis in a Political Environment

What does the CBO experience with policy analysis tell us about the agency's ability to provide useful information to Congress and for that information to influence public policy? Although this book has made no attempt to do a comprehensive analysis of the effects of every product produced by CBO, a few conclusions can be reached.

- The existence of an in-house analytical capacity for Congress has strengthened the ability of Congress to challenge the president.
- CBO itself has become one of the major producers of policy analysis in the federal government; its products are widely available outside the legislative branch, including to the general public.
- The two parts of CBO—budget analysis and policy analysis—can work together toward a common purpose but institutional barriers make that difficult. There are major exceptions however, as will be chronicled in the next two chapters.
- Despite all of this, there is no way for any analytical institution to promote or ensure good public policy if political winds to which decision-makers attend are blowing in a different direction.

Providing Institutional Capacity

The selection of Alice Rivlin over Sam Hughes (see chapter 2) reflected a conscious decision by Congress to promote policy analysis in addition to a more narrow focus on budget analysis. But, as noted, this required explicit effort. CBO had to promote its policy analysis capacity in ways that were not necessary on the budget side. A couple of examples highlighted in this book—the Carter energy policy and the Clinton health plan—are clear cases in which a president proposed a major reform and Congress needed to respond. Congress was always able to respond politically to such proposals. The effect of CBO has been to help Congress respond substantively.

Further, a key indicator of the responsiveness of any analytical organization is whether its analyses are timely. In the case of CBO analysis, it is important for the work products to be available when Congress is being asked to make legislative decisions. There is an unavoidable tension between doing the most thorough analysis possible (because analytical work is never finished) and providing information at the point when it is most likely and necessary to inform decisions. The examples presented clearly indicate that CBO analyses were available when Congress was interested in taking action (health care reform, Carter energy, the comprehensive CBO GSE study in 1991) or long before (CBO's other GSE work). This book does not attempt a comprehensive evaluation of the timeliness of CBO work, but evidence reviewed for this book clearly indicates that CBO directors have paid substantial attention to not only the quality of analytical work, but also its usefulness.

Expanding the Government's Supply of Policy Analysis

Nowhere in the statutes or in the debate surrounding the creation of CBO will you find the argument that CBO was intended to perform a public education role. That is, Congress—quite appropriately—seems to have been focused on its own ability to have information necessary for decision making. Nonetheless, by making a decision that its work products would be publicly available, CBO has done more than just educate Congress. It has educated the general public, either directly through its studies or indirectly through the news media.

This public education capacity and role has only expanded over time. As the Internet developed as a source of information for the public, CBO began to make use of it to disseminate information. Virtually all CBO reports, even those written in the first years of CBO's existence, are now available online. Those that are not are available in hard copy, by request. Further, director Orszag began in 2007 to communicate with the public through a blog, which enhanced the ability to disseminate CBO products in a user-friendly way. Elmendorf has continued this practice. Finally, CBO has always paid attention to the language of its reports, putting a premium on having them written in a clear style accessible to a more general audience.

Interaction of Budget Analysis and Policy Analysis

As discussed in chapter 2, one of the main issues that confronted Alice Rivlin in setting up CBO was the question of whether budget analysis and policy analysis should be organizationally separate. As second CBO director Rudy Penner said,

> as an outside observer when Alice organized CBO, I thought it very odd to do it that way. I couldn't really fully understand why she did it. But when I came to CBO, I thought it important to have a very open mind about the organization, and when I actually got on the ground, I thought it was the only way to do it. If everything would have been mushed together, the cost estimating

function would have driven out policy analysis. . . . You have to have . . . some separation between the two functions. So after the first week or so, I had no doubt about the wisdom of the idea.[108]

The greatest challenge, however, of a separate policy analysis function was to keep its work relevant and timely. There might be the natural tendency of the policy analysts to produce studies based on their own interests that were not directly responsive, or did not provide information to Congress on a timely basis. A certain amount of tension has continued, particularly because the policy analysts have sometimes had a luxury that BAD does not have, which is to prepare a thorough analytical product outside of the time pressures of current legislation. This can create, and has at times created, some resentment on the part of the CBO cost analysts. This has been tempered by the fact that the cost analysts are pretty sure that the work they are doing is more important and more in demand than that of the policy analysts.[109]

Recent director Douglas Holtz-Eakin confronted this issue even as he took over the agency in 2003:

You want to make sure that the program divisions stay in touch with the issues, stay in touch with the staffs, know what they're interested in, so that they can write the papers that are useful for them. . . . The other issue is internally is some sense of cohesion. You don't want to have two classes of CBOers. . . . I just decided to make the program division's life as miserable as BAD's, and that removes all tension . . . and the serious part was, to the extent to which there was some truth, I thought it resulted from risk aversion. The institution felt much better putting the paper out after the issue had passed. . . . First of all, they wanted it perfect, and if in the pursuit of perfection, the issue came and went, then they got less heat. Whereas the BAD guys don't have that luxury. They're working on a deadline, and they get the heat. So my rule of thumb should be that the study should come out in time for the decision to be made. And that has pushed them somewhat, and properly so . . . and the pushback I've gotten from the staff is that "we're going to make mistakes if we do it on that timetable." And the answer is "yes you will." I acknowledge that. The objective should not be zero mistakes. The objective should be to get it to Congress in time to make a decision.[110]

There have been spectacular successes of cooperation at some points. The cases of the Clinton health care reform, outlined in chapter 6, and the Obama health care reform, outlined in chapter 7, are clear cases in which the resources of both BAD and various program divisions were brought together to produce a comprehensive evaluation of a policy change that involved both a complex cost estimate and the need to understand the broader effects of a policy on the overall economy. There has also been substantial cooperation between BAD and FAD concerning the cost of various financial market interventions.

The most apt conclusion, then, is that, compared with a world in which budget analysis drives out policy analysis, the kinds of tensions and challenges that exist as a result of the separation of the two seem like a small cost to pay, given the increased capacity for policy analysis and the improved public education.

Using Policy Analysis to Influence Policy

Of course, perhaps the largest question (but the most difficult to answer), is what difference this all makes? That is, if Congress has all this information on the effect of policies, does it make the policies any better? It would seem that there are three types of possible impacts:

- The information coming from CBO contributes to encouraging Congress to do things that it does not think it is in its political interest to do, perhaps by giving Congress cover for politically unpopular decisions.
- The information coming from CBO enables Congress to take something that Congress is going to do and make it better.
- The information coming from CBO stops Congress from doing something stupid.

The challenge is identifying which impacts have occurred and how frequently. Let's start with what is perhaps obvious. Neither CBO nor any other analytical institution can do much to get a political body such as the U.S. Congress to do something it does not want to do. The discussion of the GSE case seems to be an example of where CBO information had a very uneven impact. Arguably, the 1991 study and its counterparts emboldened Congress to further regulate the GSEs. Subsequently, however, in the face of a consistent cry for stronger regulation, and warnings about the possible effects of inaction, Congress chose not to act. This is certainly not an isolated case.

If, however, Congress, or committees in Congress, intend to do something, CBO can make it better, or provide political cover. The earliest case cited is an example. Certainly the Carter energy proposal changed as a result of CBO analysis. Certainly, as discussed in chapter 7, the health care reform enacted in 2010 was different than it would have been without the CBO analysis. Other examples could be cited as well. In these cases, to the extent that CBO analysts are consulted by congressional committees—as in-house experts—Congress may use this expertise to shape public policies in an attempt to make them effective [for the country as a whole. It is plausible that without such analysis it would be more likely that Congress would instead craft legislation only with an eye toward particular interests].

Notes

1. Internal staffing data provided by CBO.

2. Penner, interview.

3. Percentages calculated from U.S. Energy Information Administration data, *Annual Energy Review*, Table 5.24 (June 26, 2009), www.eia.doe.gov/aer/petro.html. Although slightly less dramatic, the inflation-adjusted cost increase of 25 percent per gallon had extensive economic and political ramifications.

4. Robert Rankin, "Carter's Energy Plan: A Test of Leadership," *Congressional Quarterly Weekly* (April 23, 1977): 727.

5. Elder Witt, "Carter's Proposals: A More Unified Framework, but Many Familiar Elements from Earlier Debates," *Congressional Quarterly Weekly* (April 23, 1977): 728–29.

6. Ray Scheppach, interview with the author, October 3, 2003.

7. Everett Ehrlich, interview with the author, June 23, 2004.

8. Ibid.

9. Scheppach, interview.

10. Congressional Budget Office, *President Carter's Energy Proposals: A Perspective* (Washington, DC: GPO, June 1977), iii.

11. Scheppach, interview.

12. Congressional Budget Office, *President Carter's Energy Proposals*, xiii.

13. Ibid. Assuming savings from the portions of the proposal not analyzed by CBO would be at the level estimated by the administration, total daily saving as estimated by CBO was 3.6 million barrels instead of 4.5 million barrels.

14. Ibid., xvii–xix.

15. Alice Rivlin, interview with the author, October 23, 2003.

16. Scheppach, interview.

17. Alice Rivlin, Statement to Senate Committee on Energy and Natural Resources, May 13, 1977; to Senate Committee on Energy and Natural Resources, May 19, 1977; to House Subcommittee on Energy and Power, Committee on Interstate and Foreign Commerce, June 1, 1977; to House Committee on Ways and Means, June 6, 1977; to House Ad Hoc Committee on Energy, June 7, 1977; to House Task Force on Distributive Impact of Budget and Economic Policies, Committee on the Budget, 1977; and Richard Morgenstern, Statement to House Committee on the Budget, June 29, 1977.

18. Rivlin, interview, 2003.

19. Michael Telson, interview with the author, October 21, 2003.

20. Scheppach, interview.

21. Raymond C. Scheppach and Everett M. Ehrlich, *Energy-Policy Analysis and Congressional Action* (Lexington, MA: D. C. Heath and Co., 1982), vii.

22. Ibid. Each of these adjectives comes directly from the text of the foreword.

23. Ehrlich, interview.

24. Rivlin, interview, 2003.

25. Ibid.

26. Ehrlich, interview.

27. Congressional Budget Office, "Long-Term Economic Effects of Chronically Large Budget Deficits," *Economic and Budget Issue Brief*, October 13, 2005; Donald B. Marron,

Letter to the Honorable William H. Frist, M.D., and the Honorable Judd Gregg, "A Potential Influenza Pandemic: Possible Macroeconomic Effects and Policy Issues," May 22, 2006, revised July 27, 2006.

28. See, for example, Peter Orszag, Testimony before the House Committee on Education and Labor, "The Effects of Recent Turmoil in Financial Markets on Retirement Security," October 7, 2008—in which CBO concluded that the recent financial meltdown had resulted in a loss of approximately $2 trillion in retirement assets.

29. Dennis, interview.

30. Ibid.

31. Primus, interview.

32. Susan Irving, interview with the author, July 15, 2004.

33. See, for example, Peter Orszag, Letter to the Honorable Kent Conrad, "Long-Term Effects of Indexing the Alternative Minimum Tax and Extending the Tax Reductions of 2001 and 2003," July 17, 2008, www.cbo.gov/doc.cfm?index=9568&zzz=37740.

34. Rosemary Marcuss, interview with the author, March 22, 2005.

35. Lew, interview.

36. Marcuss, interview.

37. Lew, interview.

38. Primus, interview.

39. See Congressional Budget Office, *Historical Effective Federal Tax Rates,1979 to 2006* (Washington, DC: GPO, April 2009).

40. Congressional Budget Office, *Changes in the Economic Resources of Low-Income Households with Children* (Washington, DC: GPO, May 2007).

41. For a recent example, see Peter Orszag, Testimony before the House Subcommittee on Health, Committee on Ways and Means, "Evidence on the Costs and Benefits of Health Information Technology," 110th Cong., 2nd sess., July 24, 2008.

42. Bruce Vavrichek, interview with the author, February 24, 2005.

43. Ibid.

44. Peter Orszag, Letter to the Honorable Gene Taylor, "Resource Implications of the Navy's Fiscal Year 2009 Shipbuilding Plan," June 9, 2008; Letter to the Honorable Kent Conrad, "Analysis of the Growth in Funding for Operations in Iraq, Afghanistan, and Elsewhere in the War on Terrorism," February 11, 2008.

45. Congressional Budget Office, *Long-Term Implications of the Fiscal Year 2010 Defense Budget* (Washington, DC: GPO, January 2010).

46. Robert Hale, interview with the author, April 21, 2006.

47. Ibid.

48. Michael O'Hanlon, interview with the author, June 23, 2006.

49. Hale, interview.

50. O'Hanlon, interview.

51. Hale, interview.

52. O'Hanlon, interview.

53. Hale, interview.

54. Ibid.

55. O'Hanlon, interview.

56. Ehrlich, interview.

57. Each report produced by CBO (Washington DC: GPO), on respective dates noted. All CBO publications are available at the agency's website: www.cbo.gov.

58. Roger Hitchner, interview with the author, February 22, 2005.

59. David Moore, interview with the author, March 2, 2004.

60. Hitchner, interview.

61. Congressional Budget Office, *Characteristics and Pay of Federal Civilian Employees* (Washington, DC: GPO, March 2007).

62. Congressional Budget Office, *The Risk Exposure of the Pension Benefit Guarantee Corporation* (Washington, DC: GPO, September 2005).

63. Richard Emery, interview with the author, July 8, 2004.

64. Roy Meyers, interview with the author, July 12, 2004.

65. Congressional Budget Office, *CBO's Budgetary Treatment of Fannie Mae and Freddie Mac*, Background Paper, January 2010, 8, www.cbo.gov/ftpdocs/108xx/doc10878/01–13-FannieFreddie.pdf.

66. Jonathan G. S. Koppell, "Hybrid Organizations and the Alignment of Interests," *Public Administration Review* 61, no. 4 (2001): 469–70.

67. Ibid.

68. Marvin Phaup, "Federal Use of Implied Guarantees," *Public Administration Review* 69, no. 4 (2009): 652–53.

69. Koppell, "Hybrid Organizations."

70. W. Scott Frame and Lawrence J. White, "Fussing and Fuming over Fannie and Freddie: How Much Smoke, How Much Fire?" *Journal of Economic Perspectives* 19, no. 2 (2005): 164.

71. Congressional Budget Office, *Government-Sponsored Enterprises and Their Implicit Federal Subsidy: The Case of Sallie Mae* (Washington, DC: GPO, December 1985).

72. Robert Reischauer, interview with the author, January 7, 2010.

73. Ibid.

74. Robert D. Reischauer,, Testimony before the House Subcommittee on Oversight, Committee on Ways and Means, *Testimony on Controlling the Risks of Government-Sponsored Enterprises*, May 22, 1991, 1.

75. Ibid.

76. Ibid., 4.

77. Stephen Labaton, "More Supervision Is Being Sought for Government-Backed Lenders," *New York Times*, April 28, 1991, A1.

78. Congressional Budget Office, *Assessing the Public Costs and Benefits of Fannie Mae and Freddie Mac* (Washington, DC: GPO, May 1996), preface.

79. Ibid., xiv.

80. Ibid., 44.

81. Albert B. Crenshaw, "CBO Faults Subsidies for 2 Finance Firms: Report Stokes Fannie Mae, Freddie Mac Debate," *Washington Post*, May 30, 1996, D9.

82. Leland C. Brendsel, Testimony before the House Banking and Financial Services Committee, Subcommittee on Capital Markets, Securities and Government-Sponsored Enterprises, July 31, 1996, 195.

83. Robert E. Zoellick, Testimony before the House Banking and Financial Services Committee, Subcommittee on Capital Markets, Securities and Government-Sponsored

Enterprises, "Oversight of the Federal National Mortgage Association (Fannie Mae)," July 31, 1996, 201.

84. Reported quote from June O'Neill on Panel of former CBO directors. Verified in email correspondence with O'Neill.

85. Zoellick, "Oversight of Fannie Mae," 101.

86. Ibid.,184. Note that this latter case is exactly what happened in 2007 and 2008.

87. Ibid.,185.

88. Congressional Budget Office, *Federal Subsidies and the Housing GSEs* (Washington, DC: GPO, May 2001), 2.

89. Daniel Crippen, Letter to Franklin D. Raines, "Regarding CBO's Draft Study on the Housing GSEs," June 21, 2001, 4.

90. Daniel Crippen, Letter to the Honorable Richard H. Baker, "Regarding CBO's May 2001 Report on the Housing GSEs," July 11, 2001, 1.

91. Richard Stevenson, "The Velvet Fist of Fannie Mae," *New York Times*, April 20, 1997, sect. 3, 1.

92. John Tierney, "Privileged Life for 2 Mortgage Giants," *New York Times*, June 17, 2003.

93. Binyamin Appelbaum, Carol D. Loennig, and David S. Hilzenrath, "How Washington Failed to Rein in Fannie, Freddie: As Profits Grew, Firms Used Their Power to Mask Peril," *Washington Post*, September 14, 2008, A1.

94. "More Disclosure," *Washington Post*, June 27, 2003, A28.

95. Douglas Holtz-Eakin, interview with the author, January 5, 2010.

96. David Hilzenrath, "White House Fire for Fannie, Freddie," *Washington Post*, November 17, 2003, E3.

97. Wayne Passmore, "The GSE Implicit Subsidy and the Value of Government Ambiguity," *Real Estate Economics* 33, no. 3 (2005): 465.

98. Alan Greenspan, Testimony before Senate Committee on Banking, Housing, and Urban Affairs, "Government-Sponsored Enterprises," 108th Cong., 2nd sess., February 24, 2004.

99. Ibid.

100. Patrice Hill, "Greenspan Hits Fannie Mae, Freddie Mac: Warns Rising Debts Will Hurt Economy," *Washington Times*, February 24, 2004, 1.

101. John W. Snow, Statement before the Senate Committee on Banking, Housing and Urban Affairs, 108th Cong., 1st sess., April 7, 2005.

102. Letter to the Honorable William H. Frist and the Honorable Richard C. Shelby, May 5, 2006, http://mccain.senate.gov/public/index.cfm?FuseAction=Files.View&File Store_id=98b5364d-b206–4b22-bf6d-13c73a238f17.

103. Peter J. Wallison and Charles W. Calomiris, "The Last Trillion-Dollar Commitment: The Destruction of Fannie Mae and Freddie Mac," *Financial Services Outlook Series* (Washington, DC: American Enterprise Institute for Public Policy Research, September 2008), 1.

104. Darrell Delamaide, "Beyond the Fannie, Freddie Rescue: Real Reform Will be Difficult," Darrell Delamaide's Political Capital, Marketwatch.com, September 10, 2008, www.marketwatch.com/story/beyond-the-fannie-freddie-rescue-real-reform-will-be-difficult.

105. Richard Rahn, "Surprised by the Obvious," *Washington Times*, September 23, 2008, A20.

106. Holtz-Eakin, interview, 2010.

107. Ken Dilanian, "How Congress Set the Stage for a Meltdown: Moves by Republicans, Democrats, Helped Fuel the Calamity," *USA Today*, October 13, 2008, 1A.

108. Penner, interview.

109. Ibid.

110. Douglas Holtz-Eakin, interview with the author, August 11, 2004.

Chapter 6

Clinton Health Plan: Bringing It All Together

UNTIL 2009 AND 2010, CBO did not at any point in its history have a higher profile than it did in the months leading up to February 1994. That month, CBO released its analysis of President Bill Clinton's health care reform plan. This plan was the centerpiece of Clinton's domestic agenda. The CBO conclusions—that the plan would add to the deficit and that the transactions under the plan should be counted in the federal budget—were credited (or blamed) at the time and continued to be cited more than ten years later as important factors in killing the Clinton health plan.

The decisions involved in the analysis were at the center of a defining moment for the agency. The moment itself was at the intersection of a presidential imperative, congressional ambivalence, and sudden light on the relatively routine and normally invisible process of determining costs and applying budget concepts. In the end, the episode raised questions about presidential-congressional relations, the role of policy analysis in Congress, and the use of analysis in the political process. It also represents an apt illustration, in a single case study, of the intersection of macro budgetary forces, cost estimating, and policy analysis tied up in the analysis of a single policy.

Clinton Election Promises

President Bill Clinton came into office having pledged to reform the health care system. The economy in general had been the key theme of his campaign. Early efforts to promote investment spending in 1993 failed in deference to a strategy that focused on eliminating the deficit (see chapter 3). But this focus on the deficit and on overall budget policy was largely designed to clear the way for what was hoped would be the key legacy of the Clinton presidency—comprehensive health care reform.

The goals of the health care program were anything but modest. At the time Clinton took office, an estimated 37 million Americans had no health insurance. At the same time, national health care spending had been growing substantially, with an inflation rate in the double digits. In this context, the Clinton health care reform sought to serve two goals—cost containment and insuring the uninsured population—simultaneously. Clinton proposed to succeed where many presidents since Harry Truman had failed. Enacting comprehensive health care reform was intended to continue the social insurance commitment begun with Social Security and continuing with Medicare and Medicaid. It was designed to do nothing less than "finish the New Deal," in the words of one of the participants.[1]

As ambitious as the program was, however, it needed to accede to real political constraints. Americans were skeptical of any effort that could be characterized as nationalizing health care. A Canadian- or Scandinavian-style health insurance program had neither broad public support nor the votes in either house of Congress to pass. So the challenge—to contain costs, serve the uninsured, and avoid the appearance of a large government-operated health system—created substantial challenges for anyone attempting to design a comprehensive health care reform plan.

Further, the Clinton plan was being proposed on the heels of the 1993 deficit reduction agreement, which had barely squeaked by in Congress without any Republican support. Moreover, Clinton's advisors believed that his reelection hinged in part on an ability to appeal to a significant number of people who had not voted for him and were more likely respond to a fiscally conservative agenda than to more traditional Democratic themes. In this context, a health care reform plan that added to the deficit was viewed as simply not politically feasible. An administration official noted later that the environment in which the reform plan evolved was one where "OMB scoring mattered, CBO scoring mattered. There was no money. The challenge was how to do this enormous program where you can do a list of your sources of revenue or savings, a list of how you're going to spend it, and have the two be equal with a big part of it not counting as a budgetary expenditure. We were pretty confident that if it was viewed as a program spending hundreds of billions of dollars that that wasn't going to advance our cause."[2]

Genesis of the Clinton Plan

In 1993, still preoccupied with attempting to pass its larger deficit reduction legislation (see chapter 3), the Clinton administration had already begun to think about both the policy and strategic implications of health care reform. In fact, five days after the president's inauguration, he announced the creation of the President's Task Force on National Health Care Reform. In an unconventional and somewhat controversial move, the first lady, Hillary Rodham Clinton, was chosen to spearhead the health care reform effort. Ira Magaziner, a key White House staff member who had been a management consultant, was made her deputy.[3] Together with an army of private consultants and government policy analysts in the White House, OMB, and the Department of Health and Human Services (HHS), they developed the outlines of what would become the Clinton plan.

As it turned out, the task force created many logistical and legal problems. Lawsuits were filed by a group of conservative physicians who charged that the deliberations of the task force violated the Government in the Sunshine Act. In fact, because of the lawsuit, Hillary Clinton did not attend any task force meetings subsequent to the filing of this lawsuit.[4] Moreover, Haynes Johnson and David Broder note that it was an unconventional strategy to try to handle the development of policy through a task force rather than the normal policy process, in which interest groups, federal agencies, and congressional committees take charge.[5]

In Congress, Republicans were developing a strategy to equate the Clinton plan with big government. Conservative House Republicans, led by Newt Gingrich, viewed opposition to the Clinton plan as a necessary prerequisite to their eventual takeover of the House of Representatives. Believing that the Clinton proposal was out of step with the majority of Americans' views of government, Gingrich stated that "these folks were committed to a government-controlled, left-wing version of America."[6] In the Senate, Bob Dole, who had long advocated some kind of health care reform, had his sights on the White House in 1996, which created an imperative to oppose the Clinton health plan.

Two larger constraints, therefore, faced the administration: the plan could not be thought of as governmental, and the plan needed to be deficit neutral. It would be even better if it actually reduced the deficit. The administration had reportedly understood this since the presidential campaign when, faced with a proposal to finance health care reform with a payroll tax, they balked because of concerns that such a tax would be powerful ammunition in the hands of their opponent, President George H. W. Bush. For this reason, a September 1993 article described the plan as having been "constructed from a political corner."[7]

Early reactions, even among those sympathetic to the goals of health care reform, suggested the problems ahead. According to Johnson and Broder, CBO director Robert Reischauer warned Magaziner in early 1993 that the plan was too ambitious to expect the Congress to be able to swallow. Reischauer suggested that an incremental approach would be more likely to succeed.[8] Reischauer himself recalled the conversation.

> When the administration came in, Ira came over to see me. We had a meeting in which we bet lunch—which was probably totally inappropriate. He came over . . . he tells me what they are going to do. I said "Ira, if you go and do that, I'll betcha that there is neither fundamental health care reform nor will there be incremental reform in your first term." I said "Ira, what you're really trying to do is go to the moon without building the Kennedy Space Center

first. . . . You should let President Chelsea Clinton take us to the moon." This is a long and complicated thing and barring a total meltdown—which he thought there was going to be—the politics are too confusing.[9]

Second, from the start, there were those even within the administration who doubted that the goals of the plan could be realized without additional revenues. HHS official Judy Feder, who had been part of a group within the administration that analyzed the cost of the health care reform proposal, had developed estimates that seemed to show that the plan was much more expensive than the administration had assumed. In fact, the memo Feder prepared for the president argued that in the long run significant savings would be achieved, but that in the short run the plan would add to the deficit unless rigid price controls were implemented. Rather than heeding the warning, however, Clinton dismissed the report as another example of "inside the Beltway" thinking.[10] Feder was apparently not alone in the view that the goals of the plan could not be achieved in a manner that was deficit-neutral. According to an April 1993 *New York Times* article, "in February, Ira C. Magaziner . . . said in a memorandum that 'universal access could mean $30 billion to $90 billion of additional annual expenditures by the Government by 1997.'" This conclusion led to the consideration—and rejection—of proposals for new taxes to finance the plan, including a value-added tax.[11]

Alice Rivlin, then deputy director of OMB, in an interview ten years later echoed the view that the financing was a bit fragile.

> I was always nervous about the cost estimates because they depended on a lot of things and there was a lot of uncertainty but there was clearly a lot of incentive within the administration to minimize the cost. And the part of it that I remember arguing about was the potential for the managed competition reducing the rate of growth. . . . I think it wasn't off the charts to think that we would get a one-time reduction in health care spending, although you might not get it all at once. And in fact that happened in the nineties, but the notion that it would permanently reduce the rate of growth seemed to me quite fanciful—and more fanciful the longer that you went out.[12]

Third, substantial difficulties might be created by attempting to bypass Congress rather than working with the congressional committees with jurisdiction over health programs. Eventually, a coalition would need to be formed that involved all of the players in the health game—the committees and the interest groups, primarily. Further, if draft legislative language was shared it could be vetted for both its political and fiscal implications. The administration worried, on the other hand, that if details began to leak out the plan would be killed before it saw the light of day.

Unveiling the Plan

Finally, on September 22, 1993, in a speech before a joint session of Congress, Clinton unveiled his health care reform plan. In the speech, the president outlined the key components of comprehensive health care reform. They included, principally, providing universal coverage for all Americans, focusing on the estimated 37 million without health insurance. Because of the concern for the budgetary effect of covering the uninsured, the plan would contain cost containment measures. In the end, the president said, the Clinton plan would not add to the deficit but would reduce it.

This September speech had provided the broad outlines of the plan, but the draft legislation necessary to implement the plan was not yet ready. During September and October 1993, White House staff and staff in key departments (such as HHS) worked on drafting the language necessary to convert the president's goals to specific legislation. The bill that was ultimately sent to Congress in October was detailed. At 1,364 pages, it was one of the longest pieces of legislation that many participants in the policy process had ever seen. It attempted to make good on the twin commitments to contain costs and provide universal coverage. Specifically, several specific provisions in the bill were aimed at satisfying these priorities:[13]

- A guarantee of health insurance coverage would exist for every citizen of the United States, as well as certain other noncitizens.
- The health insurance package guaranteed under the plan would include a standard package of benefits, including (but not limited to) hospital services, service health professionals, home health care, prescription drugs, and vision and dental care.
- A new system of regional purchasing alliances would be created; most people who worked for firms with fewer than five thousand employees would have purchased their insurance through these regional alliances. Larger firms, some group plans, the US Postal Service, and various other organizations would have been permitted to establish separate corporate alliances.
- All employers would be required to pay a portion of the premiums for their employees to these alliances. Individuals insured by the alliances would also need to pay premiums, but low-income individuals would have their premiums reduced because of subsidies provided by the federal government.
- A national health board would have been established, and it would have been responsible for interpreting the benefit package, determining eligibility, and implementing cost containment procedures, among many other things.
- As a cost control mechanism, the bill would rely first on the market. It would have established a system where higher-cost plans faced pressure to reduce their costs in order to protect their market share.

- As a backstop to these market forces the bill would establish limits on the growth of premiums (so-called premium caps); these caps would permit premiums to grow at a level that exceeded the consumer price index by from 1.5 percent (in 1996) to zero (in 2000).

Congress considered the president's plan, along with many other plans, in the fall of 1993 and into early 1994. The president renewed his call for enactment of his plan in his State of the Union address in January 1994, pledging to veto any legislation that did not guarantee universal coverage.[14] In the Republican response to the president's speech, Senator Bob Dole used a chart that laid out the various new entities created by the plan, to reemphasize its complexity. He made two points in this response. First was that the country faced no health care crisis and that there was no immediate urgency to act. Second was that the president's plan was clearly government-run health care and a substantial government intrusion in the private economy. The chart that he used seemed to emphasize this point, with its labyrinth of created alliances, boards, and plans.[15]

CBO's Role in Analyzing the Plan

Since the early deliberations on the health care reform plan, the administration was acutely aware that CBO would have a role to play in analyzing the plan for Congress. Because of this, efforts were made both to brief CBO on the outlines of the plan and to draft the plan with an eye toward how CBO would score it—that is, what the five-year cost estimate would be.[16] In fact, many of the characteristics of the plan existed partially because of the need to have something in place that CBO would score as at least deficit neutral, if not outright reducing the deficit. For example, the Clinton plan included explicit (and controversial) cost controls—in the form of premium caps—explicitly because it did not believe that CBO would score the bill as producing sufficient savings without those controls in place.[17]

It soon became apparent that the CBO analysis would be of potential importance on two issues. The first, the cost estimate, was obvious. It was CBO's statutory responsibility (see chapter 4) to provide Congress with an estimate of the five-year cost of any legislation reported out of a congressional committee. But health care reform was so complex that CBO dared not wait for the bill to be reported. A major presidential initiative such as this would need to be scored, if only because some congressional committee would need to consider it as legislation, which meant that a CBO cost estimate was required.

The second issue was less apparent, and much more arcane. An integral part of the plan involved the creation of new entities—called health alliances—through which much insurance in the country would be purchased and provided. The White House intended that all the transactions of these alliances would be private, that is, that they would not be counted in the budget. They viewed the employer mandate (the requirement that employers make compulsory payments into these alliances) as regulatory, that is, little different than mandatory automobile insurance premiums required in most states.

CBO routinely (though not frequently) needed to evaluate such claims, not on the basis of what a given president or member of Congress said they were doing, but based on the substantive result of the activity. A similar issue, in fact, faced CBO in the mid-1980s (see chapter 3), when attempts were made to place the savings and loan bailout off-budget by creating a government-sponsored enterprise to act as a conduit for the necessary transactions. In this case, CBO would evaluate the Clinton plan based on the nature of the health alliance transactions. For the relatively few people who follow such CBO estimates (usually associated with the budget committees, OMB, GAO, or CBO) it was a foregone conclusion that the CBO analysis would have to confront this issue. In evaluating the administration's claims that the transactions were not budgetary, CBO (as it always did) needed to rely on budgetary concepts and budgetary precedents.

This second issue came as somewhat of a surprise to some within the administration. This CBO role was certainly not a revelation to either Leon Panetta or Alice Rivlin, both of whom were seasoned congressional players with decades of experience with CBO. Both Rivlin and Jack Lew, who worked on health care reform in the White House and was later OMB director, thought that some on the White House staff gave too much emphasis to the CBO analysis. Lew thought that "there was always enough of a risk that they would go their own way on that that we should have found a way to marginalize it as opposed to make it something that the whole world—including ourselves—was putting so much weight on. You can always declare victory if it comes out confirming your view."[18]

For the administration, the budgetary treatment question was potentially more explosive than the cost question for two reasons. First, it was uncontrollable. The administration had made an effort to draft the plan to gain favorable CBO scoring of the cost, but the budgetary treatment question was all or nothing. This relates to the second reason for its importance. If the CBO said that these transactions were budgetary, it would provide congressional Republicans and other opponents of the plan with powerful ammunition to label the plan as a huge expansion of government and the compulsory payments to the alliances as large new federal taxes.

CBO's analysis was awaited with great anticipation, not just by the White House and Congress, but by the news media as well. CBO's position of prominence at this point in the health care reform debate probably stemmed from several factors.

- The preoccupation with the deficit that had started in 1985, but had continued through 1990 with the BEA and 1993 with the Clinton plan, elevated questions of the deficit impact of any piece of legislation to higher status. The drafters of earlier major social legislation (Social Security, Medicare) did not have to confront these kinds of evaluations of their costs.

- The cumulative credibility of CBO developed since the Reagan era, and the corresponding loss of credibility for OMB (see chapter 3), had elevated CBO's stature with the news media both because of the effectiveness of the first three directors as spokespeople for the agency, and because its nonpartisanship was rarely questioned, at least by the media. In short, the media believed that CBO (and perhaps CBO alone) would tell it like it saw it.
- A self-inflicted wound came from the Clinton administration itself, in that President Clinton had unwittingly contributed to CBO's credibility by pledging to use CBO numbers in his initial budgetary proposals (again see chapter 3). He had done so to avoid having to debate economic and budgetary assumptions, but had in the process elevated CBO to a position of even greater prominence in many economic and budgetary matters.[19]

Development of the CBO Report

CBO was already hard at work analyzing potential health care reforms prior to the introduction of the Clinton health care reform legislation. The agency had decided to develop a working group to analyze health care reform proposals. Although it was not common practice in many cases for analysts from BAD to work with analysts from the program divisions, for health care reform Reischauer decided that the most effective way to evaluate these proposals was to combine the cost experts with the policy experts. At least five divisions within CBO were involved in the analysis, including staff not only from BAD and the Health and Human Resources (HHR) program division, but also from program divisions focusing on macroeconomic analysis (on issues related to broader economic effects), national security (concerning veterans' health), and special studies (on the budgetary treatment question).

The Clinton health care reform plan was simultaneously nothing new and (because of its scope and level of detail) something that had never been seen before. In fact, the sheer size and reach ended up involving many more people within CBO than any plan before it. The lead for the development of the CBO analysis was taken by Paul Van de Water of BAD and Linda Bilheimer, who was the lead health analyst within HHR. Under their leadership, CBO went to work on evaluating two main aspects of the reform: the effect of the proposal on the economy (primarily national health spending) and the federal budget; and the budgetary treatment of the proposal.

Economic Effects and Cost

CBO director Reischauer had been expressing his skepticism for some time concerning the capacity of health care reform plans to generate savings for the federal budget. In a February 1993 appearance (a full year before the analysis of the

Clinton health plan, and only two weeks after Clinton took office) before the House Ways and Means Subcommittee on Health, he testified that there was little likelihood of short-term savings. He was more optimistic about longer-term savings, but noted that many of these might lie outside of the five-year cost-estimating window.[20] A March 1993 *Chicago Tribune* editorial noted that "every now and then, someone in Washington says something so obviously sensible that he or she is forthwith banned from the nicer social circles for having told us something that we didn't wish to hear. Last week the offending party was Robert D. Reischauer, head of the Congressional Budget Office. The message we didn't wish to hear? That cutting the cost of health care may mean getting less health care."[21]

Within CBO, the development of the cost estimate involved complex modeling of the impact of managed competition on health spending, and assumptions about future premiums. This latter estimate was particularly important because the level of the subsidy provided to employers under the plan was driven by the level of premiums required to be paid without the subsidy.

Although in the first decade of its history, health reform was not a major emphasis within Congress or CBO, the agency had had some recent experience in developing health cost estimates. In July 1993, well before the Clinton plan was formally introduced, CBO had published a report that summarized cost estimates on health care proposals from the 102nd Congress (1991–92).[22] This report was issued in part to lay the groundwork for the estimate of the Clinton plan, including estimating national health spending. This was particularly critical in the case of single-payer plans, but other plans also had characteristics that CBO had not yet analyzed.[23] Perhaps as critical, the core group of cost estimators from both BAD and HHR who eventually estimated the budgetary effects of the Clinton plan had effectively cut their teeth as analysts on these other plans.

CBO made no effort to bring in staff from outside of CBO in developing the cost estimates of the Clinton plan. It was not clear why the agency made the judgment not to involve people from the outside; contracting with outside experts was done periodically, primarily when CBO felt that it lacked the capacity to fully evaluate a proposal. In this case, CBO may not have involved outsiders for any of a number of reasons. First, there was not enough time, particularly given the arcane issues at the intersection of health care reform and cost estimating. Second, there may have been a concern that involving non-CBO staff would increase the probability that the analysis would come out in the press. Finally, it is possible that, given the large number of people working for the administration in the development of the proposal (or already enlisted by groups opposed to it), there were simply no (or next to no) good impartial health analysts left. Perhaps most important, CBO staff had renewed the relevant professional literature and the agency felt that its in-house analytical capacity was sufficient.[24]

Back and forth between the administration and CBO as the CBO estimate was developed was significant. According to Reischauer, "we met with them a number of times during this process and they were very forthcoming in sharing their methodology and their data with us. They were desperate to get us to come up with a number like theirs."[25] According to Paul Van de Water, CBO staff knew which administration staff worked on the cost estimate, and these people were available to CBO staff and could respond to questions, if necessary.[26] At no point, though, did CBO share its conclusions about the cost of any aspect of the reform package with these people.

Although data and methodological information were shared between the administration and CBO, there was not much lobbying at the staff level. Much of the interaction there, both on the Clinton plan and on other bills, came from those wanting to provide inputs to the cost estimating process on a technical level, and almost never because they wanted to convince CBO about the desirability of a particular policy.

CBO was aware of the potential for differences in estimates between it and the administration, but was confident that its data sources were legitimate. According to Reischauer, "we were using different data sources than what they were doing. We had developed a data base that was coming out with different numbers and I have every reason to believe that our people were at least as skilled as their people were in doing this kind of thing."[27]

Budgetary Treatment

The CBO decision on the budgetary treatment of the proposal involved a completely different group of people than the health experts. Van de Water was involved in both, but the budgetary treatment analysis involved mainly individuals in BAD and in Bob Hartman's SSD, which had jurisdiction over reform in budget concepts. Within SSD, the two staff who played key roles were probably Robin Seiler, who had headed CBO's 1991 GSE study, and Tom Cuny, who had a long history of working with budget concepts at OMB. The first reported reference to the CBO process after the introduction of the plan was in mid-October, when the *Washington Post* noted that "the Congressional Budget Office is considering whether the money employers and employees would be required to pay for medical coverage under the president's health plan should be entered on federal budget books as a tax. The issue, although seemingly arcane, is politically dangerous for President Clinton. He specifically rejected proposals to finance his health plan using broad new taxes . . . because Clinton was certain it would be a political kiss of death."[28]

Almost immediately after the president's proposal was introduced, CBO staff began to consider arguments for and against including the finances of the health alliances in the federal budget. In fact, relatively early in the process (almost immediately after the president's speech) emails were exchanged between CBO staff on the issue. The subject was an unsigned OMB staff memo that had found its way to CBO outlining the OMB staff recommendation that the transactions of the health alliances be included in the budget; OMB staff had been overruled by senior staff at OMB or the White House on either political or substantive grounds, and perhaps both.[29]

Particularly because the OMB staff position was not the official position of the executive branch, this analysis obviously did little to lessen the burden on CBO to present its own justification. At most, it may have provided some comfort in the knowledge that other budget technicians had concluded that the transactions were budgetary. Over the next two months (until late December), there were numerous (at least weekly, and normally daily) email, spoken, and written exchanges at the staff level attempting to resolve the issue of the correct budgetary treatment of the alliances using traditional budget concepts.

The details of all of the CBO deliberations are perhaps too tortured and arcane to detail here (or anywhere) but it is clear that there was a careful consideration of past precedents and budget concepts, primarily those developed by the 1967 President's Commission on Budget Concepts. This commission, which had been established to address a real problem stemming from the inconsistent application of budgetary principles, included specific language intended to guide discussions of what would be considered budgetary transactions and what would be considered private transactions (for example, regulatory actions which, though they might cost individuals money, were not considered part of the federal budget). These arguments were played out in discussions and email exchanges among CBO staff. Reischauer himself took the unusual step of composing a detailed memorandum laying out the arguments pro and con concerning the budgetary treatment question.

In short, the arguments against including the alliance transactions in the federal budget stemmed from whether they were in fact regulatory (the equivalent of state requirements that individuals purchase automobile insurance) or represented compulsory payments required by and to the federal government (the equivalent of taxes). An important point is that all of the evidence points to deliberations by CBO based on what relevant CBO staff viewed to be the substance of the proposal. In fact, Paul Van de Water, who was at the center of the discussions, acknowledged ten years later that the budgetary treatment question "became easier as we thought more about it."[30]

Although that may have been true substantively, tremendous pressure was being applied on Reischauer from both the advocates of the president's plan (in the executive branch and Congress) and opponents in Congress. In their book *The System*, Haynes Johnson and David Broder describe the pressure on Reischauer as "intense, personal and abusive."[31] Reischauer confirmed when interviewed that people from inside the administration contacted him to talk about the proposal.[32]

The White House allegedly believed, both because Reischauer came from a Democratic family, and because he had worked for Rivlin, that he could be swayed to "do the right thing." Johnson and Broder reported that Senator Edward Kennedy called Reischauer at his home to express his outrage because

Reischauer, a "minor staff official" was about to "bring down the Clinton administration."[33]

An example of public pressure from the other side came on October 28, 1993, when a proposal was made in the House of Representatives to direct CBO to count the premiums as taxes. The proposal to direct OMB, CBO, and the JCT to count mandated premiums as taxes was defeated on a largely straight party line vote of 252 to 170. Republican Whip Newt Gingrich summed up the Republican view on the issue by saying that "if the government requires you to pay it, if the government is going to make you take it out of your wallet, if the government is going to ensure that the money is gone from your choice, if the government is going to control the expenditure of your money, that is called a tax."[34] House Budget Committee chair Martin Sabo called that thinking "nuts," adding that the health alliance transactions "are clearly private expenditure, not public expenditures."[35] Subsequent to this, a letter was sent to CBO on November 19 signed by Republican committee chairs with jurisdiction over health care matters reiterating the arguments in favor of counting the transactions as part of the budget.

As if the pressure wasn't already intense enough, a story appeared on December 2, 1993, on the front page of the *Washington Post*, the lead sentence of which was "the Congressional Budget Office has agreed to the Clinton administration's strong plea that the bulk of the spending included in the president's health care plan be kept off the federal budget, according to informed congressional sources."[36] These congressional sources were (in retrospect) almost certainly Republicans who were attempting to leak word (incorrectly) that Reischauer had caved to increase pressure on him not to cave; that is, to stand up to the pressure from the administration. The article included the obligatory (but correct, given that Reischauer's own memo on the issue had not yet been delivered to CBO staff) denial from Reischauer, who said the issue "has not been fully resolved. If people think it has, that's their interpretation."[37] This *Post* story was not the only example. The next day, a similar story appeared in the *St. Louis Post-Dispatch* noting that CBO had "agreed to President Bill Clinton's plea that most of the spending in the president's health-care plan be kept out of the federal budget."[38] In a December 3 story in the *Washington Times*, Reischauer denied explicitly that the decision had been made; he repeated this assertion to House Republican leaders in a meeting the following week.[39]

In the end, the judgment of the CBO staff, affirmed by Reischauer, was that the transactions of the health alliances were by rights budgetary transactions, and should be included in the budget. Reischauer, however, gave the staff a last opportunity to (possibly) avoid the eye of the storm by choosing to exclude the chapter on budgetary treatment, as well as another titled "Other Considerations" (which effectively called into question whether the plan could work), from the CBO report. Johnson and Broder, in their book on the Clinton health plan, described an extraordinary meeting called by Reischauer in which he assembled the CBO executive staff and asked them to vote on whether to make the most controversial parts of the report public.[40] Deputy Director Jim Blum, who was at this meeting (and collected the scraps of paper on which the votes were cast), recalled that

> Reischauer said that we could just provide a more narrow cost estimate instead of the broader report that had been prepared. He told us that he had been threatened about counting the transactions of the health alliances as on-budget items and that CBO as an institution could be affected. While he wasn't ultimately concerned about his own job security, CBO could end up with a different kind of director and that a lot of us could lose our jobs. The effectiveness of the institution could be compromised if we caved to political pressure, although we would still be an institution that provides good and useful things. But in proceeding with this broader report, we would be taking another step in providing good and useful analytical information at a higher level that would be expected to be continued in the future. Reischauer wanted us to vote on whether to go broad or narrow, and we all voted "full speed ahead."[41]

Until the very end, CBO did an extraordinary job of keeping its conclusions secret. One CBO staffer recalled that this extended to staff going through their garbage to avoid having anything leak that would provide evidence of CBO's deliberations and conclusions.[42] And up to the end, many in Congress and the administration did not know where CBO would come out, particularly on budgetary treatment. An interview with several people who had worked intimately on the proposal confirmed that the administration did not know what the report was going to say about premiums or anything else before it came out. Reischauer recalled an incident that illustrates the point well.

> There was the famous interaction with John Kasich [the ranking Republican on the House Budget Committee], who the day before I testified, I was up there doing something, and he runs into me in the hall, and he puts his arm around me, and he said, "I know what you're going to do tomorrow, and I know that you don't have any leeway at all—I mean, I understand that. I know the way this world works, and I know because we've talked about it, that the Republicans are going to introduce a resolution to kick you out, but I want you to know I'm going to speak on your behalf. I'm going to defend you, and I think I can get some others to go along with me." And I thanked him profusely. There were a lot of people who were surprised.[43]

Release of the CBO Report

The CBO report on the Clinton health care reform plan was released on February 9, 2004, setting off a flurry of testimony, political spin, press reaction, and speculation. The report highlighted each of the issues that CBO focused on in their deliberations. Concerning the budgetary impact of the plan, CBO concluded that it would add approximately $70 billion to cumulative deficits between 1995 and 2000, rather than reducing these deficits by $60 billion as the administration had claimed. CBO noted that "the difference between these estimates is small, however, compared with the uncertainty surrounding the budget projections."[44] CBO noted that about half of the difference between CBO and the administration stemmed from different assumptions about subsidies for employers; because CBO assumed higher premiums, its subsidy estimates were higher.

CBO presented a table within the report that summarized the difference between the administration and CBO on the five-year cost estimate. The difference between CBO and the administration was approximately $130 billion; of this difference, $72 billion was in subsidies for employers.[45]

Further, CBO noted that it believed that the administration's proposal, when fully implemented, would reduce both national health care costs and the federal deficit. As to the former, although CBO thought that national health spending would be higher under the Clinton plan than under the CBO baseline through 1999, it believed that, after 1999, national health spending would decrease.[46] Further, though CBO's estimates found that the plan increased the federal deficit through 2004, the declining effect of the proposal on the deficit in the later years of this period led CBO to conclude that "after 2004, the proposal could potentially reduce the deficit."[47]

Second, CBO assumed that though overall health care spending would eventually drop because of the Clinton plan, there would likely be substantial redistribution of expenses between individuals and between sectors of the economy. CBO argued that the proposal would encourage some people—Medicaid recipients, for example—to enter the work force, and others to leave the labor force because they no longer needed to work to be guaranteed insurance.

On the question of the budgetary treatment of the proposal, CBO came down on the side of putting the transactions in the budget, using typically careful language. The language, in fact, is so careful that it is worth quoting at length.

> This issue of budgetary treatment is not unique to proposals to restructure the health care system. Every time the Congress considers or enacts a bill that establishes a new program, the Congressional Budget Office and the Office of Management and Budget must consider whether and how it should be treated in the federal budget. For most pieces of legislation, the call is a relatively easy one. But for some bills, such as major health care reform proposals, some ambiguity and considerable complexity accompany that assessment. In this case, CBO strongly believes that the president and the Congress should address the budgetary treatment of the proposal explicitly through legislation. CBO's role in the decision is strictly advisory.
>
> In answering such questions, budget analysts normally consult two sources for guidance. One is the 1967 Report of the President's Commission on Budget

Concepts. The other is budgetary precedent. Because of the unique features of the Administration's health proposal, however, neither source provides a definitive answer.

Considering the Administration's proposal in its entirety, CBO concludes that it would establish both a federal entitlement to health benefits and a system of mandatory payments to finance those benefits that represents an exercise of sovereign power. In administering the proposed program, regional alliances, corporate alliances, and state single-payer plans (if any) would operate primarily as agents of the federal government. *Therefore, CBO believes that the financial transactions of the health alliances should be included in the federal government's accounts and the premium payments should be shown as governmental receipts rather than as offsets to spending.* (emphasis added) Nonetheless, because of the uniqueness and the vast size of the program, the budget document should distinguish the transactions of the alliances from other federal operations and show them separately, as is the practice for Social Security.[48]

CBO did not hide its conclusion that the health alliances created by the Clinton plan belong in the budget. It tempered this conclusion, however, with two caveats. First, that these transactions should be shown in the budget separately, thus allowing them to be included or excluded, depending on one's view of them. Second, that Congress and the president should legislate the budgetary treatment, rather than leaving the conclusion to CBO.

Other Considerations

It was well understood that any CBO analysis would evaluate the budgetary and economic effects of the proposal. Somewhat late in the CBO analytical process, however, the agency decided that its report must include a discussion of the operational viability of the proposal. That is, the analysis would include a discussion of whether the various institutions created by the plan would carry out their functions as intended. This evaluation of the public administration of the plan was intended to move beyond CBO's more traditional role of cost to a discussion of the institutional viability of the plan.

This ultimately resulted in the inclusion of a chapter in the CBO report titled "Other Considerations." Paul Van de Water talked about the genesis of this chapter: "I think it was something that just evolved as we learned more about the plan and read about people's reactions to it and thought about how we might be helpful. It was clear that there was need for . . . this final chapter for which we produced this terribly unhelpful name called 'Other Considerations.' . . . We just felt that in order to help people understand the proposal and think through the issues, it was important to get this stuff on the table."[49]

This chapter began by reiterating that the health care reform proposal "provides a blueprint for restructuring the entire health care system, complete in almost every particular of the design."[50] The chapter noted that whether the plan would actually work or not was dependent on whether the changes could be implemented in the time frame planned, and whether "unintended consequences" would thwart any of the goals of the plan. The chapter questioned, among other things

- whether the National Health Board could recruit the large, skilled staff they would need, and whether they would be able to make decisions under the extremely ambitious schedule envisioned;
- whether it would be possible to establish adequate information systems that could provide the required data on cost and quality of care within the required timeframe;
- the capacity of the alliances to perform the many functions prescribed for them; and
- practical problems associated with trying to limit growth in premiums.[51]

It did not take much reading between the lines to capture CBO's main conclusion concerning the institutional prospects for the plan; in short, CBO believed that it was optimistic to assume that the plan would work as proposed, regardless of how much it cost and whether its transactions were in the federal budget.

Testimony and Reaction

Reischauer testified during the entire second week of February 1994 before various congressional committees with jurisdiction over the proposal, including the House Committee on Ways and Means and the Senate Committee on Finance. The Ways and Means testimony, on February 8, was the first and most critical of the testimonies, as it was the public unveiling of the CBO analysis.[52]

The core of the testimony was simply a summary of the major CBO conclusions, on cost, budgetary treatment, and other considerations. Perhaps the most extraordinary part was the way Reischauer closed. His closing remarks, which were reprinted in the *Washington Post* two days later, provided a classic example of an effort by a policy analyst to try and caution his employers about the limitations and potential misuse of policy analysis. It is worthy of being quoted at length.

With your indulgence, I would like to close my remarks on a more personal note than is typical for the testimony of the director of the Congressional Budget Office. I have appeared before committees and subcommittees of the Congress well over 100 times. On each of these occasions I have started with some customary remarks concerning how pleased I was to have the opportunity to testify.

I did not start off that way today. I did not because I have considerable foreboding that the information contained in my statement and in the CBO report might be used largely in destructive rather than constructive ways. . . . I have not been encouraged by the recent debate, which at times has degenerated into semantic mud wrestling and name calling. Do we face a "crisis" or just a large problem? Should the payments made to the alliances be labeled a "tax" or a "premium"? Are pharmaceutical companies and health insurers behaving in unconscionable ways or are they the jewels of our free enterprise system? The American people—particularly those ill-served by our current health care system—deserve better.[53]

He went on to remind committee members of the seriousness of the national health care problem, that many past presidents who had attempted health care reforms (Truman, Nixon, Carter) had not been successful, and that a reform would require bipartisan solutions. Reischauer closed his statement with a story about an earlier trip he had made with the House Ways and Means Committee to the LBJ Presidential Library in Texas, where committee members had reflected on the importance of the 1965 Medicare Act, and the pride that (in 1994 Ways and Means chair, but in 1965 junior congressman) Dan Rostenkowski had felt in being a part of this legislation.

I wonder whether any of those who are now junior members of the committee someday will be able to tour a presidential archive and say to a grandchild that they may have in tow: "That's my signature on the legislation that helped to make America's health care system more equitable, more efficient, and less costly." I hope so. Where the solution that you develop on this committee builds on the framework proposed by the administration or on some other approach is not as important as that some substantial step forward be taken now that the president has created this opportunity.[54]

The White House had been prepared for the conclusions of the CBO report to go against them, but until the morning of the release, they did not know the specifics of the CBO analysis. Len Nichols, an administration official who had worked on the reform, reported that he attended a briefing at CBO the day the report was released and that, by the time he returned to the White House, a number of people had read it, and Magaziner said that he believed it had dealt a major blow to health care reform.[55]

Reaction to the report and the Reischauer testimony was predictable. Certainly the press anticipation of the CBO analysis had been palpable. One report noted that "the analysis is being viewed by many experts as the equivalent of a Supreme Court ruling on health care."[56] Ironically, an article by David Broder (who had announced two months earlier that CBO had acceded to the wishes of the administration) in the *Washington Post* the morning of the release of the report noted that administration officials were gearing up for a ruling that was not going their way.[57]

The press reaction focused on the two key questions—differences in the cost estimates and the budgetary treatment of the health alliances. Much attention was paid to what was advertised as a large difference ($130 billion) between the administration and CBO on the cost.[58] Others reported (accurately) that CBO (and Reischauer in testimony) had emphasized that there were really only small differences between CBO's numbers and those of the administration's, given the magnitude of national health spending.[59] Some (albeit not many) also noted the "other considerations," noting that the CBO argued that "the myriad old and new government agencies required to implement the plan may not be up to the task."[60]

The administration and its allies scrambled to find positives in the CBO report. Administration cost estimators noted that CBO found that the plan did work (it did achieve universal coverage) and that the cost differences were really about how fast savings could be achieved, not whether they could be achieved.[61] Clinton himself was dismissive, arguing that the inclusion of the transactions in the federal budget "is not a problem. That's a Washington policy wonk deal. No serious person out in the real world would be troubled by it."[62]

In terms of the cost estimate, in particular, many people who worked closely on the scoring on both sides viewed both the CBO and OMB cost estimates as well within the typical margin of error for cost estimates. Health cost estimates were particularly difficult to nail down. But the sign—given the political context—was important.

People within the administration, however, were unhappy with some aspects of the CBO cost estimate. Many were still unhappy more than ten years later. The particular issue surrounded the estimate of future premiums, which (as noted) accounted for more than half of the difference between the administration and CBO. Analysts from the executive branch considered the way CBO did the calculation to be out of line with the way both economists and actuaries do these analyses. In fact, they noted that even without the Clinton health plan, it was four years before premiums got as high as they were assumed in the CBO cost estimate.[63]

Editorial writers and columnists also had widely varying responses. The *New York Times*, though acknowledging the political damage resulting from the CBO analysis, also emphasized the limitations of the CBO analysis, dismissing it as largely technical and not addressing the fundamental health care issues.[64] Others hailed the report as a triumph for "truth in government."[65] Paul Gigot of the *Wall Street Journal* went so far as to praise Reischauer as one of two "honest liberals" in Washington.[66] Robert Samuelson actually criticized the CBO report on methodological grounds, arguing that the picture it painted was too rosy because the assumption that cost controls would be 100 percent effective was wildly optimistic.[67]

Reaction in Congress was along partisan lines. Senator Kennedy, who had tried to dissuade Reischauer from allowing CBO to take the position it took, went to the Senate floor on the day of the release of the CBO report to tout it as good news for the administration. "After all the ideological smoke dissipates," he argued, "it will be clear that CBO's analysis is a solid vote of confidence in the administration's plan. . . . The CBO report specifically confirms that the long-term effect of the President's plan will be to reduce the federal deficit."[68]

Conversely, Republicans seized on the report to argue that it confirmed what they knew all along—that President Clinton was proposing a vast new expansion of government. Representative David Dreier (R-CA) tweaked the administration for dismissing the conclusions of the CBO report when it had argued for "using the independent numbers of the Congressional Budget Office" when unveiling the Clinton economic program in 1993.[69]

Some—from both sides of the aisle—specifically acknowledged the pressure that CBO had been under. Representative Pete Stark (D-CA), a single-payer advocate who chaired the Ways and Means health subcommittee, said that "the White House was merciless in the pressure they put on Bob Reischauer to get him to change his testimony."[70] Senator Pete Domenici, clearly somewhat surprised by the CBO conclusion, took to the Senate floor to praise Reischauer as "a very, very courageous employee of the U.S. Government."[71] Senate minority leader Bob Dole noted that CBO "put together a very objective and comprehensive analysis under very difficult circumstances."[72]

Conclusion: What Difference Did the CBO Report Make?

Ultimately, we are left with the question—what difference did it make? What did the CBO report add to the process? Did the CBO report kill the Clinton health care reform? These are very difficult questions to answer, even more than fifteen years later. We can at least speculate on some of these issues.

What do we know for sure? We know that the fact that CBO existed, and therefore did an analysis, had at least two effects on the process. First, it required all plans (including the administration's and others) to be evaluated against a common standard. Certainly people could disagree with the appropriateness of that standard, and the weight given to these cost and budgetary treatment considerations, but no one argues that CBO did not apply the same rules to all bills. This is one of the main effects in general of having CBO, and clearly it applied to health care reform. For example, perhaps the leading alternative plan to the Clinton plan, one backed by Congressman Jim Cooper (D-TN) and Senator John Breaux (D-LA), was also found lacking in key respects. The Cooper-Breaux bill would have cut long-term deficits, according to CBO, but would still have left 24 million Americans without health insurance.[73] Second, it affected the way that the administration crafted the legislation. That is, the proposal might have been different (but only in details, not in its basic outline) without the prospect of CBO scoring.

Did the CBO report kill health care reform? A group of Clinton veterans gathered to commemorate the ten-year anniversary of the health care reform effort. In an informal poll, they reportedly listed the CBO report as the number 2 factor that killed the health care reform effort: failure to work adequately with Congress was number 1.[74] Jack Lew speculated on the impact of CBO's role:

> The employer mandate ultimately killed health care reform. If CBO had said it wasn't a tax, it probably still would have killed health care reform, but there would have been a slightly higher probability that we could have overcome the resistance. If you look at the politics of it, it came down to one vote in the Energy and Commerce Committee to move on to the next stage of the process, so we weren't miles away from getting where we needed to go.

Others interviewed for this book reached a different conclusion. In fact, it is striking the extent to which virtually all Clinton administration officials or advocates of health care reform cite the CBO analysis as an important factor, which virtually everyone who was within CBO or people who had no particular vested interest view the CBO report as relatively unimportant. This latter group of individuals tends to cite (in no particular order): the general lukewarm reaction in Congress, the fragmented nature of Congress, poor strategic decisions in working with Congress, the opposition of the health insurance industry (generally), and the "Harry and Louise" ads (specifically). One observer described the CBO report as "just another nail in the coffin. . . . I think the legislation was already headed downhill."[75]

Two other questions should be asked as well. First, was CBO's analysis ultimately correct on the two main questions—cost and budgetary treatment? Second, did CBO play too important a role in the debate over reforming health care?

On the first question, it is impossible to judge whether it was correct in estimating the cost of a reform that did not become law. On the question of whether CBO's estimates were better than the administration's, some of the administration's supporters noted that on the key difference between CBO and the administration—the estimate of premiums—they viewed the fact that actual premiums grew more slowly than assumed by CBO for the rest of the 1990s as evidence that the administration estimate was more correct.

The budgetary treatment question is far more metaphysical. Differences remain (and will remain) among key players about whether CBO reached the correct conclusion. Reischauer and other former CBO staff interviewed more than ten years later felt strongly and unanimously that CBO had gotten the analysis correct. Reischauer himself noted that "I didn't even think it was a close call because . . . the fact that some individual living clipping coupons in Northwest Washington who did not have a job would be forced to pay premiums and join one of these things is an act of sovereign power, and there's no way around it, I don't think. It's no different from my telling him he has to pay taxes, is the point. Telling him that it is for the public good, and the social welfare of the country— well, does that make a difference?"[76]

The Reischauer view was echoed by others interviewed for this book, including Paul Van de Water, Jim Horney, and Barry Anderson.[77] Alice Rivlin felt the opposite equally strongly, saying, "I thought it was wrong. I thought you could make a very good case for not scoring the alliance premiums as taxes. And I remember arguing things like there are lots of compulsory payments. . . . There are lots of kinds of examples of that—things that are mandatory but not scored as taxes, not counted anywhere. I didn't buy the argument that the alliance premiums had to be taxes."[78] This view was echoed by Richard Kogan, who at the time of the CBO report had been on House Budget Committee Democratic staff.[79]

Even though agreement was not universal on whether CBO reached the right conclusion, there does seem to be a general consensus that it would not have been desirable for CBO to simply duck the question. Such a strategy would have had political consequences for the agency, and would have detracted from its usefulness and credibility as an analytical institution. On the first point, Jim Horney spoke to a point raised by several people when he argued that, had CBO punted on the budgetary treatment question, "the Republicans would have screamed bloody murder and it would have been even harder subsequently to convince them that CBO was an impartial, responsible organization."[80] On the second, the prevailing view—even among those who had served in the Clinton administration—was that CBO needed to offer its opinion, whatever it was.

Did CBO have too much influence in the health care reform debate? Certainly comprehensive health care reform did not fare well in the fifteen years after the Clinton plan went down to defeat. Some argue that it represented the best chance for meaningful reform, and its failure did irreparable harm to the country, in terms of both the larger public welfare and the country's fiscal condition.

Where did CBO's influence come from? First, the context in which the analysis was conducted made a lot of difference. President Clinton had in 1993 shepherded a comprehensive deficit reduction plan through Congress. In that context, a health plan that added to the deficit was untenable. Given this, there would be a focus on the price tag of the plan, and, because CBO analyzes costs, that would elevate CBO.[81]

Second, the president himself had elevated CBO to budget oracle status early in his administration by promising to use CBO numbers for his deficit reduction plan. Although this seemed expedient at the time, it raised the stakes with respect to any CBO analysis of an administration proposal. Further, as some in the administration noted later, there were those in the administration who were preoccupied with what CBO would say; perhaps had they placed less emphasis on CBO in advance of the CBO report, it would have had less of an impact.

Third, the administration's strategy may have been flawed in two respects, both of which gave greater weight to the CBO analysis. First, they chose to drop a fully developed plan in the lap of the Congress, instead of going through congressional committees to develop it. In the latter case, they would have had the benefit of CBO pre-scoring components of the plan in private, rather than CBO providing what one former Clinton official referred to as an "imperial judgment" on the whole plan.[82] Paul Van de Water suggested that it clearly could have made a difference to take the plan through the Congress, at least in terms of the cost estimate: "That is exactly CBO's normal way of operating. . . . There was Senator Chafee, and Breaux, and another group of people who were putting together a bipartisan proposal—that was exactly what we did—they [the staff] were down in my office at eight o'clock on various nights as we went back and forth with stuff to discuss how they could adjust the proposal. . . . No one knows, but clearly had that kind of back and forth gone on [with the Clinton plan], they could have eliminated any of the differences they wanted to eliminate."[83]

Further, neither Congress nor the Clinton administration allowed explicitly for the budgetary treatment of the plan in the legislation. This might have forced CBO to treat the health alliance transactions as nonbudgetary flows, despite whatever substantive characteristics, because of what the law called them. According to Van de Water, CBO

> recognized that ultimately the Congress and the administration can write the law to treat anything in the budget any way they want to, and that was again the opening that we had given to the administration, saying "Don't ask us for our opinion on this; tell us how to do it!" Because under these circumstances there's enough uncertainty that if you say it shouldn't be included in the budget that would create a presumption that that's the way it should be treated. And we never understood why they didn't do that . . . at least I never did.[84]

Finally, members of Congress may have used CBO to mask their own ambivalence to the Clinton plan. Even those from the president's own party who supported health care reform did not necessarily support the president's plan. These included Representatives Cooper, Stark, and McDermott, and Senator Breaux. It may have been easier for these people to emphasize CBO's analysis rather than to challenge the president directly.

The common denominator here is that the CBO analysis was important not because of any efforts on the part of CBO to elevate the importance of either the agency or the analysis, but because the agency found itself as the center of a perfect analytical storm. It had developed credibility over the years as an objective analyst, it had been asked a set of questions that it had the responsibility and expertise to answer, and the answer was provided in a political context in which CBO's analysis was given maximum weight. Then–CBO deputy director Jim Blum put it well when he said, "Both the Congress and the administration were looking to CBO to pronounce. If we had too much importance, they gave it to us. Now we could feel reluctant that such a little agency should have such importance . . . but . . . we are a creature of the Congress. They gave it to us."[85]

Notes

1. Len Nichols, interview with the author, February 6, 2004.

2. Lew, interview.

3. Haynes Johnson and David Broder, *The System* (Boston, MA: Little, Brown, 1996), 96–103.

4. Ibid., 111–12.

5. Ibid., 112.

6. Ibid., 304.

7. Greg Gordon, "Health Plan; The Tax That Dare Not Speak Its Name," *Minneapolis Star-Tribune*, September 13, 1993, 1A.

8. Johnson and Broder, *The System*, 116–18.

9. Robert Reischauer, interview with the author, March 23, 2004.

10. Johnson and Broder, *The System*, 109–10.

11. Robert Pear and David Rosenbaum, "As Health Plan Comes Together, Big Price Tag Comes into Focus," *New York Times*, April 19, 1993, A1.

12. Rivlin, interview.

13. The following specific provisions are summarized from Congressional Budget Office, *An Analysis of the Administration's Health Proposal* (Washington, DC: GPO, February 1994), 1–24.

14. Johnson and Broder, *The System*, 267.

15. Ibid., 270–71.

16. Virtually everyone interviewed who had worked on the plan, including Alice Rivlin, Jacob Lew, and Ken Thorpe, among others, agreed that the plan was drafted with CBO scoring in mind. Both Lew and Rivlin argued, however, that the broader issue was that the bill needed to reduce rather than add to the deficit because of the broader fiscal environment. There was also a universal understanding within CBO that the drafting of the bill was done with an eye toward CBO scoring.

17. Peter Gosselin, "Health Plan Debaters Await Reischauer Word: Budget Office Head Downplays Role," *Boston Globe*, January 31, 1994, 1.

18. Lew, interview.

19. Rivlin, interview, 2003.

20. Robert Pear, "Budget Official Sees No Savings in Clinton's Health Care Plan," *New York Times*, February 3, 1993, A16.

21. Otis Pike, "Healthy Debate Isn't Popular," *Chicago Tribune*, March 9, 1993, 25.

22. Congressional Budget Office, *Estimates of Health Care Proposals from the 102nd Congress*, CBO paper, July 1993.

23. Van de Water, interview.

24. Van de Water, interview.

25. Reischauer, interview, 2004.

26. Van de Water, interview.

27. Reischauer, interview, 2004.

28. Clay Chandler and Dana Priest, "Hill Budget Experts May Stamp 'Taxes' on Health Premiums," *Washington Post*, October 17, 1993, A20.

29. Barry Anderson, interview with the author, March 10, 2005.

30. Van de Water, interview.

31. Johnson and Broder, *The System*, 283.

32. Reischauer, interview, 2004.

33. Johnson and Broder, *The System*, 284–85.

34. Bureau of National Affairs, *Daily Tax Report*, November 1, 1993, G-7.

35. Ibid.

36. David S. Broder, "Health Plan Spending to Be Off-Budget; Congressional Agency's Assent Seen as Major White House Victory," *Washington Post*, December 2, 1993, A1.

37. Ibid.

38. "Budget Office Backs Clinton Plan; Health-Care Funding Won't Count as Taxes," *St. Louis Post-Dispatch*, December 3, 1993, 3E.

39. Ralph Hallow, "Health Plan's Budget Spot Remains a CBO Question," *Washington Times*, December 8, 1993, A1.

40. Johnson and Broder, *The System*, 285–86.

41. James L. Blum, email communication, November 6, 2010.

42. Gail Millar, interview with the author, February 12, 2004.

43. Reischauer, interview, 2004.

44. Congressional Budget Office, *An Analysis of the Administration's Health Proposal* (Washington, DC: GPO, February 2004), xiii.

45. Ibid., 36.

46. Ibid., 26.

47. Ibid., 27.

48. Ibid., xiv–xv.

49. Van de Water, interview.

50. CBO, *An Analysis of the Administration's Health Proposal*, 69.

51. Ibid., 69–77.

52. Robert Reischauer, Testimony to House Ways & Means Committee, "The Administration's Health Care Proposal," 103rd Cong., 2nd sess., February 8, 1994.

53. Robert Reischauer, "Don't Let This Chance Go By," *Washington Post*, February 11, 1994, A25.

54. Ibid.

55. Nichols, interview.

56. James Risen, "Budget Office Report Crucial for Health Plan," *Los Angeles Times*, February 7, 1994, A1.

57. David Broder and Dana Priest, "White House Girds for Ruling Counting Health Fees in Budget," *Washington Post*, February 8, 1994, A4.

58. Steven Pearlstein and David Broder, "Clinton and the Analysts: A $133 Billion Difference of Opinion," *Washington Post*, February 9, 1994, A4.

59. Dana Priest and Spencer Rich, "Health Plan Will Swell Deficit, Hill Office Says," *Washington Post*, February 9, 1994, A1.

60. Steven Pearlstein and David Broder, "Clinton and the Analysts: A $133 Billion Difference of Opinion," *Washington Post*, February 9, 1994, A4.

61. Richard Wolf and Judy Keen, "Is the Plan DOA or Still Breathing?" *USA Today*, February 9, 1994, 1A.

62. Priest and Rich, "Health Plan Will Swell Deficit."

63. This point was made by two people interviewed for this book. Linda Blumberg, interview with author, February 6, 2004; Nichols, interview.

64. "Propagandizing a Health Report," *New York Times*, February 10, 1994, A22.

65. Jim Wooten, "Mandatory Premiums Definitely Are Taxes," *Atlanta Journal and Constitution*, February 9, 1994, A10; also see "CBO's Straight Health Plan Report," *Chicago Sun-Times*, February 10, 1994, 47.

66. Paul Gigot, "In Praise of Honest Liberals (Sorry Bill)," *Wall Street Journal*, February 11, 1994, A12. For the record, the other was Congressman Jim McDermott, the lead sponsor of the House single-payer bill. Gigot viewed him as honest because he was willing to acknowledge that his bill was government-run health care, which the Clinton administration was not.

67. Robert Samuelson, "CBO's Wishful Thinking," *Washington Post*, February 16, 1994, A19.

68. Senator Edward Kennedy (D-MA), addressing the Senate on CBO's *Analysis of the Administration Health Proposal*, 103rd Cong. 2nd sess., February 8, 1994, *Congressional Record*.

69. Representative David Dreier (R-CA), addressing the House on CBO's *Analysis of the Administration Health Proposal*, 103rd Cong. 2nd sess., February 10, 1994, *Congressional Record*, xxx.

70. Carolyn Lochhead, "New Setback for Clinton's Health Plan," *San Francisco Chronicle*, February 9, 1994, A1.

71. Senator Peter Domenici (R-NM), addressing the Senate on CBO's *Analysis of the Administration Health Proposal*, 103rd Cong. 2nd sess., February 8, 1994, *Congressional Record*, S1137.

72. Senator Robert Dole (R-KS), addressing the Senate on CBO's *Analysis of the Administration Health Proposal*, 103rd Cong., 2nd sess., February 8, 1994, S1135.

73. David Rogers and Hilary Stout, "Rival Health Plan Would Cut Deficits but Fall Short on Coverage," *Wall Street Journal*, May 4, 1994.

74. Jeanne Lambrew, interview with the author, May 7, 2004.

75. William Hoagland, interview with the author, March 26, 2004.

76. Reischauer, interview, 2004.

77. Van de Water, interview; Horney, interview; Anderson, interview.

78. Rivlin, interview, 2003.

79. Kogan, interview.

80. Horney, interview.

81. Richard Wolf, "The Office That Roared in Health Debate," *USA Today*, September 1, 1994.

82. Nichols, interview.

83. Van de Water, interview.

84. Ibid.

85. Blum, interview.

Chapter 7

Obama Health Care Reform

ON MARCH 23, 2010, President Obama signed HR 3590 (PL 111-148).[1] When combined with a second and smaller bill approved a week later, this law is the most sweeping federal entitlement legislation in almost half a century—since, in fact, the passage of Medicare and Medicaid in 1965.[2] This result was far from inevitable, even after the election of Obama in 2008. Over the fourteen months between the president's inauguration and passage of the bill, health care reform had a great many births, deaths, and rebirths. To an even greater extent than in 1994, CBO was in the middle of the debate—writing advance papers to provide guidance, producing cost estimates, working behind the scenes to advise Congress on the cost of various proposed changes. It is clear that the structure of the health care reform that passed was fundamentally influenced by CBO's advice. That is, without CBO, the health care reform that passed would have—for better or worse—looked fundamentally different.

Three factors contributed to enhance CBO's position in the 2009 debate. First, as important a role as CBO had played in 1993 and 1994, its role at that time took some by surprise. By 2009 everyone who followed health care reform (or Congress generally) knew that CBO would eventually play an important role if Congress considered a bill with large revenue and spending effects—which of course describes health care reform. Second, Obama had (as Clinton had before him) given CBO a role because of his pledge that the health care reform bill would reduce the deficit. Any such pledge necessarily raises the profile of the scorekeepers. The mood of the country—in light of substantial increases in federal spending and deficits over the previous two years—made a deficit-reducing health care bill more than simply a promise of President Obama. A deficit-reducing bill was a political necessity if majorities in Congress were to be put together to pass the legislation. Third, that a tactical decision was made to work through the congressional process meant that CBO would play its normal role at the center of the give-and-take, or at least estimating the results of the give and take.

This chapter outlines the role that CBO played in the process of passing this landmark health care reform, starting with the preparatory work in advance of the proposed bills, moving to the role that the agency played in the legislative process, and reaching several conclusions on the effect that the agency played on the process and the result.

Health Reform, 1994–2008

In the wake of the failure of the Clinton health care reform, some in Congress continued to push the same agenda. Political realities, however, dictated that any realistic chance needed to wait for another day. After the Democrats lost control of Congress in the 1994 midterm elections, Clinton necessarily played defense for the remainder of his term. As outlined in chapter 3, the necessity to focus on deficit reduction, and that the Republicans had won control with a strategy that opposed any health care reform efforts, meant that no reform would occur as long as the Republicans controlled Congress. The election of George W. Bush to the presidency only reinforced that reality, and even after the Democrats regained Congress in 2006, any health care reform would have faced a major hurdle in the form of a presidential veto. In fact, the only significant health-related legislation enacted in the Bush administration was the Medicare prescription drug bill passed in 2003 (see chapter 4).

The fiscal reality, however, was that some change in the health care system—in cost if not coverage—seemed inevitable. Although health care costs totaled one-seventh of all costs in the US economy in the early 1990s, they were slowly edging upward, and were projected to reach one-sixth of spending by 2005. During this interim period CBO attempted to prepare by continuing to do research on those issues likely to surface when the next health care reform was considered.

When Peter Orszag took over as director of CBO in January 2007, he was almost single-mindedly committed to having the agency well-prepared to serve Congress when the reform came about. One practical step was to lobby Congress, now controlled by Democrats more likely to be sympathetic to health care reform, to increase the number of CBO staff working on health care reform issues. The agency, which had been at approximately 230 authorized staff since the early 1990s, received permission in 2008 to increase by almost 10 percent, all dedicated to health sector research and analysis.[3] The infrastructure that would permit CBO to better respond to the next wave of health care reform was thus put in place.

What was the agency doing during this interim period? Relatively early, much of CBO's work surrounded the Bush administration proposal (eventually signed into law) to provide a prescription drug benefit for Medicare. As discussed in chapter 4, uncertainty and controversy surrounding the cost estimates for the Medicare Part D program were substantial. Between 2001 and 2005, according to the publications listing on the CBO website, four studies or reports concerning the prescription drug benefit were released, four testimonies on the issue given before congressional committees, and eleven letters sent to members of Congress providing information on the costs and effects of the benefit.

In terms of the nonprescription drug related studies over the period, a sampling of the types of studies issued between 2000 and 2008 included the following:

The Impact of Social Security and Medicare on the Federal Budget (November 2002)
How Many People Lack Health Insurance and for How Long? (May 2003)
Limiting Tort Liability for Medical Malpractice (January 2004)
Financing Long-Term Care for the Elderly (April 2004)
High-Cost Medicare Beneficiaries (May 2005)
Consumer-Directed Health Plans: Potential Effects on Health Care Spending and Outcomes (December 2006)
Costs of Covering More Children in Medicaid and SCHIP (March 2007)
Challenges of Health Care Costs (June 2007)
Health Care Issues and Challenges for Reform (October 2007)
Research on the Comparative Effectiveness of Medicare Treatments: Issues and Options for an Expanded Federal Role (December 2007)
Geographic Variation in Health Care Spending (February 2008)
Evidence on the Costs and Benefits of Health Information Technology (May 2008)

The Obama Election and Its Immediate Aftermath

President Obama ran for election on a platform including comprehensive health care reform. Once he was elected it was inevitable that health care reform would become a major part of his agenda. He signaled this, in part, by his selection of Orszag to be his director of OMB. Obama's argument, during the campaign and after his election, was that it was not possible to separate health care reform from two other urgent matters facing the country—the long-term health of the broader economy and the substantial future fiscal imbalance in the federal budget.

Health care reform would have to wait, however, at least for a few months. The economy Obama inherited in 2009 was in crisis. In the short run, the collapse of the financial sector choked off the capital necessary for everything from business operations to mortgage lending. In addition, housing values plummeted in many areas of the country. All of this combined to create the most severe recession in seventy years, and led to a series of probably necessary but unpopular moves to shore up the financial system, and to save the economy from immediate collapse. It also forced Obama to spend precious time and political capital dealing with a crisis that was not of his own making, while necessarily moving his signature policy efforts—such as health care reform—to the back burner.

Thus, Obama was well into his third month in office before he established the White House Office of Health Care Reform to coordinate administration efforts on health care reform. Part of the delay certainly was that administration personnel to spearhead the effort were not in place. In particular, Obama suffered a major personnel setback when his first choice to lead HHS, former senator Tom Daschle, had to withdraw when it came to light that he had failed to pay required income taxes in a timely manner. But an even larger part of the delay stemmed from the fact that it was just not possible for the administration or Congress to focus on health care reform when there were more immediate crises to deal with.

The Obama administration made one explicit tactical decision that would substantially influence the trajectory of the reform effort in 2009 and 2010. Unlike the Clinton administration, which had drafted a mammoth health care reform bill and dropped it in the lap of Congress in late 1993, the Obama administration decided that it would allow the normal congressional process to play out, and would provide inputs into congressional legislation rather than be tied to any one piece of legislation.

CBO: Preparing for Health Reform in 2008–9

The CBO activity culminated in two rather extraordinary documents issued in December 2008, just after the Obama election. Although the release date may not have been coincidental, it resulted from a decision on the part of (by that time) former director Orszag that CBO should take as much of the mystery out of the health care reform estimating process as possible. The preface to the report lays this out nicely: "This report describes some of the key assumptions that the CBO would use in estimating the effects of key elements of [health care reform] proposals on federal costs, insurance coverage, and other outcomes; the evidence on which those assumptions are based; and—if the evidence points to a range of possible effects rather than a precise prediction—the factors that would influence where a proposal falls within these ranges. In doing so, it also reviews many of the major issues that arise in designing such proposals."[4]

This detailed 200-page document, then, provided Congress with a road map that could be used by congressional committees to make an educated guess concerning CBO scoring of many crucial reform issues. Before doing this, however, it repeated what was by this point an oft-heard admonition: that the future economic state of the country, and specifically national fiscal stability, depended on reforming health care. The first page of the report's summary noted that "those problems cannot be solved without making major changes in the financing or provision of health insurance and health care."[5] Given the need for reform, the report went on to discuss the most important issues Congress would face in designing, and CBO in estimating costs of, a reformed health care system. It covered the following elements:

- how CBO would analyze the effect of proposals on the number of uninsured people;

- the factors that affect insurance premiums, and how CBO would frame analysis of efforts to limit those premiums;
- how CBO would think about proposals affecting the choice of insurance plans;
- what factors, in CBO's view, would most affect the supply and price of health care services;
- how proposals to modify health habits and medical practices (including issues such as application of certain procedures, the use of information technology, or changes in malpractice laws) might affect health care costs; and
- how to analyze health care costs vis-à-vis the role of the federal budget in the national economy.

The report directly addressed the issue that had been most controversial in 1994: that is, identifying when a health care reform proposal created a new or expanded federal program and when it simply proposed regulation of private behavior. In signaling what it might do about the budgetary treatment of such proposals, CBO stated very clearly what its practices would be:

> Proposals might require that individuals or businesses make payments directly to nongovernmental entities. Depending on the specific provisions of such proposals, CBO might judge that payments resulting from federal mandates should be recorded as part of the federal budget even if the funds did not flow through the Treasury. The extent of federal control and compulsion is a critical element in determining budgetary treatment. *In general, CBO believes that federally mandated payments—those resulting from the exercise of sovereign power— and the disbursement of those payments should be recorded in the budget as federal transactions.*[6] [emphasis added]

A later document, issued in May of 2009, summarized the CBO view on budgetary treatment. The conclusions listed in this document are summarized in box 7.1.

In addition to this document, CBO issued a separate report in the same month, outlining various options for health care reform, and the costs associated with those options.[7] This continued a practice that CBO had been engaged in for twenty-five years—presenting budget options for Congress to choose from in reducing federal spending or increasing taxes—but was the first time that such options had been presented in a volume devoted solely to health. In all, this volume presented 115 options for reforming the health system, associating estimates of the federal costs or savings with each option. As a result, committees considering these options later were already armed with substantial information concerning how CBO would estimate their budgetary effects.

These two documents, together, point to a substantial difference between the 1993–94 version of health care reform and the 2009 version. In 1993–94, the

■ **Box 7.1** The Budgetary Treatment of Health Reform in 2009

On May 27, 2009, CBO released an issue brief which reviewed the major provisions of the bills under consideration to that point, and outlined the implicit budgetary treatment questions associated with them.[1] In doing so, CBO attempted to signal to decision-makers the factors that would lead a particular activity or provision to have its transactions counted in the federal budget. As the report on the Clinton health care reform had fifteen years earlier, CBO noted that its guiding principle is in one sense simple. In accord with recommendation of the 1967 president's budget concepts commission, if an activity is federal, it belongs in the budget. CBO had not lost sight of the fact that the commission did also note that "the boundaries of the federal establishment are sometimes difficult to draw."[2] Intended to reduce potential ambiguity, the brief specified how various aspects of health care reform efforts should be assessed vis-à-vis the budget. Key CBO judgments were as follows:

- If the federal government makes a payment to an individual or reduces that individual's taxes, such as would be true for a subsidy to offset the cost of purchasing insurance, that type of transaction is budgetary.
- If a public plan were created, and the federal government stood behind that plan (bore the financial risk) the transactions of that plan should be part of the budget, regardless of whether the plan was administered by a federal entity or not.
- The cash transactions of private entities can be a part of the budget if the private entity is acting as an agent of the federal government (this happens now with some programs, such as the Coal Industry Retiree Health Benefits Program, and for the transactions of the Universal Service Fund).
- The existence of a federal mandate on a private individual or entity does not, by itself, justify the inclusion of that activity in the budget, any more than (for example) the costs resulting from the requirement that businesses pay a minimum wage belong in the budget.
- If the mandate is making health insurance an essentially government program, however, "tightly controlled by the federal government with little choice available to those who offer and buy health insurance" then those transactions belong in the budget. What would matter, in this case, is choice—of plans, of coverage, or of companies.
- The transactions flowing through the insurance "exchanges" would be budgetary if payments were made to the exchanges (rather than to insurers directly) and if the exchanges were acting as federal entities. This question—whether they are federal entities—would itself depend on the duties, products, and oversight responsibilities associated with the exchanges.
- The income from premiums—if counted as budgetary—should count as revenues and spending, rather than as offsetting receipts or collections (revenues counting as offsets to spending with no apparent net budgetary cost) if there is a requirement for the purchase of health insurance coupled with tight controls on the market for insurance.[3]

Notes

1. Congressional Budget Office, "The Budgetary Treatment of Proposals to Change the Nation's Health Insurance System," *Economic and Budget Issue Brief*, May 27, 2009.

2. Report of the President's Commission on Budget Concepts (Washington, DC: GPO, 1967), 24.

3. CBO, *Brief*, May 2009.

Clinton administration and congressional reformers did not have explicit notice from CBO on the two key elements on which CBO scoring would eventually matter—the cost and the budgetary treatment. Between these two December 2008 documents, Congress had substantial advance information on how CBO would approach various reform options. CBO had thus taken much of the guesswork out of the congressional drafting process, in advance.

First Bills: Spring and Summer 2009

The first congressional committee to unveil a specific health care reform proposal was the Senate Health, Education, Labor and Pensions (HELP) Committee. On June 9, 2009, this committee released the Affordable Health Choices Act. CBO's preliminary cost estimate of this bill was released, in a letter to Senator Edward Kennedy (D-MA) on June 15. In this preliminary estimate, CBO put the ten-year cost of the bill (increase in the deficit) at $1 trillion, and estimated that it would cover only 16 million of the 46 million uninsured Americans.

In addition to the HELP Committee, the Senate Finance Committee was hard at work in the summer of 2009 drafting health care reform legislation. This involved, as was true in every case, lots of back and forth between CBO and the committee concerning the specific provisions, and their costs. Most of these interactions flew underneath the public radar. In mid-June, however, it was reported that the Senate Finance Committee had delayed its markup because the preliminary number that it had received from CBO did not meet its desired target in terms of either cost or deficit reduction.[8]

In the House, the three committees (Ways and Means, Education and Labor, and Energy and Commerce) with jurisdiction over health care reform issued a discussion draft on June 19. Ultimately, H.R. 3200, the America's Healthy Choices Act of 2009, was introduced by the House leadership on July 14, 2009.[9] Three days later CBO released a preliminary cost estimate of that proposed legislation. According to this estimate, the provisions of H.R. 3200 that would increase insurance coverage would add $1.042 trillion to spending over ten years, offset by spending reductions of $219 billion and revenue increases of $583 billion. Taken together, this meant that H.R. 3200 would have added $239 billion to deficits between 2010 and 2019.[10]

These bills had a number of provisions, but they highlighted the analytical and estimation issues CBO would have to confront during the rest of the congressional debate and consideration of these health bills (in addition to the budgetary treatment question, highlighted in box 7.1). Exemplifying the demands placed on the CBO, the bill that became law included the following types of provisions, each of which had budgetary effects requiring estimation:

- changes in insurance coverage requirements—including provisions requiring that companies permit dependents up to age twenty-six to continue to be covered on their parents' policies, constraining limits on coverage, and removing exclusions due to preexisting conditions;

- subsidies to individuals—based on income, to enable them to better afford insurance premiums;
- expanded eligibility for Medicaid—a cost shared between the federal government and the states;
- penalties for individuals without health insurance, and for employers with more than fifty employees not offering health insurance coverage;
- insurance exchanges at the state level through which individuals and businesses could buy policies;
- various taxes to finance increases in coverage, including principally an excise tax on high-end health insurance plans; and
- mechanisms designed to control costs for Medicare, including primarily a new Independent Payment Advisory Board.[11]

The analytical issues involved in estimating these effects principally involve predicting the behavior of individuals and firms in response to these provisions. How many individuals and businesses will choose to pay the penalties? How many people will enroll in the insurance exchanges? What will be the effect on insurance premiums, and thus on subsidies? How successful will the Medicare cost control provisions be? How many more people will be enrolled in Medicaid, and what effect will that have on federal and state budgets? The range of possible outcomes is large, as therefore are uncertainties associated with estimating. In addition, CBO was increasingly asked to offer its opinion not just on the first ten years (the typical estimating window) but the eleven- to twenty-year time frame as well. In addition, bills proposed early in the process included other provisions needing estimation, including variations of a more expansive public option.

Given the number of assumption decisions that need to be made in preparing these estimates, it was understandable that there was considerable concern in some circles over their accuracy. Part of this wariness stems from the problem that CBO has with many estimates and projections. Essentially, they are asked for point estimates when in fact it is possible only to estimate ranges. In October 2009, lead CBO health analyst Phil Ellis was quoted as saying, "We're always putting out these estimates. This is going to cost $1.042 trillion exactly. But you sort of want to add, you know, 'Your mileage may vary.'"[12]

Beyond problems inherent in presenting point estimates for what everyone knows are ranges was a more fundamental issue. Some stakeholders just did not agree with the estimates themselves. This included both people who thought CBO was being too cautious, and those who thought the agency was understating the cost of various proposals. In the former case, the White House and other health care reform supporters believed that CBO was being overly conservative in not giving credit for key cost containment proposals: OMB Director Peter Orszag, writing in his blog and appearing on CNN, criticized CBO for its position that the

Independent Medicare Advisory Council (IMAC), designed to set Medicare payment policies and decrease costs, would likely not save much, and wasn't strong enough to effectively reduce spending. Orszag called IMAC a game changer and suggested that CBO had a "bias toward exaggerating costs and underestimating savings." He suggested that by "providing a quantitative estimate of long-term effects without any analytical basis for doing do, CBO seems to have overstepped."[13]

John Gabel of the University of Chicago similarly argued that CBO had consistently overestimated costs in the Medicare program, arguing that when savings are unknown (for example, because there is no experience with a cost-control mechanism) the CBO tendency was to assume that there would be no savings. Gabel contended that such conservatism put health care reform in jeopardy, because it "leads Congress to think that politically unpopular cost-cutting initiatives will have, at best, only modest effects."[14] This would force Congress to pay for health care reform with tax increases, thus making it harder (if not impossible) to pass.

Senator Christopher Dodd (D-CT) was among those who believed that CBO did not give enough credit to preventive interventions: "How they evaluate costs and benefits is very frustrating. They can tell you how much a treadmill costs, but they're unwilling to calculate what the benefit is if somebody actually uses it, loses weight and therefore reduces premium costs. So you get a kind of one-dimensional view of budgeting."[15]

Other observers thought that the CBO was substantially understating the costs of key proposals. For example, the agency said in July that only about 12 million people would opt for the public option included in the House bill, but the Lewin Group (referred to in a *Washington Times* article as "a health research firm owned by an insurance company") put that number at 100 million. This difference would have dramatic implications for cost, given that the more people that opt for public insurance, the higher the public cost of the plan.[16] Others criticized the Medicare reductions as unlikely to be sustained by future Congresses.[17]

CBO Profile Raised in July

July 2009 saw two high-profile events involving CBO director Elmendorf. The first occurred at a Senate Budget Committee hearing July 16 (the day before the analysis of the House bill was released), at which the CBO director was appearing to discuss his agency's long-term budget outlook. He had recently sent a letter to Senator Conrad (D-ND) and Senator Judd Gregg (R-NH, the ranking Republican on the committee), in response to questions they raised concerning ways to effectively control health care costs. After Elmendorf finished delivering his prepared statement, Conrad (also a member of the Senate Finance Committee) immediately launched into the question that was most on his mind.

CHAIRMAN CONRAD: Dr. Elmendorf, I am going to really put you on the spot
   because we are in the middle of this health care debate, and it is critically

important that we get it right. Everyone has said—virtually every one—
that bending the cost curve over time is critically important and one of the
key goals of this entire effort. From what you have seen, from the product
of the committees that have reported, do you see a successful effort being
mounted to bend the long-term cost curve?

MR. ELMENDORF: No, Mr. Chairman. In the legislation that has been reported,
we do not see the sort of fundamental changes that would be necessary to
reduce the trajectory of Federal health spending by a significant amount.
And, on the contrary, the legislation significantly expands the Federal responsibility for health care costs.

CHAIRMAN CONRAD: So the cost curve, in your judgment, is being bent, but in
the wrong way. Is that correct?

MR. ELMENDORF: The way I would put it is that the curve is being raised,
so there is a justifiable focus on growth rates, because of course, it is the
compounding of growth rates faster than the economy that leads to these
unsustainable paths. . . . It is very hard to look out over the very long term
and say very accurate things about growth rates. . . . But the changes that
we have looked at so far do not represent the kind of fundamental change
on the order of magnitude that would be necessary to offset the direct
increase in Federal health costs from the insurance coverage proposals.[18]

Observers saw this exchange not as an accident, but as a carefully orchestrated
effort to affect the trajectory of health care reform by a member of one of the key
committees. Former CBO director Douglas Holtz-Eakin explained it this way:
"Kent Conrad asked [Elmendorf] before the Senate had a product, to make sure
the House product was dead. It was classic. He is the budget chairman. He called
the hearing. He asked Elmendorf point blank. He smiled and said, 'Well, OK,
then we need a new product.' And people think that Doug Elmendorf just got up
and decided to say that. It's not his job. It's not what he did."[19]

Although that is certainly true, former CBO director Robert Reischauer noted
that there were many ways to answer Conrad's question, and that perhaps the
particular words Elmendorf chose (intentionally or unintentionally) had a greater
effect than would have resulted from a more nuanced, less direct response (such
as, for example, the second response to Senator's Conrad's inquiry).[20]

Members of Congress, who were still aiming to enact health care reform legislation before the August recess, were reportedly startled by the Elmendorf revelation.[21] When told of this exchange, according to one press account, majority
leader Harry Reid snapped, "Maybe what he should do is run for Congress."
Speaker Pelosi had a similar reaction, which the New York Times noted was "the
legislative equivalent of arguing balls and strikes in baseball. The budget office is
supposed to be an impartial scorekeeper, and the White House has said that the
legislation has to be paid for in accordance with budget office rules."[22] Leading
Republicans predictably jumped on the Elmendorf assessment as an indictment

of the entire health care reform effort. House Republican leader John Boehner (R-OH) argued that "the director of the Congressional Budget Office today confirmed that the Democrats' government-run plan will make health care more costly than ever, making clear that one of the Democrats' chief talking points is pure fiction."[23]

The second July event had to do with Elmendorf being invited— along with other health care experts—to the Oval Office to brief the president on options for health care reform. There is no record of, nor could anyone recall, any previous instances of a sitting CBO director being invited to meet with the president at the White House. When Elmendorf decided to accept the invitation, it alarmed some as evidence that the president was trying to pressure CBO to come up with the appropriate numbers to favor Democratic health care reform proposals. Elmendorf suggested, immediately afterward and later, that this was not true. Sufficient attention was paid to this meeting that he felt the need to reassure CBO groupies, on the director's blog, that this was not an effort to intimidate CBO:

> The president asked me, and other experts in the room, for our insights into possible ways to reduce the nation's health care spending. The very capable staff at CBO has thought a lot about this subject, and I shared those thoughts with the president. Although the audience was unique, my comments were no different from what we have said publicly on numerous other occasions. . . . Across the range of topics we study, we deliberately spend a lot of time explaining our thinking to policymakers, because we believe that such openness is a responsibility of our agency and can help policymakers to reach better-informed policy decisions. But we never adjust our analysis or conclusions to please our audience (as the reaction to various CBO reports amply demonstrates).[24]

In a later interview, Elmendorf expanded on these points:

> I guess what I would say offhand is that CBO aims to be very transparent in its analysis and I have gone and talked with lots of members individually in their office and in groups . . . about health care reform and how our analysis works—what we think the evidence shows. I got an invitation to go meet with the president and to offer that explanation and it seemed appropriate to accept that invitation just as I had accepted similar invitations all year from people on the Hill. . . . I don't regret going. It is true that people got worried that somehow I had been taken to the woodshed—that somehow the independence that CBO had exhibited thus far in the health care reform debate would not continue. I think it is pretty clear to everyone now that it has continued just as it had before. So I think in retrospect this issue is not such a big deal. But at the time I think people on the Hill were concerned to protect CBO's independence because they think it's important and I am delighted

that they recognize the importance of CBO's independence. I just don't think that my offering explanations of how we are analyzing health care reform is a threat to that independence and I think the experience since then has confirmed my views.[25]

Alice Rivlin, who was one of the other invited experts, confirmed the substance of what went on in the meeting.

Well, I was in that meeting. And it wasn't at all an effort to strong-arm Doug. It was a moment at which the president and his team were saying we've got to show that we can bend the long-run cost curve. And they're saying there's nothing in the bill that will do that. Let's get some people in to talk about what we should do. And so they invited in David Cutler and me (and others) . . . and Doug was considered one of the outside experts. And I'm sure the fact that he was the head of CBO was noticed but . . . there was nothing in the meeting that suggested attention to his scoring.[26]

It is hard to find anyone who believes that Elmendorf should have turned down the president, once he was invited. Former director Reischauer indicated that "if Hillary had invited me you can believe that I would have gone. It would have been fun."[27] Former director Holtz-Eakin, while agreeing that Elmendorf had to go once invited, did opine that he thought it was a bad idea for the White House to invite him, calling it "a terrible misstep. . . . The White House put him in a terrible position. . . . From that point forward, the minority had more suspicions."[28]

It seems significant, given the history of CBO and Elmendorf's desire to have the agency be nonpartisan and aboveboard, that it would be naïve at best to assume that he, or the agency, could be intimidated this way.[29] In the end, if there was an issue, it was about appearance rather than reality.

President Sets a Marker, Congress Goes Home, President Turns Up the Heat

On July 22, 2009, President Obama held a nationally televised news conference called specifically to talk about progress with health care reform. At this news conference, he urged swift action by Congress. He promised, however, not to sign a bill unless it met certain core principles. Specifically, he noted that he had "pledged that health-insurance reform will not add to our deficit over the next decade, and I mean it. In the past eight years, we saw the enactment of two tax cuts, primarily for the wealthiest Americans, and a Medicare prescription program, none of which were paid for. And that's partly why I inherited a $1.3-trillion deficit. That will not happen with health-insurance reform. It will be paid for."[30]

In the House, reform moved forward in July as House Democratic leaders agreed with fiscally conservative Democrats (known as Blue Dogs) on negotiations to trim the bill's cost and exempt many small businesses from having to provide health coverage to their employees. Late in the evening of July 31, 2009, the House Energy and Commerce Committee voted 31 to 28 (largely along party lines), to pass health care legislation. The measure was intended to cover up to 95 percent of Americans and included a new government-run plan. There was no action in the Senate.

As Congress adjourned for its August recess, no bill had become law; in fact, no bill had passed in either the House or the Senate. Health care reform looked very much in doubt, in particular because of major differences between House and Senate approaches. The biggest single difference was the inclusion of a public option in the House bill. It was generally agreed that the Senate would be unable to secure enough votes for a public option to pass that body.

Back home in their districts, many members of Congress faced loud, angry crowds opposed to health care reform. Coming on the heels of the unprec-edented government involvement in other parts of the economy, such as the automobile and banking sectors, these individuals expressed their opposition to what they called a government takeover of health care. Spurred on by radio and television talk show hosts, they shouted down members of Congress in town hall meetings and other events across the country. This effort was clearly designed to threaten the health care reform effort by raising fears that voters would take out their anger on supporters in the 2010 midterm elections.[31]

President Obama, observing this phenomenon from Washington, and con-cerned that the entire health care reform effort was about to fizzle and die, de-cided that it was time to attempt to take control of the debate. Accordingly, he planned to address a joint session of Congress shortly after Congress returned from the recess. This speech, given on September 9, was intended to rejuvenate the reform effort. In his speech, in addition to exhorting members of Congress to enact health care reform, he laid out some basic principles that would need to be met for him to sign any legislation. These included providing more security and stability to those with health insurance by, for example, preventing people from being denied insurance because of pre-existing conditions; providing health insurance to the vast majority of those legally in the country but without insur-ance; and slowing the growth of health care costs.

He addressed directly the budgetary effect of any proposed legislation:

> Finally, let me discuss an issue that is a great concern to me, to members of this chamber, and to the public—and that's how we pay for this plan. And here's what you need to know. First, I will not sign a plan that adds one dime to our deficits—either now or in the future. (Applause.) I will not sign it if it adds one dime to the deficit, now or in the future, period. And to prove that I'm serious, there will be a provision in this plan that requires us to come forward with more spending cuts if the savings we promised don't material-ize. (Applause.) Now, part of the reason I faced a trillion-dollar deficit when I walked in the door of the White House is because too many initiatives over

the last decade were not paid for—from the Iraq war to tax breaks for the wealthy. (Applause.) I will not make that same mistake with health care.[32]

Armed with these principles, both the House and the Senate moved to pass health care legislation before the adjournment of the Congress in 2009. In the Senate, all eyes were initially on the Finance Committee, the only committee with jurisdiction over health care reform that had yet to report a bill. Reportedly several members on this committee were awaiting the CBO analysis to decide how to vote. A CBO score estimating either that the overall scope of the bill exceeded $900 billion or that it added to the deficit in the first ten years might have been enough to prevent it from being able to emerge from committee.[33] Ultimately, the CBO cost estimate of the bill passed both tests—the cost came in at $829 billion and was projected to reduce deficits by $81 billion over ten years. It was also estimated to cover 94 percent of Americans under age sixty-five.[34]

Senator Reid, who two months earlier did not sound like a card-carrying member of the CBO fan club, announced that the Finance Committee could now vote on its plan:

> The nonpartisan Congressional Budget Office confirmed that the Finance Committee plan—which is one of five plans before Congress to reform the way health insurance companies treat people in this country—will reduce the deficit. It didn't say it will keep the deficit the same; it didn't say it will increase it, not even by a penny. It said, in black and white, that the Finance Committee's bill will reduce our deficit not just in the short term, but over the long term as well. That's something progressives, conservatives and everyone in between can applaud.[35]

Although conservatives did not applaud, this was enough to allow the Finance Committee, on a largely party-line vote—with Maine Republican Olympia Snowe the lone senator to break ranks—to send the bill out of committee.

House and Senate Pass Their Bills

The House of Representatives became the first of the two bodies to pass a health care reform bill when, on November 7, the Affordable Health Care for America Act passed by a vote of 220 to 215. Only one Republican crossed party lines and voted with the Democrats; thirty-nine Democrats opposed the bill.[36] The bill, which passed only after substantial last-minute lobbying from the House Democratic leadership and the White House, included an individual and employer mandate, a public option, and the establishment of state-level insurance exchanges. The CBO estimated that this bill would increase federal spending over ten years by $891 billion, and reduce deficits over that same period by $138 billion. This overall reduction in deficits resulted from offsetting the $891 billion in increases due to insurance coverage provisions with reductions of $456 billion in direct spending reductions and $574 billion in revenue increases.[37] The bill was financed primarily by a health care surcharge, an income tax on individuals making more than $500,000 per year ($1 million for joint returns). This provision, by itself, was estimated to raise approximately 80 percent of all of the revenues raised by the legislation.[38]

Senate Majority Leader Harry Reid put together a package that combined elements of the HELP and Finance Committee bills, but, in a bow to liberals, put in a limited public option provision. A CBO analysis of the bill estimated that, because premiums would be higher than private competitors and because it would permit states to opt out of the public plan, this limited public option would attract only 4 million subscribers.[39]

The Senate debate, as was to be expected, took longer than the House debate. As the Senate began to consider the reform, CBO delivered an additional piece of welcome news. Contrary to claims by the insurance industry that the legislation would cause premiums to rise dramatically, the CBO analysis asserted that because of hefty federal subsidies premiums would be reduced by nearly 60 percent on average for low- and middle-income families. Premiums would rise in the individual market, where the self-employed obtain insurance, but coverage would improve as well.[40]

As debate in the Senate continued, efforts commenced to put together a package that could satisfy Democrats across the political spectrum, as there were literally no votes to spare if the Senate was to be able to obtain the sixty votes necessary to close off debate. One issue under consideration was one to allow Medicare to expand to people aged fifty-five to sixty-four who did not have insurance. Senators, such as Charles Schumer (D-NY), were largely mute as they waited for official word from CBO on the budgetary effect of the provision: "I can't say what there is, because we're not allowed to talk about what's submitted to CBO. . . . I think when people see the details, they're going to be pretty happy with it. I think that many of the concerns that have been voiced, when we get a CBO score and see the details, will be allayed."[41]

Finally, after two weeks of debate, the Senate passed a health care reform bill on December 24 by a straight 60 to 39 party line vote. Because of the need to appeal to moderate Democratic senators, the final bill did not include a public option, and also did not include the Medicare expansion to individuals fifty-five to sixty-four.[42] CBO ultimately estimated that the bill would reduce deficits by $118 billion over the first ten years, and would add a total of $836 billion worth of coverage provisions.[43]

Therefore, by the end of 2009, a bill had passed the Senate and another the House. Although they had differences that would certainly be difficult to work out in conference, both chambers adhered to the basic principles that President Obama had spelled out in September. In fact, the outlines of a compromise were beginning to become clear. On January 11, the *New York Times* reported that "as

White House and Congressional negotiators work toward an agreement on a final version of sweeping health care legislation, they seem likely to push the ten-year price tag closer to the $1.05 trillion cost of the House-passed bill while relying on new taxes proposed by the Senate, probably including a bigger increase in the Medicare payroll tax than currently proposed."[44] Getting there would not be easy, particularly given the close margin in the House and the need to preserve sixty votes in the Senate, but it seemed reasonable to assume that a bill would be sent to the president's desk early in the new year.

The Massachusetts Election: Failure Again?

Any expectation that health care reform was near the finish line evaporated in January 2010. Massachusetts held a special election to fill the seat of Senator Edward Kennedy, who had died in August 2009. This seat had been assumed to be safe in Democratic hands—thus preserving the sixty votes needed in the Senate to block a filibuster of the conference agreement. But in a stunning upset, Massachusetts voters elected moderate Republican Scott Brown in the January 20 election, thus throwing the entire future of health care reform into question. No longer was it an issue of simply finding a compromise between the two houses. The entire political calculation of health care reform had changed. Some declared the reform to be dead.[45]

Unquestionably, avoiding a repeat of the Clinton failure of 1994 would take some political and procedural maneuvering. The surest path to success—defined as passing something—was to simply have the House vote to pass the Senate bill. That approach was a nonstarter, according to Speaker Nancy Pelosi (D-CA). The distrust between the House and Senate was palpable, and enough House members found some of the Senate provisions objectionable that it was presumed to cost the Speaker enough votes to keep the bill from passing.[46]

Ultimately, the White House settled on a three-part strategy. First, change the subject until it could decide how to proceed. Thus, the State of the Union address, which was coming up in only a week, would only tangentially mention health care reform. Its main focus would be on job creation. Second, attempt (or at least appear to attempt) to gain bipartisan support. Third, depending on whether any moderate Republican senators could be convinced to vote for health care reform, work out a strategy for final approval.

The second of these three was the most immediate concern. In early February the president announced that he would hold a bipartisan summit at the White House to discuss areas of compromise and potentially adopt some Republican ideas. In advance of this summit, the administration, for the first time, released a draft of a health care reform bill that included key elements of both the House and Senate legislation. It represented what the conference report might have looked like if the House and Senate had been able to agree on such a report. It was closer to the Senate bill than the House version; the most striking difference from the House bill was the exclusion of a public option, an omission bound to make such a bill more difficult to pass in the House. According to the White House, the bill would cost $950 billion and reduce the deficit by $100 billion over ten years.[47]

The summit itself was little more than political theater, providing Republicans with an opportunity to paint the Democratic plan as a dangerous government takeover of health care, and allowing the president to paint Republicans as obstructionists. It also gave the White House a chance to (at least apparently) reach out to Republicans so that when (almost inevitably) the legislation ended up as partisan (that is, supported by no Republicans) they could argue that the president made a good faith effort and was rebuffed.

Once the summit was concluded, however, Democrats moved immediately to try and figure out how they could overcome the twin obstacles of House opposition to the Senate bill and the lack of sixty votes in the Senate to pass a conference report. Increasingly it became apparent that the only real chance of success would come if the House adopted the Senate bill (as passed) and then adopted a separate set of changes as a part of the budget reconciliation process—which has the virtue of not being subject to filibuster in the Senate.[48] Congressional leaders had earlier rejected the use of reconciliation to pass health care reform in its entirety, largely because of limitation placed on the content of a reconciliation bill by the Senate's Byrd rule. Some Republicans argued that this was an inappropriate use of reconciliation, but in fact reconciliation had been used many times before to enact changes in law, including by Republicans to enact the Bush tax cuts in 2001 and 2003.[49]

As February moved into March 2010, it became increasingly clear that the White House was prepared to implement its "Senate bill first, then reconciliation" strategy. There was no guarantee, however, that the House—deeply distrustful of the Senate and its approach—would go along. The president's key challenge was to convince enough wavering House members to vote for both bills in order to allow health care reform to become law. Because the Senate had already passed the main reform bill, and needed only a simple majority for the reconciliation bill, Senate approval seemed more likely.

In the House, Obama faced a delicate calculation as factions of House members had reservations over different provisions of the bill. Some progressives didn't think the bill went far enough in terms of benefits. Some conservative Blue Dogs thought it went too far. Abortion foes were concerned that the antiabortion language was weaker in the Senate version than in the House bill.[50]

CBO, which had already provided revised estimates of the Senate-passed legislation, needed to assess the cost of the reconciliation provisions as well. The revised estimate of the December 24 Senate bill was $875 billion over ten years, and CBO indicated it would reduce deficits by $118 billion over that same period. As had been true for other provisions, these estimates were potentially going to force changes to the final bill. "Clearly we're looking at the Medicare tax," said

Representative Sander Levin (D-MI). "Would that need to be increased? Depends on what the score is."[51] This process was made more complicated by the fact that the Congressional Budget Act requires a reconciliation bill to produce greater deficit reduction over a five-year period than the legislation it amends. This meant that the reconciliation bill had to be projected to reduce the deficit by more than the $104 billion in deficit reduction estimated for the Senate bill over the same five-year period.[52] Ultimately, the CBO cost estimate of the entire package, including both the Senate bill and the reconciliation changes, put the final cost at $938 billion over ten years, with total deficit reduction of $143 billion over that same period.[53]

That the CBO estimate of the cost was below $950 billion and the deficit reduction was above $100 billion put the numbers at better than the Obama administration's targeted levels. This apparent show of fiscal responsibility appeared to

---

■ Box 7.2 Health Care Reform Legislative Timeline 2009–10

2009

April 8: President Obama establishes the White House Office of Health Reform to coordinate administrative efforts on national health reform.

June 9: Senate Health, Education, Labor and Pensions (HELP) Committee releases Affordable Health Choices Act draft of 615-page bill. Senator Christopher Dodd (D-CT) led committee efforts in the absence of HELP Chair Edward Kennedy (D-MA).

June 15: CBO says Senate HELP committee proposal could cost $1 trillion, and would cover only 16 million of the 46 million Americans now uninsured.

June 19: House Tri-Committee (House Ways and Means, Energy and Commerce, Education and Labor Committees) releases Health Care Reform Discussion Draft.

July 15: The U.S. Senate Health, Education, Labor and Pensions (HELP) Committee orders reported the Affordable Health Choices Act. The bipartisan bill includes more than 160 Republican amendments accepted during the month-long markup, one of the longest in congressional history.

July 16: CBO director Douglas Elmendorf tells Congress that none of the bills he has seen contain "the sort of fundamental changes that would be necessary to reduce the trajectory of federal health spending by a significant amount."

July 17: The House Committee on Education and Labor approves legislation 26 to 22 in the morning after an all-night session. The House Ways and Means Committee approves health care reform legislation by a 23 to 18 vote.

July 22: President Obama addresses the nation in a nationally televised health care news conference and urges swift action by the Congress but promises not to sign a bill that will increase the nation's deficit or, in his view, will not work.

July 23: Senate Majority Leader Harry Reid (D-NV) announces that the Senate will be unable to pass a reform bill until after the August recess.

July 31: The House Energy and Commerce Committee votes 31 to 28, largely along party lines, late in the evening to pass health care legislation. The new legislation is intended to cover up to 95 percent of Americans and includes a new government-run plan.

September 9: In a nationally televised speech to the joint sessions of Congress, President Obama presents a detailed outline of a plan he said will provide more security and

sway some members, such as Representative Bart Gordon (D-TN)—an earlier opponent who said he would vote for the bill after the CBO estimate was released.[54] President Obama used the CBO numbers on the short- and long-term deficit reduction effects to attempt to sway other wavering House members.[55]

On March 21, 2010, the House approved—without change—the legislation passed by the Senate on Christmas Eve. The vote was 219 to 212. Subsequently, the House adopted a package of changes to that bill (this was the reconciliation legislation) by an almost identical vote of 220 to 211. The first bill was signed into law by President Obama two days later, on March 23. The second bill was approved, with amendment (two minor provisions were stripped out under the Byrd rule), by the Senate on March 25. This was approved again by the House on March 25, and signed into law by the president on March 30.[56] With these two bills President Obama achieved victory in launching health care reform.

---

stability to those who have health insurance, provide insurance to those without coverage, and slow the growth of health care costs for families, businesses, and the government.

September 16: Senate Finance Committee Chairman Max Baucus (D-MT) introduces his long-awaited health care bill (America's Healthy Future Act of 2009).

October 13: The Senate Finance Committee votes along party lines to approve its health care bill. Republican Senator Olympia Snowe of Maine is the sole GOP supporter.

November 7: The House passes its health bill late Saturday night, by a 220 to 215 margin. The CBO cost estimate of this bill puts the total additional spending at $891 billion, with a reduction in deficits of $138 billion over ten years.

December 24: After clearing a procedural hurdle three days earlier, the Senate passes health care overhaul bill by a vote of 60 to 39.

2010

January 4: House meets to begin discussing plans to combine health bills.

January 20: Scott Brown's Senate victory in Massachusetts may cost Democrats their thin advantage in the health care overhaul.

February 22: The White House releases a summary of President Obama's health care reform proposal.

February 25: President Obama's health care summit does not appear to bring Democrats and Republicans any closer to a bipartisan solution.

March 13: CBO releases revised cost analysis of Senate health bill that passed December 24, 2009—putting the price tag at about $875 billion over ten years, an increase of about $4 billion from the previous estimate.

March 18: CBO releases cost analysis of health bill with House changes. It is estimated to cost $938 billion over ten years and projected to reduce the deficit by $143 billion over the same period.

March 21: House approves H.R. 3590, the Senate-passed health overhaul, sending the bill to Obama.

March 23: President Obama signs the Patient Protection and Affordable Health Care Act (H.R. 3590—PL 111-148), which includes the main provisions of health care reform.

March 30: President signs the Health Care and Education Affordability Reconciliation Act of 2010 (H.R. 4872—PL 111-152) making changes to health care and student loan programs.

Deficit Reduction: Did CBO Get It Right?

Despite the CBO cost estimates showing that the health care reform as signed into law would reduce the deficit, the public, according to a Quinnipac University poll, remained skeptical. In this poll, featured in a column by David Broder (*Washington Post*, November 22, 2009), respondents were asked the following question: "President Obama has pledged that health insurance reform will not add to our federal budget deficit over the next decade. Do you think that President Obama will be able to keep his promise or do you think that any health care plan that Congress passes and President Obama signs will add to the federal budget deficit?" Fewer than one in five respondents thought that the president would be able to keep this promise. Nine of ten Republicans, and even four of seven Democrats, thought that the legislation would add to the budget deficit rather than reduce it.[57]

This skepticism was echoed by Republicans at the White House health summit and on the editorial pages of the *New York Times* and the *Wall Street Journal*, leading up to the final vote on March 21, 2010. Skepticism about whether the bill would actually have the effect on the deficit estimated by CBO led to responses refuting these claims—first from the White House and then from the Center on Budget and Policy Priorities (CBPP). Those arguing that the CBO estimates painted too rosy a picture were extraordinarily careful not to appear to be criticizing CBO even as they argued that they did not believe their cost estimates. Paul Ryan, ranking Republican on the House Budget Committee, said that though staff at CBO were "great professionals" who "do their jobs well, . . . their job is to score what is placed in front of them. And what has been placed in front of them is a bill that is full of gimmicks and smoke-and-mirrors."[58]

Austin Smythe, the staff director on the Republican side for the House Budget Committee, amplified the position expressed by Ryan, both respecting CBO's numbers and doubting estimates will come true: "His point was that [the Democrats] had manipulated the legislation to get what they wanted out of CBO. . . . We don't agree with CBO on all their numbers in terms of those being the numbers that we would produce, but when we look at what they do. . . . it is rational and supported . . . we're confident that they're doing their best. That's the reason Paul says that. He has tremendous confidence in Director Elmendorf and tremendous confidence in the institution . . . to meet its objective to provide objective nonpartisan analysis."[59]

There were five main elements of arguments and counterarguments concerning the results of the CBO cost estimates:

The bill includes ten years of tax increases and only six years of costs, which is the only reason that it saves money over ten years. Because most parts of the bill that spend money—such as the new insurance cooperatives—do not become fully effective until 2014 or later, whereas most provisions that raise money take effect within the first year, opponents argue that the $143 billion in ten-year savings are illusory. They contend that the bill actually has a significant cost over the first ten years, and that the intent of the bill is to use the time-honored gimmick of back-loading costs in order to hide its budgetary effect.[60] The counterargument, offered by Budget Director Orszag and echoed by the CBPP, is that the bill was structured this way to allow necessary transitions associated with the complexity of the bill. They point out that if the reform were a budget buster the savings would not go up in the second ten years, as CBO says they will.[61]

The bill leaves out the cost of discretionary spending, thus understating the spending and deficit effects. The policies enacted by the bill will need to be administered, and these administrative costs would be appropriated—or discretionary—spending. Although CBO acknowledges that it will be necessary for future Congresses and presidents to fund these discretionary costs, it does not include them in its cost estimates. One estimate put these costs at $114 billion over ten years.[62] The counterargument is that it is standard CBO practice to exclude these costs from estimates for the simple reason that they are discretionary. That is, it is not possible to know now whether they will add to future deficits or not without knowing future legislation. Congress, in the annual appropriations process, routinely cuts some programs in order to fund others. Unless it is known now that Congress will increase the amount of funding available for appropriations explicitly because of the health care reform bill, it is not possible to assign this cost to the health care reform bill.[63]

The cost estimate does not include the cost of a permanent fix to the sustainable growth rate (SGR) for physicians. This so-called doc fix was enacted by Congress each of the previous seven years before 2010 to prevent a payment reduction included in law from taking effect. If allowed to take effect, the law would cut payments to doctors by 21 percent, according to Ryan, who estimated that a permanent fix would have added $371 billion in cost to the bill.[64] The CBPP analysis notes that this cost is "unrelated to health care reform; all of its cost would remain if health care reform were repealed tomorrow."[65] In other words, fixing the SGR formula is akin to the annual "fix" to the AMT. We know Congress is going to do it, but that doesn't mean that every tax bill should include its cost as part of that bill. Further, costs of the doc fix are not made larger (or smaller) by the health care reform bill.

The bill relies on future Medicare cuts, which may not be approved by future Congresses. Because Medicare is a very popular program that Congress may be reluctant to cut in future according to this argument, the $463 billion in Medicare cuts are unlikely to be realized.[66] There certainly are well-publicized cases where Congress has failed to enact Medicare savings (the $270 billion in cuts proposed in 1995–96 discussed in chapter 3 come to mind). In other cases, Congress has even repealed unpopular changes, such as tax increases that had been enacted to prevent senior citizens from being bankrupted by spending on catastrophic care.[67]

The CBPP analysis countered that the claim that Medicare savings were not allowed to go into effect was "thoroughly refuted by the historical record," based on a review of cuts enacted in 1990, 1993, 1997, and 2005.[68]

The bill includes some things that reduce its deficit effects, such as savings from Social Security and premiums from long-term care insurance that have nothing to do with health care reform. This includes additional Social Security taxes paid by people who will earn higher wages because employers may shift some compensation from health insurance to cash wages. No substantive counterarguments to this case have been put forth, except the claim that the bill would reduce the deficit over ten years even if these savings were not included.[69]

In the wake of this inside-the-Beltway food fight over the effect of health care reform, Elmendorf felt the need to "stand by the CBO's assertion that the health-care reform package would reduce the budget deficit over the next 10 years—and in the 10 years after."[70] Writing on his blog, however, Elmendorf cautioned that the accuracy of the estimates was dependent on the law being implemented as written, but that "the legislation maintains and puts into effect a number of policies that might be difficult to sustain over a long period of time" including reducing the growth rate for Medicare spending, the change in the indexing rate for exchange subsidies after 2018, and the tax on so-called Cadillac insurance plans after 2018.[71]

Conclusions: What Lessons from the Obama Effort?

In the end, as in the 1994 experience, a number of lessons can be drawn from CBO's role in the Obama health care reform effort. First, and most obvious, is that the CBO's role was substantial and dispositive. It is completely unchallenged that CBO was viewed as the health care reform oracle (mostly on costs, but also on coverage) and that its analyses were viewed as more or less holy writ by the media and public. In a July *Wall Street Journal* article, David Wessel pointed to CBO's role, noting that "in a city riddled with dysfunctional institutions, the CBO survives as a call-it-as-we-see-it outfit that rarely bends to political winds."[72] In short, had it not been for the significant role played by CBO, the bill that became law would have (for better or worse) been much different. There are several reasons for this.

Because of the experience of 1993 and 1994, there was never any question about whether CBO had an important role to play in health care reform, or about what the outlines of that role would be—estimating costs and determining the position of various plans relative to the federal budget.

As in 1994, that role was elevated by a stated policy goal of the sitting president—first Clinton and then Obama—that health care reform needed to reduce the federal budget deficit. Further, the administration's position in 2009 was that the bill needed not just to "bend the cost curve" in the long run, but to reduce the deficit in the first ten years. Once that became a bottom-line goal, it was inevitable that CBO's analysis would be seen as critical.

Again, as in 1994, the president was complicit in pointing to CBO as the oracle for budgetary effects of the legislation. Rather than openly picking fights with CBO about whether the administration's or CBO's estimates were correct (on issues such as preventative care, where clearly many in the administration did not agree with CBO), he accepted the CBO conclusions almost without challenge.

Perhaps most important, by embracing a strategy of working through Congress in enacting the legislation, the administration virtually assured that its cost and deficit goals would be achieved. Because of CBO's standard practice of working informally with committees to permit them to tweak legislation to meet budgetary targets (see chapter 4), there was no question that the estimates were going to eventually be consistent with Obama's parameters.[73]

Second, there is no question that the substantial investment Orszag made—and Elmendorf reinforced—to establish and maintain the capacity of CBO to do health care analysis and estimates was critical to the ability of the agency to deliver timely, quality analysis of the many proposals that were considered by Congress. Perhaps the end result, in terms of budgetary and insurance effects, was changed substantially by the investment of CBO in additional analytical capacity for health. This not only affected analyses of the plans as they proceeded through Congress. It also enabled the CBO to lay better groundwork for reform proposals up front, evidenced by production of the twin analytical reports in December 2008.[74]

Third, much to the chagrin of some proponents of the legislation, CBO behaved like a budget office in the debate: they appeared skeptical of claims by proponents and opponents alike in the absence of evidence to back up those claims. This was true whether the claim was that health care reform would drive tens of millions out of private insurance plans, or that specific health prevention programs would more than pay for themselves. As Holtz-Eakin said, "The way I characterize it is that every advocate comes to CBO and their null hypothesis is that they are right and they think CBO's null hypothesis is that CBO is right: but that's not CBO's null. CBO's null is you're wrong."[75] On the other hand, there is at least one example of the CBO changing its position to give credit for cost savings in the face of new evidence. For years, CBO had frustrated Republicans by arguing that tort and malpractice reform would have at most limited, if any, effect on health care spending. On October 9, 2009, however, the agency sent a letter to Senator Orrin Hatch informing him that, in light of additional evidence concerning the savings that could result from medical malpractice reform, the agency had reconsidered its previous position, which was that such malpractice reform efforts were unlikely to save money.[76]

Although CBO's role was critical in the ultimate development of the specific health reform bill that passed, two criticisms of CBO's work—one substantive and one procedural—were identified by sources interviewed for this research.

On substantive grounds, it was noted that—on this as well as many other analyses—the federal budgetary costs may trump the larger economic effects. That is, in the case of health care reform, the dominant analytic focus should have been on likely effects of various proposals on the overall health care system or the broader economy, rather than its attacks on the federal budget.[77] Again, this narrow focus of analysis is not peculiar to health care reform—and may be unavoidable given CBO's mandate, which is largely to provide input regarding budgetary issues. However, considering health care reform will result in reworking one-sixth of the economy, consequences may be regrettable.

On a more procedural note, former director Holtz-Eakin, though he praised CBO for having "the best year in its history," did observe that some Republicans felt slighted by CBO at particular points in the process because CBO did not place a priority on the analysis in which they were most interested: "In providing supplementary information, they provided what the majority wanted but not what the minority wanted. The minority cared about the cost of insurance for the covered already (but the focus was on) how many people were covered. . . . It took them until the very end . . . to provide information on the cost to those with insurance."[78]

In the end, this was certainly less about the desire of CBO to rig the game in favor of the majority, and more about a rational need to prioritize products required. The reality was that Republicans did not have alternative proposals in most cases, and where they did, they were highly unlikely to become law. Although there is little credible evidence that CBO does its analyses to give the majority what it wants, there is some suggestion that the majority (as the majority, and therefore the party in control of the agenda) is in a more powerful position in terms of getting answers to its questions.

As in the Clinton health care reform effort, whatever influence CBO had in the 2009–10 health care reform debate was partly of the agency's doing and partly a result of specific political and economic circumstances. Had it not been for the development of CBO's credibility over thirty-five years, it would not have played as important a role. Had it not developed the ability to respond in terms of both analytical products and timing—by increasing its capacity to conduct health research—it might have been less influential. Perhaps most important, however, had cost and deficit effects not been a central focus, a budget agency's analysis might not have mattered nearly as much. It is worth repeating that the reason the deficit mattered was related to factors that had nothing to do with CBO. The deficit mattered because in the wake of unprecedented federal deficits brought about by the recession and the government's response to it, public angst concerning the size and reach of the federal government was considerable. It also mattered because the president, responding to this angst, laid down a marker that inevitably was going to give CBO's conclusions more weight.

On this last point, Elmendorf, when asked whether focus on the deficit gave CBO's analysis more weight, responded, "That's certainly right. When you pledge to do something on a balanced budget or better than balanced budget basis then the cost estimates that we produce are more important. . . . Both this time and seventeen years ago were moments of a lot of concern about budget balance and a lot of concern about what the deficit effects of health care reform might be."[79]

Notes

1. *Patient Protection and Affordable Health Care Act*, Public Law 111–148, 111th Cong., 2nd sess., H.R. 3590, March 23, 2010.

2. Part of the health care reform was contained in the *Health Care and Education Reconciliation Act of 2010* (P.L. 111–152, 11th Cong., 2nd sess., H.R. 4872, March 30, 2010), which the president signed a week later.

3. Douglas Elmendorf, interview with the author, February 2, 2010.

4. Congressional Budget Office, *Key Issues in Analyzing Major Health Insurance Proposals* (Washington, DC: GPO, December 2008), preface.

5. Ibid., ix.

6. Ibid., xxiii.

7. Congressional Budget Office, *Budget Options I: Health Care* (Washington, DC: GPO, December 2008).

8. David Herszenhorn and Robert Pear, "Democrats Work to Pare Cost of Health Care Bill," *New York Times*, June 17, 2009, A15.

9. *America's Affordable Health Choices Act of 2009*, 111th Cong., 1st sess., H.R. 3200, July 14, 2009.

10. Douglas Elmendorf, Letter to the Honorable Charles Rangel from Congressional Budget Office, "Presenting preliminary cost estimate on H.R. 3200, the America's Health Choices Act of 2009," July 17, 2009, www.cbo.gov/ftpdocs/104xx/doc10464/hr3200.pdf.

11. Marilyn Werber Serafini, "The Plan: A Closer Look," *National Journal Online*, March 22, 2010, www.nationaljournal.com/njonline/hc_20100322_5094.php.

12. Lori Montgomery, "In Health Debate, Those Numbers Are Just Numbers," *Washington Post*, October 19, 2009, A1.

13. Jason Plautz, "The Price Is Debatable," *National Journal Online*, August 18, 2009, www.nationaljournal.com/njonline/hc_20090817_4051.php?mrefid=site_search.

14. Jon R. Gable, "Health Care Numbers Don't Add Up," *New York Times*, August 26, 2009, A23.

15. Sheryl Gay Stolberg, "Capital Holds Breath as He Crunches Numbers," *New York Times*, November 17, 2009, A1.

16. Jennifer Haberkorn and S. A. Miller, "CBO Gives Boost to Obama's Health Plan; Says Proviso Won't Kill Private Insurers," *Washington Times*, July 28, 2009, A1.

17. Jennifer Haberkorn and David M. Dickson, "Deficit Math Questioned in Health Care Reform," *Washington Times*, October 20, 2009, A1.

18. Senate Committee on the Budget, *Concurrent Resolution on the Budget FY2010*, 111th Cong., 1st sess., July 16, 2009, 859–60.

19. Holtz-Eakin, interview.

20. Reischauer, interview.

21. Lori Montgomery and Shailagh Murray, "Lawmakers Warned about Health Costs; CBO Chief Says Democrats' Proposals Lack Necessary Controls on Spending," *Washington Post*, July 17, 2009, A1.

22. David M. Herszenhorn and Robert Pear, "Budget Office Questions Controls on Costs in Current Health Care Legislation," *New York Times*, July 17, 2009, A12.

23. Greg Hitt, "Budget Blow for Health Care Plan—Congress's Chief Fiscal Watchdog Warns of Overhaul's Cost; Ammunition for Critics," *Wall Street Journal*, July 17, 2009, A1.

24. Douglas Elmendorf, "CBO Is One of the Best Places to Work in the Federal Government," *CBO Director's Blog*, July 23, 2009, http://cboblog.cbo.gov/?cat=22.

25. Douglas Elmendorf, interview with the author, February 2, 2010.

26. Alice Rivlin, interview with the author, January 8, 2010.

27. Reischauer, interview, 2010.

28. Holtz-Eakin, interview, 2010.

29. This point was made by two former directors of CBO: Reischauer, interview, 2010; Holtz-Eakin, interview, 2010.

30. Transcript of Obama News Conference, July 22, 2009, www.nytimes.com/2009/07/22/us/politics/22obama.transcript.html?pagewanted=2&ref=politics.

31. Kaiser Health News, "Anger at Town Halls Continues, Sides Trade Barbs," August 13, 2009, www.kaiserhealthnews.org/Daily-Reports/2009/August/13/More-Town-Halls.aspx.

32. White House, Office of the Press Secretary, "Remarks by the President to a Joint Session of Congress on Health Care," September 9, 2009.

33. Shailagh Murray and Scott Wilson, "Vote on Key Health Bill Delayed for Cost Report," *Washington Post*, October 6, 2009, A5.

34. Drew Armstrong, "Better-than-Expected CBO Score Buoys Senate Finance's Health Bill," *CQ Today Print Edition*, October 7, 2009.

35. Robert Pear and David M. Herszenhorn, "Health Care Bill Gets Green Light in Cost Analysis," *New York Times*, October 9, 2009.

36. Alex Wayne, "House Passes Health Care Overhaul Bill," *CQ Today Online News*, November 9, 2009, www.cqpolitics.com.

37. Douglas Elmendorf, Letter to the Honorable John Dingell, "On HR 3962, the Affordable Health Care for America Act," November 20, 2009.

38. Alex Wayne, "House Passes Health Care Overhaul Bill."

39. Lori Montgomery and Shailagh Murray, "Reid Pushes for Votes on Health-Care Bill; CBO Analysis of Public Option Is an Obstacle," *Washington Post*, November 20, 2009, A1.

40. Lori Montgomery, "Senate Health Bill Gets a Boost; Measure Wouldn't Increase Insurance Costs for Most, CBO Says," *Washington Post*, December 1, 2009, A1.

41. Drew Armstrong, "Senators Await CBO Report," *CQ Today Online News*, December 13, 2009.

42. Drew Armstrong, "Senate Passage of Health Bill Sets Stage for Talks with House," *CQ Today Online News—Health*, December 24, 2009.

43. Douglas Elmendorf, Letter to Honorable Harry Reid, "Providing Cost Estimate of HR 3590, the Patient Protection and Affordable Care Act," March 11, 2010.

44. David M. Herszenhorn, "Higher Price Tag Enters Negotiations," *New York Times*, January 11, 2010, A10.

45. Ceci Connolly, "61 Days from Near-Defeat to Victory; How Obama Revived his Health Care Bill," *Washington Post*, March 23, 2010, A1.

46. Ibid.

47. Alex Wayne, "White House Posts Revised Health Bill," *CQ Today Online News*, February 22, 2010, www.cqpolitics.com.

48. Shailagh Murray and Lori Montgomery, "Democrats Already Look Past Health Summit," *Washington Post*, February 25, 2010, A1.

49. "Reconciliation and Truth: Using the Congressional Procedure Might Be Unwise, but It Would Not Be Unfair," *Washington Post*, February 25, 2010, A22.

50. Alex Wayne and Edward Epstein, "High-Speed Drive for Health Overhaul Votes," *Congressional Quarterly Weekly* (March 8, 2010): 567.

51. Rebecca Adams, "Price Tag Is One Focus of Health Care Talks, Levin Says," *Congressional Quarterly Online News*, March 10, 2010, www.cqpolitics.com.

52. Alex Wayne, "Budget Math Slows Health Timeline," *CQ Online News*, March 17, 2010, www.cqpolitics.com.

53. Douglas Elmendorf, Letter to the Honorable Nancy Pelosi, "On the Amendment in the Nature of a Substitute to H.R. 4872, the Reconciliation Act of 2010," March 20, 2010. Newspaper stories published at the time put the deficit reduction figure at $138 billion; this was the original number, but was revised upward by CBO in its March 2010 estimate presented in the letter to Speaker Pelosi.

54. Greg Hitt and Janet Adams, "Bill Gets Boost from New Cost Estimate: Obama Delays Trip for Weekend Vote," *Wall Street Journal*, March 19, 2010, A1.

55. Ceci Connolly, "61 Days from Near-Defeat to Victory," *Washington Post*, March 23, 2010, A1.

56. Alex Wayne and Edward Epstein, "Obama Seals Legislative Legacy with Health Insurance Overhaul," *Congressional Quarterly Weekly* (March 29, 2010): 748.

57. David Broder, "A Budget-Buster in the Making," *Washington Post*, November 22, 2009, A19.

58. Paul Ryan (R-WI), comments on health inflation at White House Health Summit, February 25, 2010. Taken from CQ transcriptions.

59. Austin Smythe, interview with the author, April 30, 2010.

60. Douglas Holtz-Eakin, "The Real Arithmetic of Health Care Reform," *New York Times*, March 21, 2010, A12.

61. Peter Orszag, "Fiscal Realities," *The White House Blog*, March 21, 2010, www.whitehouse.gov/blog/2010/03/21/fiscal-realities; Paul N. Van de Water and James R. Horney, "Health Care Reform Will Reduce the Deficit," *Center on Budget and Policy Priorities*, March 25, 2010.

62. Holtz-Eakin, "The Real Arithmetic."

63. Van de Water and Horney, "Health Care Reform."

64. Ryan, comments at White House Health Summit.

65. Van de Water and Horney, "Health Care Reform," 4.

66. Holtz-Eakin, "The Real Arithmetic."

67. For an account of this, see George Hager and Eric Pianin, "Rosty's Wild Ride," in *Mirage: Why Neither Democrats Nor Republicans Can Balance the Budget, End the Deficit, and Satisfy the Public* (New York: Random House, 1997), 73–98.

68. Van de Water and Horney, "Health Care Reform," 3.

69. Ibid.

70. Linda Feldman, "CBO Chief Stands by Claim: Health Care Reform Will Reduce Deficit," *The Christian Science Monitor*, April 8, 2010.

71. Douglas Elmendorf, "The Effects of Health Reform on the Federal Budget," *CBO Director's Blog* (April 12, 2010), http://cboblog.cbo.gov/?p=650.

72. David Wessel, "Man Who Wounded Health Care Effort Could Also Save It," *Wall Street Journal*, July 23, 2009, A4.

73. David M. Herszenhorn, "The Numbers Come Out Just Where Obama Wanted, with No Magic Involved," *New York Times*, March 19, 2010, A16.

74. Congressional Budget Office, *Key Issues in Analyzing Major Health Insurance Proposals* (Washington, DC: GPO, December 2008); *Budget Options I: Health Care* (Washington, DC: GPO, December 2008).

75. Holtz-Eakin, interview, 2010.

76. Douglas Elmendorf, letter to Senator Orrin Hatch, "Concerning CBO's analysis of the effects of proposals to limit costs associated with medical malpractice," October 9, 2009.

77. Philip Joyce, "Congressional Budget Reform: The Unanticipated Consequences for Federal Policymaking," *Public Administration Review* 56, no. 4 (1996): 317–25.

78. Holtz-Eakin, interview, 2010.

79. Elmendorf, interview.

Chapter 8

An Excellent Skunk?

CBO HAS PERHAPS never been—before or since—in as precarious a position as it was in early 1995. Newt Gingrich and the Republicans had taken over Congress for the first time in forty years, and the new speaker threatened to clean CBO out. This was based on a view that CBO had really been just a tool of the Democratic majority, and that the only way to make the agency responsive to Republicans was to replace not only the director, but the majority of the professional staff as well. This was painfully ironic, in a sense, as it came on the heels of CBO dealing a potentially mortal blow to the central domestic priority of the Clinton administration less than a year earlier. Nonetheless, the threat was acknowledged in a February 17, 1995, *Washington Post* editorial reminding readers that the important role CBO had played was that of "the skunk at the congressional picnic."[1] It reassured its readers (perhaps hoping that if it said so, it was true) that the new director, June O'Neill, had not been selected to destroy CBO: "Mr. Reischauer was an excellent skunk, as were his Democratic-and-Republican-appointed predecessors and as his successor will likely be too."[2]

This, in effect, suggests that Alice Rivlin, the first director, and her successors had been spectacularly successful in establishing CBO as a strong, independent voice in the budget process. This view of CBO's role went back at least to the first organizational meeting Rivlin had called to outline her vision for CBO. At this meeting, she had articulated three clear organizational goals.

a. The agency should be highly respected and nonpartisan.
b. Initiative should be kept within CBO. The agency should not just be responsive to Congress, but instead should retain the right to initiate its own studies where appropriate to the performance of its mission.
c. Its major products—the annual report (tracking what happens over the budget cycle) and policy analyses (of particular issues) should be presented "in a form readable by Congressmen."[3]

Others at the meeting articulated a similar vision for CBO. One said that the agency would be successful if it had respect from Hill staff, if this respect extended beyond a particular director, and if it had an impact on the executive branch. Hugh Heclo suggested, in a paper written in 1975 and distributed to new CBO staff, that the agency was attempting to develop "neutral competence" in its support for Congress, much as Heclo had argued OMB provided neutrally competent advice for the president.[4] If anything, CBO's job in this respect was harder than OMB's.[5] CBO was trying to serve Republicans and Democrats simultaneously; OMB only had to serve one party at a time.[6] Moreover, all of this was intended to contribute to one larger goal, which was to have an operating budget procedure on the Hill.

Chapter 1 laid out a number of questions for this book to answer. In this final chapter, I return to these questions and review what has been learned.

- Has CBO assisted Congress in countering the trend toward greater executive branch dominance in the budget process and allocation that existed before 1974?
- What has the creation and growing importance of CBO meant for the ability of Congress to compete with the executive branch in the policy arena, and for presidential-legislative relations in general? More broadly, to what extent is there evidence that CBO has significantly influenced public policy—that is, are there policies that might be different had CBO not existed?
- What is the role of leadership (particularly, the leadership of CBO directors) in establishing a vision and a continuing culture for the agency?
- Has CBO in fact engaged in nonpartisan analysis? That is, to what extent has CBO produced "honest numbers"?
- How has CBO assisted Congress in the congressional budget process, and assisted the public (through the media or independently) in understanding the choices that face the country, and the effects of those choices?
- Given the importance Alice Rivlin placed on doing policy analysis, what can we say about CBO's performance and its identifiable influence in this area?
- What role has CBO played in educating Congress and the general public, and what difference has this made?
- How does the story of CBO, as documented in this book, fit within existing theories of the role of expertise in the political process?
- What, if anything, do these lessons tell us for the future of CBO, for policy analysis in general, or about policymaking in the federal government?

CBO and the Executive Branch

As discussed in chapter 1, CBO has become such an important tool in holding the executive branch responsive and in checking executive budgetary power that it has positively alarmed some observers. Examples of CBO's influence in this role abound in this book, but probably the three most prominent are the 1981 response to the Reagan economic plan, the 1993 report on the Clinton health reform, and congressional Republican insistence in 1995 and 1996 that President Clinton present a balanced budget plan using CBO assumptions (a stance resulting in two relatively lengthy government shutdowns).

A number of other cases come immediately to mind as well, such as the Carter energy policy, the controversy over the savings associated with Vice President Gore's reinventing government initiative, and the flap over the cost of the Medicare prescription drug bill. In each of these cases, at issue was a presidential proposal to change the status quo (although, in the case of the Clinton balanced budget plan, the impetus for change came from Congress).

From almost the beginning, the Obama administration fell into this same pattern of proposing, and then waiting for CBO to pronounce. As Congress and the new president worked on the details of an economic stimulus package, CBO's analysis of the components of the package being crafted by the House suggested that it fell short of its stated goals. Specifically, the analysis suggested that only about 40 percent of the items included in the package could provide stimulus to the economy by the end of fiscal year 2010—that is, within a year and a half of projected enactment. There was significant mismatch between administration and CBO analyses, in spite of the fact that Obama's budget director had until recently been director of CBO. Later, the CBO response to the Obama health plan, as recounted in chapter 7, was another spectacular example of CBO's influence on federal budget-making. Once the president laid down the marker that any bill had to be deficit neutral—and identified CBO as the arbiter of that—he (in the words of one participant) "just . . . handed CBO the keys because no policy was going to be acceptable if it didn't meet the CBO test."[7] That the president took the step of inviting Elmendorf to the Oval Office—a first for a CBO director—provides some indication of the importance of CBO from the perspective of the Obama administration.

Arguably, then, the highest-profile situations involving CBO have not been associated with internal workings of Congress, but when the executive has proposed a change in policy and CBO has been asked to analyze it. This is the strongest indication that the main goal of creating CBO—that is, to support Congress in asserting its independence from the president in the budget process—has been effectively achieved. In fact, it has sometimes worked better than the president's own party in Congress would prefer.

Jack Lew, who—as a former high-level congressional staffer and a former director of OMB—should know, put it extraordinarily well:

> In terms of the relationship between Congress and the White House on budget issues, CBO has empowered Congress in a way that is very significant. OMB is an institution that is inherently half policymaking half analytic. . . . it's unambiguously a partisan policymaking body, and it's unambiguously the

arbiter of an awful lot of analytic responsibility. I actually believe that it balances those roles extraordinarily well most of the time . . . CBO having only the analytic capacity and being the only place in Congress that is not under direct partisan control has given the Congress the ability to police the White House's ability to define the terms of engagement on economic issues . . . just the fact that it's a check on the White House empowers Congress. It creates a choice. A choice of how you measure, a choice of the size of the problem, a choice of comparing options on terms that can be tested.[8]

In addition to affecting the broad relationship between the executive branch and Congress, CBO has also had effects on OMB. More accurately, two significant institutions have influenced each other. Susan Irving observed that "before CBO was created, OMB was the only game in town. It had developed a certain amount of credibility, but it was largely understood that OMB necessarily worked for the president. So, if a member of Congress wanted a cost estimate for a bill, he or she had to send it to OMB. And, although I couldn't prove this, I suspect that if the administration didn't like the proposal, it could be amazing how long it might take for the member to hear back from OMB."[9]

CBO changed all that. Those interviewed for this book—including three former OMB directors—agreed that one effect of CBO was to keep OMB honest. CBO has substantially influenced OMB because it creates bounds for OMB analysis: there are just limits beyond which OMB cannot reasonably go. If OMB is going to be substantially different from CBO on any issue, there has to be a good reason why.[10] Probably the clearest illustration of this was during the Reagan administration, when the OMB rosy scenarios were widely seen as optimistic in their economic projections, largely because there were no CBO numbers against which to compare them.[11]

Van Ooms, who was on the House Budget Committee staff from its inception in 1977 until 1990, argued that the emergence of CBO as the credible arbiter of budget numbers was one of the most important lasting effects of the Budget Act. According to Ooms, CBO "replaced OMB as being the place where you go to get the quote 'right numbers.' That certainly was not foreseeable at the time that I arrived in Washington, and it gradually developed over the years."[12]

There is clearly a down side to having two sets of numbers. It creates confusion. Members of Congress do not know which numbers are right, and policy advocates can pick and choose among numbers that best support their policy positions.[13] Perhaps no incident in CBO's history illustrates the tension inherent in this situation as well as the fight in 1995 over whether the administration would use CBO or OMB numbers in putting together its budget plan. The resulting impasse ultimately precipitated the longest government shutdown in American history (see chapter 3).

Another effect of CBO's ability to challenge OMB is that it may generate some advantages for OMB career staff—who sometimes find it difficult to convince their political masters to embrace what staff view to be an analytically superior (albeit politically inferior) position. According to Jim Horney, "I know for a fact that OMB staff use CBO to argue to their superiors to do stuff the right way. They'll say, 'Well, obviously you can tell me to do it this way but CBO's going to do it the other and everybody's going to know that's the right way to do it. We're going to look like fools.' And it works."[14]

Dick Emery, formerly the top career official at OMB, agreed. He cited a couple of specific examples, including the Boeing tanker lease. OMB career staff wanted the arrangement viewed as an operating lease before they were overruled by political advisors in the George W. Bush administration. Emery indicated that "the reality is that we and CBO frequently use each other as a foil."[15] Sometimes, if OMB and CBO agree with each other on budget concepts, elected officials can be convinced to embrace analysts' point of view: "Having the institutions working for the Congress and the executive branch that have the same general point of view has really helped. The development of scoring rules which was something we did collectively I think both reflects the realities that we deal with but it helps improve the quality of the debate—prevent nonsense to a certain extent, and that's a real plus."[16]

This raises another key point. One reason for consistent interaction—even agreement—between CBO and OMB career staff is that they speak the same language, hold the same general professional views, and have the same orientation. Jim Blum, who worked in both agencies, explained it this way:

> It is the role of budget institutions to be skeptical. Certainly both OMB and CBO share this, in the sense that they are constantly on the lookout for someone who is trying to put one over on them. In the case of the Clinton health plan, it is possible that the reason CBO reacted the way that it did was because it saw itself as the protector of budget concepts. That is, if you are trying to be cute and make something that could be called a tax look like something else, it is the tendency of the scorekeepers to see themselves as the gatekeeper—protecting the public against obfuscation by elected officials.[17]

In fact, there has been a history of some personnel movement between the two institutions, because many of the skills required are the same. According to Dick Emery,

> Almost to a person, a person who will be effective here will be effective at CBO. I think there may be more people who come to work at OMB who move on. . . . I mean, our turnover rate is higher, and we may have a few more people who go on to stardom than CBO does. CBO is by definition a behind the scenes enterprise. OMB, in contrast—the OMB budget examiners deal with agency counterparts who are frequently Assistant Secretaries when they're GS-9 budget examiners. That gives them an entree to mobility that

they wouldn't have if they didn't have a function that provided them with that kind of exposure.[18]

Finally, requirements imposed on the two institutions by budget legislation, particularly after the deficit became the focus of the budget process after 1985, forced them to communicate collegially. As discussed in chapter 3, both Rudy Penner (director of CBO in the late 1980s) and Barry Anderson (a top career official at OMB at the same time) referred to the importance of Gramm-Rudman (and later the BEA) in forcing CBO and OMB to talk to each other. These two agencies needed not only to talk to each other, but also to understand each other's assumptions. This occurred because they were required to explain not only that they differed, but why their assumptions differed.

CBO and Lessons of Leadership

A second lesson to emerge from the study of CBO has to do with the importance of leadership in creating and maintaining an organization that remains true to its mission. Returning to the goals articulated for CBO in the initial organizational meeting—respected, nonpartisan, independent, and communicative—review of evidence appears to indicate that it has been a spectacular success on all of these fronts. This did not just happen. It resulted from conscious choices, particularly on the part of CBO's directors, to keep it that way. It is a tribute to the organizational culture of CBO—created by Alice Rivlin, affirmed by Rudy Penner, and emphasized in a generally consistent fashion by subsequent directors.

The Importance of Alice Rivlin

A key lesson to be drawn from the history of CBO is simply that a leader with a strong vision can create a sustainable culture, provided that subsequent leaders and employees commit to that culture. CBO never had a strategic plan. It never really had a mission statement—that is, unless you count the unofficial motto "On the one hand . . . on the other." Nevertheless CBO developed a very clear mission and work ethic consistent with the foundational statute: CBO directors and staff are to be selected to be neutrally competent. CBO was extremely fortunate to have Alice Rivlin as its first director. Rivlin had three attributes essential to CBO's eventual success.

She understood that decisions concerning how to organize to produce analysis were important. The ability of CBO to engage in neutral policy analysis, which she personally valued, depended on allowing the policy divisions within CBO to have enough rope to be able to make connections with congressional committees and enough protection from the day-to-day budget work to be able to engage in longer-term analysis.

She understood the importance of institutional culture in promoting the mission of an organization—particularly a new one. In the case of CBO, she drilled the ethic of nonpartisanship into CBO employees, and she made sure (in staff selection and retention) that the ability to adhere enthusiastically to that ethic was a clear job requirement.

She was uncompromising in sticking to her vision of CBO's role in the budget process. If a senator wanted a greater role in setting CBO's agenda (as Bob Dole did, as recounted in chapter 2) she politely informed him that "the report is our report."[19] If there was pressure to go along with the Reagan economic policies, she made sure that CBO maintained an independent voice. If Congress wanted to bury CBO analyses and put the budget committees out front, she held press conferences. She intentionally looked out for the profile of the institution, even when that upset her political masters. Efforts by Rivlin to publicize CBO was part of a conscious strategy to put CBO on the map. Rivlin might have chosen another path. She might, for example, have followed the model of the Congressional Research Service—which bends over backwards to be low profile—but she chose not to.[20]

Rivlin worked assiduously to create an internal culture, and an external profile, consistent with the vision of CBO as a source of neutral competence in the budget process. As discussed in chapter 2, she negotiated the rules of the game for dealings between congressional, members, committees, staffs, and CBO. She circulated documents articulating her vision of CBO's nonpartisanship. Early on she circulated copies of letters internally that she had signed each week, so the staff could understand the types of things CBO was involved with and positions it had taken.[21] In short, it is hard to imagine where CBO would have ended up if the House had had its way and Sam Hughes, who held a much narrower vision of CBO, had been chosen the first director. It is not too much of a stretch to say that it would have been likely to be less relevant and to have exerted far less influence over the years.

Rivlin herself made this point in 2010, but emphasizing Congress's interest that CBO start as and remain a nonpartisan institution:

> As to how it really got started on that track there are really two things. One is appointing me because if they had appointed a more partisan person that might not have happened. But the other is really important and that is the bipartisan cooperation of the Senate Budget Committee. It was the Muskie-Bellman cooperation. They supported and protected the nonpartisanship. They protected me from their more partisan colleagues. And it ran through the leadership of the SBC for several iterations in the period of Domenici and Chiles . . . there were chairmen of both parties who continued that bipartisan tradition—more in the Senate than in the House.
>
> And then how did it persist? I think it was important that I was there for eight years and through three administrations. . . . By the time we got to the third

year of the Reagan administration, which is when Rudy took over, it was pretty well established. Rudy . . . was a Republican but he was like me. So by then you had twelve years so that was a pretty good base. And Reischauer was that kind of person. . . . And so it was continuity of leadership with that in mind.[22]

Subsequent Directors and CBO's Culture

In addition to CBO's good fortune in having Rivlin as the first director, it is hard to overstate the contribution made by the second director. Rudy Penner certainly made other positive contributions to the organization, but perhaps his main gift to the organization was in what he did not do. He established the practice, almost universally followed by subsequent directors, of assuming that the staff could be responsive, and that this responsiveness transcended allegiance to party or individual director: he continued and facilitated the institutional expectation of neutral competence. As discussed in chapter 2, Alan Greenspan commented, at the time of Penner's appointment, that he was a "Republican Alice Rivlin." Eloquent testimony to the most important quality in CBO directors—which is the ability to play it straight, regardless of whether you are a nominal Democrat or nominal Republican. Roy Meyers argued that "Rudy made an incredible contribution to the organization in that he was just as good as Alice, although with different skills."[23] This view was echoed by Susan Irving, who said that "if you think of the first shoe as dropping when Alice criticized Carter, the second shoe was when Penner turned out to say the same stuff that she said."[24] Once Penner, a Republican, had demonstrated that the mission of the institution needed to transcend the political affiliation of its director, it set an important precedent for subsequent directors to follow. There is ample evidence that subsequent directors did in fact take up this charge.

- Reischauer, who had deep ties to the Kennedy family, was nonetheless viewed as instrumental in helping kill Clinton health care reform over the strong objections of Senator Edward Kennedy, then chair of the Senate Health Committee.
- O'Neill, handpicked by Gingrich and Kasich to assist in the Republican revolution by cleaning out CBO and adjusting CBO scoring methods to support Republican policies, did neither.
- Crippen, though he had a rocky beginning in terms of his relationship with CBO staff, nonetheless resisted "dynamic scoring" and supported CBO's analyses that were critical of the GSEs (as detailed in chapter 5),[25] despite the fact that he had been a GSE lobbyist.[26]
- Holtz-Eakin defied Democratic expectations and was almost universally respected as a straight shooter, despite the fact that his position just before the CBO directorship had been working for President Bush's Council on Economic Advisors.

In a sense, when you think about the stature of the job and organization, it is not surprising that all of these people were, at the time of their appointment, mainstream. As Wendell Primus said, "recalling history, I mean, I thought at the time that the argument that we tried to establish (was) that we were going to go middle of the road nominal Democrat to middle of the road nominal Republican back and forth. And, so Rudy Penner fit that well, there weren't any major staff shakeups if I recall correctly. You know . . . I couldn't tell a whiff of difference . . . between Alice to Rudy to Bob. And in some ways, you know, that's the way I thought it should be."[27]

It appears there are three reasons that the organization has resisted becoming more partisan. First, there aren't many real partisans with the skills necessary to manage CBO. Jim Bates, who as Republican staff director was instrumental in the selection of Doug Holtz-Eakin, said that one thing that surprised him was the fact that in the end, the list of people actually qualified for the job was not long.[28]

Second, people who meet the minimum qualifications for the job have one other thing in common. They are professional economists, and as such operate within the intellectual limits prescribed by their profession. Put another way, they are going to think twice before doing anything that will embarrass them in the eyes of their professional colleagues. They might need the associated credibility in a future life.

Third, an important result of the CBO culture is that it actually limits the ability of directors to substantially change the organization. If a given new CBO director came in and decided that the type of analysis that CBO was doing was wholly incorrect and wanted to change it unilaterally, it would be extraordinarily difficult to accomplish without replacing a substantial number of staff. If from time to time there were individual staff that sought to promote a partisan agenda, the knowledgeable sources interviewed for this book had precious few examples they could point to of CBO directors having behaved in a partisan manner. Alice Rivlin herself—who has observed CBO with the interest of a parent—indicated that if there had been anyone who tried to move CBO in a partisan direction, then "none of those people were ever director. Dan Crippen took the most grief for it, but it wasn't really true that Dan Crippen wanted it to move in a Republican direction. Douglas Holtz-Eakin has just been terrific, and he managed to move from the White House to CBO and completely reverted to what I think must have been his original feeling, that good analysis is good analysis."[29]

Roy Meyers sums it up appropriately: "To tell you the truth, I've never been concerned about it. There are a couple of reasons. First, that Alice created a culture there, and hired so many smart people who were dedicated to doing the kind of work that CBO ended up doing—people who are a lot like academics, but they're not into teaching, they're into applied research, or applied policy. And I think it would be very difficult, if not impossible, to shift it into a partisan organization."[30]

Even the period most often cited as not fitting the CBO mold—the first year of the Crippen administration—appears to have been an anomaly. There is general agreement that the situation changed in later years and also that no lasting damage was done to CBO's credibility.[31] According to Dick Emery, who had held management positions in both CBO and OMB, and thus knew both organizations—and the players—quite well, both Crippen and his deputy Barry Anderson started out with some misconceptions of CBO in that they tried to apply an executive branch model. "It took the better part of a year or longer to change Dan and Barry to fit the CBO mold. I think it hurt CBO initially having an OMB-style political leadership for CBO. I think they ended up both of them being quite effective at CBO and reasonably well respected by the Congress, but it was a rough transition."[32]

In the end, according to a longtime CBO staff member, "if you're looking for sort of the cult of personalities, CBO is absolutely the wrong place to look for it. I don't think it changes much year in year out with whoever is sitting in the front office. It makes some difference in terms of style. Alice had an incredible influence on what happened later, but once going, it has not made really sharp departures in my judgment."[33]

CBO and Nonpartisanship

Agreement seems to be widespread that that CBO directors have largely fostered the same culture Alice Rivlin established in CBO. But what is the evidence that CBO as an agency has actually been nonpartisan? One hard to avoid general stream is that CBO directors appear to have been more likely to be done in by friends (that is, the party that most supported their appointment) than by enemies. There are many examples.

- House majority leader Jim Wright (D-TX) was livid with Rivlin (a nominal Democrat) over the analysis of the Carter energy plan. He was so upset, in fact, that he allegedly opposed the appointment of Reischauer as director because of Reischauer's involvement at the fringes in that analysis.
- Robert Reischauer, another Democrat, himself was much more heavily criticized by Democrats than Republicans during his tenure—largely because of CBO analysis of the Clinton health plan. The irony, of course, is that he was not reappointed when the Republicans took over control of the Congress because he was identified with the Democrats.
- June O'Neill, whom the Republicans chose to succeed Reischauer, was unpopular with Republicans by the end of her term. She had not done any of the things they expected that she might— including getting rid of several staff and embracing dynamic scoring.

- House Budget Committee chair Jim Nussle (R-IA) was so upset with Dan Crippen, and CBO under his leadership, that he was quoted as saying, "CBO sucks" (see chapter 3).
- Doug Holtz-Eakin, who had come from the Bush White House, and was thus looked on with great skepticism by Democrats in Congress, later surprised these same skeptics with his even-handed analysis. Republicans, particularly those on the tax-writing committees, were just as surprised—but not as pleasantly.
- Doug Elmendorf, appointed by Democrats, was criticized most strongly by those same Democrats, particularly for failing to give appropriate scoring credit for initiatives in the health care bills.

One striking phenomenon is that it seems very difficult for political officials to understand that public servants who have been associated with a political party in the past can be both neutral and competent when occupying a position that expressly requires such nonpartisan behavior. So there was genuine shock in the White House and in some quarters in the Congress that Reischauer, as a Democrat, could possibly take a position that would do anything damaging to the domestic policy centerpiece of the Clinton administration. It was especially difficult for some of the younger Clinton White House staff to believe that Reischauer, who was hired by Rivlin, would reach conclusions that would not support the administration's position. This is particularly ironic given that Rivlin's analysis of the Carter energy plan had demonstrated the capacity of the organization to be nonpartisan.

There is evidence beyond the behavior of individual directors that CBO has at times taken on powerful and entrenched interests, in spite of the fact that CBO has stood to gain little other than reputation for doing its job. Certainly this was the case in CBO's work on the GSEs discussed in chapter 5, but there are other cases as well, including analytical battles with the Department of Defense (CBO would definitely lose the more traditional kind of conflicts with DOD) and an effort by CBO to bring the Federal Reserve on to the federal budget.

There is, however, a difference between being nonpartisan and being foolish. It seems likely that CBO has paid a lot of attention to whom it serves, if not to the answer that it provides. Jim Blum said that his original design of BAD intentionally established the scorekeeping unit as a separate entity to deal with the appropriations committees, because he knew how important service to those committees was going to be.[34] CBO made sure that it was responsive to those committees, although no specific evidence indicates that this extended to actually providing the answers the appropriations committees wanted.

Moreover, in the budget process itself, at least some participants detect a tendency to respond more to the majority party than the minority party. It should be noted that this was not identified as an issue of partisanship, but as practicality. Tom Kahn, Democratic staff director of the House Budget Committee, interviewed when the Democrats had been in the minority for ten years, put it this way: "There is no question about it, our requests get answered more slowly than the majority. . . . I understand CBO's view even though I don't necessarily share it. At the end of the day, the majority writes the bill that goes to the floor and is eventually enacted into law. With very limited resources and overtaxed staff, CBO has to set priorities to manage its workload."[35]

Having said this, however, it is important to point out that staff of the budget committees who are in the minority were universal in their view that CBO did not ignore them. Even in the House, where CBO might ignore the minority party with impunity, given the institutional weakness of House minority parties, CBO has not done so. Longtime House Budget Committee staffer Jim Bates stated that he would simply have been unable to do his job when he was in the minority, which included coming up with full substitute budget resolutions, without the assistance of CBO staff.[36] And CBO offered that assistance with certainty that these substitute resolutions would never pass. Austin Smythe, who was House Budget Committee minority staff director in 2010, rejected out of hand the notion that CBO is somehow less responsive to the minority.

> If you go to CBO . . . at 11:30 on Friday, and you say I need an analysis by Monday morning, or by COB today, you're not going to get it. . . . If you give them . . . what information you need, and give them some time, they will produce an analysis. . . . You're always at a disadvantage if things are moving quickly. . . . Congressman Ryan got a letter . . . on a series of questions that we asked that CBO gave us before the (health reform) bill was considered in the House and I think that is evidence that they are responsive to our requests. . . . We talked to CBO and spent some time with them . . . and they told us what their limits were in terms of what they could produce on a timely basis. I thought they were very responsive and very timely.[37]

CBO has also continually walked a tightrope concerning whether it works for the budget committees exclusively, or other committees in Congress as well. Even though rules govern this relation, that does not preclude pressure for CBO to work for more members. In fact, increasingly, as was true in the Obama health reform process, CBO appears to work for the leadership, rather than for committees. One staff member reported that the budget committees mainly played the role of translator between CBO, the committees of jurisdiction, and the leadership.[38]

There is another contextual challenge, which is the extent to which nonpartisanship creates risks of isolation. As discussed in chapter 3, this was an issue in the case of the 1996 May surprise, when CBO revised its baseline estimates just as the White House and Congress were preparing to reach an agreement. The suggestion here is that, in an effort to remain independent, CBO may have removed itself from the political process to such an extent that it did not understand timing implications of releasing new budget figures. As a result of controversy over the release of these figures, CBO began to make public its monthly budget analyses, to preclude any possible future concerns associated with timing of the release of new figures. Another less high-profile example of this, from the Crippen years, was the change in practices in scoring the farm bill that led to the Nussle comment described earlier that "CBO sucks."

Doug Holtz-Eakin explained that there were two things that he tried to avoid being tempted to do while director. The first was falling prey to what he called analyst hubris, where you become convinced that you can get Congress to do the right thing through the way you score or analyze a piece of legislation. The second is to look beyond the current situation or piece of legislation to what comes next—that is, to score the ultimate impact of legislation, rather than the effect of the legislation itself.[39]

At the same time, it has to be acknowledged that the urge to look at every issue through a budgetary lens can result in asking rather narrow questions, and therefore missing the larger economic and social picture. It is possible that, from a desire to not be a victim or progenitor of budget chicanery, CBO gives less weight than might be warranted to these larger questions, as opposed to narrower questions of budget effects and budget concepts: "Whether these alliances (in the Clinton health reform) should be on-budget or off-budget was an important and unavoidable question for the budget agencies. You could say that CBO leadership didn't understand that CBO would be blamed for torpedoing the bill by suggesting the alliances should be on budget, but I think that is ridiculous. Where CBO's contribution wasn't as great as it could have been was that this question became a central focus rather than the larger access, quality, and cost trade-offs that should be dominating policy analysis and budgetary analysis for health policy."[40]

CBO and the Success of the Process

The main reason, of course, for the creation of CBO was to make resources to support the congressional budget process available to Congress. The CBO role in supporting the budget process can be divided into two: the high-level role of supporting the overall budget process, including the success or failure of the budget resolution, and the more specific role of informing individual budget decisions through cost estimations.

CBO and the Larger Process

The budget process itself has somewhat of a checkered history. There is no question that as the federal budget process has evolved over time, Congress has established an independent voice. The role of Congress relative to the president has been strengthened. At particular moments, the budget process has been used to enact lots of policy changes, including the Reagan and Bush tax cuts, welfare reform, the Medicare prescription drug bill, and the various efforts in the 1990s to reduce the deficit. The existence of the budget resolution and particularly the reconciliation process has facilitated these efforts.

On the other hand, there is broad dissatisfaction with the budget process. In fact, there is bipartisan and nonpartisan agreement—among participants and ob-servers—that the federal budget process is a mess. Observers do not necessarily agree on either the reasons or the worst offenses of the process, but the most prominent criticisms include the following:

The federal government does not enact its budget on time. In fact, all appropriation bills have been passed prior to the beginning of the fiscal year for only four of the past thirty-five fiscal years (including 2011). This has sometimes, but not since 1996, led to partial government shutdowns, disrupting government services and contracts.[41] Moreover, since 1999 Congress has failed five times to enact a budget resolution at all. This represents a substantial deterioration in recent years, be-cause budget resolutions were enacted every year between 1977 (the first year of the current budget process) and 1998.[42]

The federal deficit, which had been eradicated in the late 1990s, soared to historic post–World War II levels in 2009 and 2010. It is uncertain when (and how) it will be eliminated again. Under the most plausible ten-year projections for prevail-ing policies, there is no reason to believe that the deficit will disappear without action.[43]

Long-term fiscal problems associated with providing entitlement benefits to an aging population have been largely ignored by political leaders and constituents alike. This lack of attention has led key budget watchdog groups, such as the Concord Coalition and the Committee for a Responsible Federal Budget, along with former comp-troller general Walker, to conclude that the only option is to appeal directly to the voters.[44]

The budget process encourages the provision of wasteful benefits to narrow constitu-encies, most prominently evidenced by spending and tax earmarks (pork, if you prefer). According to Rubin "some of these earmarks have been revealed as rewards for financial donors, contributing to the impression that government is corrupt."[45] Earmarks have been increasing substantially, on both the tax and spending sides of the budget.[46] The practice of earmarking, though often decried as a solely legislative phenomenon, is also practiced by the executive—although perhaps even less transparently.

The budget process, instead of following international trends toward greater transpar-ency in budgeting, has recently become even less transparent.[47] This lack of transpar-ency is contributed to by the sheer complexity of the process. Choices, such as the exclusion or intentional understating of the cost of Iraq and Afghanistan war funding in presidential budgets or the routine funding of disaster relief through supplementals, have tended to make the budget process even less transparent.

Although the Obama administration has embraced transparency, it also built its fiscal year 2011 budget using multiple and confusing baselines—some of which bore little resemblance to traditional baselines.

Dissatisfaction with the budget process, even among relatively dispassionate academic observers, is nothing new. In his classic 1990 article about failures of the budget process, Louis Fisher wrote that "the current budget process followed by the Congress and the president is embarrassing both in operation and results."[48] Among the reasons Fisher cited were the relative lack of transparency of the process and its failure to encourage responsible budgeting. In his view, the 1974 reform allows the president to escape accountability for budget outcomes. Surpluses in the late 1990s may have temporarily convinced some that Fisher was wrong, but experience in the early 2000s appeared to substantiate his criticisms. Bush administration tactics certainly reflected a lack of fiscal responsibility. The Bush administration pursued policies that demonstrably worsened the deficit outlook and compounded fiscal harm by failing to exhibit leadership to confront the problem. So far, the same can be said for the Obama administration, although many of the recent policies of the last two administrations have been focused on counteracting the effects of the recession.

Given this uneven history, what has CBO done for the federal budget process, and is there anything it could have done to mitigate observable process shortcomings? First, operation of the budget process as designed would not have been possible without the role played by CBO. The budget committees could have operated, but they would have had to create some source for expertise housed in CBO—particularly related to economic and baseline budget projections. Moreover, given the realities of the Congress, each house would have needed to have this expertise. Recall that at the outset the argument was that the cost of CBO was going to be justified by the benefits derived from "providing Congress with the expert help it needs to regain its control over the federal budget process."[49]

The other value-added that CBO has arguably brought to the federal budget process is the extent to which CBO has helped Congress engage in multiyear budgeting. Multiyear budgeting is on what is a very short list of budgeting good practices. International organizations, such as the World Bank and the International Monetary Fund, encourage countries to look beyond the current budget period to plan for the future, and to provide direction to line ministries and agencies. The congressional budget process was designed to focus on multiple years through the budget resolution, and the CBO baseline estimates have been integral to accomplishing that. Longtime budget participant Richard Kogan says that the budget process has been the vehicle through which members of Congress and congressional committees have been encouraged to look at multiyear effects of policies, particularly for entitlement programs. To the extent that the focus is on the general direction of fiscal policy, and not the deficit number in a given year, that is a positive result, and the budget process has tended to encourage it.[50] On the other hand, the budget process has often not been very effective at budgeting for even one year, as evidenced by the inability to pass budgets and, especially, appropriation bills on time.

CBO has made important contributions to the unfolding of the budget process, but it has also frequently been significantly wrong in its projections. To be fair, forecasting either the economy or the budget beyond a year or two is rife with extremely difficult methodological challenges. This can, in turn, undermine effective multiyear budgeting. Perhaps the highest profile case of such errors was in 2001, when the CBO projection of $5.6 trillion in cumulative surpluses helped to pave the way for the Bush tax cuts. These projections proved overly optimistic for a number of reasons, including primarily the failure to anticipate the recession which was already under way and the unpredictable effects of September 11. Everett Ehrlich commented that "in the summer of 2000 I did an NPR piece about how the surpluses were illusory. . . . The bad CBO forecasts led to a mountain of money that led to tax cuts. On the other hand, Greenspan deserved more blame."[51] CBO has done several things to mitigate risks of seriously flawed forecasts, including presenting confidence intervals of possible outcomes. However, Congress tends to focus on the point estimates, particularly when those point estimates allow them to take actions they want to take. It should also be said that most of the reason that it has become more difficult for CBO to accurately forecast over time relates to the pressures to do longer-term estimates. It will always be true that ten-year estimates will have higher levels of uncertainty than five-year estimates.

Regardless of these drawbacks, in the end, according to Paul Posner, CBO has made the budget process better.

> I think if you didn't create it you'd have to invent it given what we've created in the budget process. Someone has to keep score, someone has to be the honest broker. I was just talking to the deputy budget director in New York state. . . . We were speculating that one of the reasons that New York is so contentious is that they don't have a legislative fiscal analyst. They have committees—each of the committees really does their own thing, and they are often really reflecting the political views of their parties. So they don't come to the table with any legitimacy. And CBO really does have that. And it's been sustained over time. It's hard to imagine the Budget Act, whatever the problems are now, even having gotten this far if we didn't have an independent arbiter like that.[52]

Jack Lew cited a perception held by some that without CBO, an administration might be tempted to take advantage of its ability to coordinate and exercise unchecked central control over the budget, because it is responding to the wishes of the president. CBO has an ability to define the starting point, through the baseline, and it is a consistent starting point for not only the budget committees, but for the entire Congress to use.[53] Without that starting point, the natural tendency of Congress to operate in a purely fragmented and decentralized way would take over, and the result would be that the president's budget would occupy a much more central role.

Cost Estimating

Separately, there is the question of CBO cost estimating. That is, regardless of what has happened in terms of macrobudgetary outcomes, what has been the role of CBO in providing Congress with the cost estimates required by the Congressional Budget Act? As discussed in chapter 4, early on it was difficult for CBO to establish the necessary cost estimating capacity. For example, CBO needed to have a way to identify what the committees were doing, so that CBO would know when a bill was reported. It was essential for CBO credibility that it develop capacity on this front quickly. That Jim Blum and others in BAD did so, and provided required estimates in a timely manner, allowed room for the policy analysis function to develop a clientele.

Congressional staff interviewed for this book uniformly both expressed admiration for the capacity of CBO to produce cost estimates and noted the difficulty of doing so. Former House Budget Committee staffer Jim Bates described the cost estimating function as excellent. There have sometimes been pressures to rely on numbers other than the ones prepared by CBO, but Bates noted that he has always supported using the CBO numbers because "at the end of the day we want an objective system" and that CBO does very well at producing a point estimate within such a system.[54] Austin Smythe agreed: "I think where they are most important is ultimately in their scoring of legislation. I think their estimates are viewed as objective and I think their numbers are just taken as a given. . . . the debate focuses not on the cost estimate of the legislation, but on 'what should we do about legislation or policy.' I think that's been a tremendously positive outcome and something CBO should be proud of."[55]

Although there is little systematic criticism concerning the substance of CBO cost estimates (most people who are dissatisfied with a given number have no analytical basis to challenge it), there have been questions raised from time to time about the timeliness of the cost estimates. Some share of any delays almost certainly relate to the difficulty in doing estimates for some sectors, such as health care. Some share may also be a reflection of the fact that the congressional workload can be a bit lumpy. If there is a farm bill this year, for example, then there is pressure on the agriculture analysts. In other years, there is much less pressure.

Barry Anderson said he didn't have an appreciation for CBO cost estimating, despite years of working at OMB, until he arrived at CBO. The main challenge, he said, is in "the difficulty in putting together cost estimates that are nonpartisan and objective. . . . I also had a much greater appreciation that independence doesn't come automatically. You really have to take it to heart and fight for it, on virtually a day-by-day basis. There isn't anything that CBO does that's important that you don't get a call, and usually multiple calls, and usually from both sides."[56]

Doug Holtz-Eakin agreed and added an important amplification, that "scoring is making sure you order things correctly, not making sure that you get the number right. More important than anything else is making sure that you order proposals in the correct way."[57] In other words, perhaps the most important thing is that you use a consistent set of assumptions, and that you treat like proposals in a consistent way, so that one bill does not end up as more expensive than another because you used different assumptions.

The other important question concerning cost estimating, of course, is how big a difference the CBO cost estimates make in actually changing congressional behavior. It seems clear that the estimates do matter. As noted in chapter 4, the Medicare prescription drug bill would have looked different had it not had a $400 billion price tag, and it was up to CBO to determine whether it had achieved this target. The health care reform bill that emerged in 2010 would have looked a lot different had there not been a focus on passing a bill that could meet the CBO test. Further, avoiding having a bill saddled with the label of unfunded mandate has changed legislation. Especially during the time when the Budget Enforcement Act was in effect (1991–2002) a CBO cost estimate could effectively decide whether politically difficult offsets needed to be found to comply with PAYGO rules. This has been particularly true in the Senate, where Budget Act points of order have far more teeth.

In the end, it would be hard to paint CBO cost estimating as anything but successful, in the sense that Congress has now what it did not have before the Congressional Budget Act created the requirements for cost estimates starting in 1977—credible, multiyear estimates on the costs of proposed legislation. Moreover, Congress must pay attention to these estimates, which has the effect of introducing greater fiscal responsibility into the process.

Support of the Budget Committees

Before leaving the discussion of CBO's relationship to the budget process, it is important to make one more point. To the extent that CBO has been successful, it certainly owes that success in no small part to the support that it has gotten from the budget committees themselves. These two institutions—the budget committees and CBO—were inexorably intertwined from the beginning. If Congress had criticisms of CBO, as illustrated in the story about the Carter energy policy, this could easily translate into problems for the budget committees. Still, if the budget committees were unwilling to support CBO and its nonpartisan mission, there would have been little chance that the agency would have lasting success.

Most important, CBO was a nonpartisan institution trying to serve partisan masters. It would have been easy for these masters to turn their back on nonpartisanship—particularly in their selection of CBO directors—but the overwhelming evidence is that they did not do that. As Alice Rivlin reported, the original bipartisan support of Senators Muskie and Bellmon was crucial to establishing CBO's credibility and culture. Later, Senator Domenici (R–NM), supported by his long-time staff director Bill Hoagland, was perhaps the most consistent and staunchest supporter of CBO. He reportedly rebuffed a Reagan administration effort to remove Alice Rivlin, and he only agreed to support June O'Neill after he became convinced that she was not going to make CBO into a partisan institution. In the House, which tends to be a much more partisan institution, CBO was supported by a number of budget committee chairmen of both parties, perhaps most notably Jim Jones, Leon Panetta, and Jim Nussle. The most recent chairs and ranking members on the budget committees—Kent Conrad and Judd Gregg in the Senate, and John Spratt and Paul Ryan in the House—have continued this bipartisan support of CBO.

CBO and Policy Analysis

Given that Alice Rivlin's vision of CBO was as a mini-Brookings internal to Congress that could weigh in on the important policy questions of the day, it seems reasonable to ask how well that has worked. Although it seems fair to say that Congress did not know exactly what that meant, it is equally clear that by choosing Rivlin as director, they were implicitly embracing that vision of CBO.

First is the view from the supply side. CBO itself has become one of the major producers of policy analysis in the federal government; its products are widely available outside the legislative branch, including to the general public. That it produces these studies either provides other organizations with the opportunity to focus on alternate work, or serves to keep those organizations honest in the studies they conduct. Moreover, in-house policy analysis capacity has declined substantially in the federal government. Often, to the extent that policy analyses are done, they tend to be contracted out.

There is also the demand perspective. Call for—and effect of—CBO policy analysis is idiosyncratic. It does enable Congress to challenge the president on his own analytical terms, such as happened in the cases of the Carter energy policy and Clinton health reform. But CBO policy analysis does not necessarily have a consistent constituency.

There is a natural existing constituency for CBO budget analysis work—that is, the budget committees. In cases where the macrobudgetary direction of the country requires the policy analysis capacity of CBO to be engaged, CBO policy analysis work has been in demand. This was true during discussion of the Clinton health care reform plan (see chapter 6), and has recently been true given the long-term health care sector challenges facing the country. Each event caused CBO to increase its health policy analysis capacity. There are likely many more cases where CBO has to sell its work to Congress, by proactively convincing a congressional committee that a particular issue is worth studying. Not surprisingly, the record is less even on whether Congress pays attention to such analysis.

One clear example of CBO's analyses becoming institutionalized as part of the congressional decision-making process involves CBO analyses of the distributional effects of policies. These began to be requested by the House Ways and Means Committee, mainly driven by Wendell Primus, in the 1980s. Primus himself noted that the goal of this was to simply answer an analytical question—that is, "who benefits from certain policy choices."[58] By the time of the 1990 BEA negotiations at Andrews Air Force Base, the distributional tables were in demand as a key element in policymaking. According to Jack Lew, "the CBO distributional analyses were the driver of much of the final shape of what was and wasn't acceptable."[59]

Sometimes CBO policy analyses empowered particular members of Congress, even when those members were destined to fight a lonely battle. For example, the GSE work that CBO carried out for almost a quarter of a century was only sporadically considered. It was, however, a key element in Representative Richard Baker's (R-LA) uphill effort to rein in the GSEs. He never could have raised the questions he raised without the CBO analysis. By the time of the collapse of the GSEs in 2008, those questions looked particularly prescient.

Finally, there is the question of how organization of CBO influenced its output of policy analysis. Was Rivlin fundamentally correct that the two sides of CBO had to be separated to preserve the ability to do policy analysis? It seems likely. Certainly all subsequent CBO directors thought so. Reflecting on this thirty years later, Rivlin herself thought that they "did have it right to begin with, and it isn't a very large organization. So the defects in the organization—such as not enough communication between budget analysis and the program divisions—can be solved without moving people around. And I think subsequent directors have said 'I've got so much to do . . . that I don't have time to worry about the organization.'"[60]

One down side of this separation is that nothing in particular prevents a given program division from losing touch with the client, if it is inclined to do so—except the desires of individual directors, assistant directors, or analysts. The program divisions do not have the same time-bound demands for responsiveness placed on them as do budget analysis units, therefore a productivity failure on the part of the program divisions would not be as readily apparent as one within budget analysis.

The main benefit of having the separate divisions—trying to prevent budget analysis from driving out policy analysis—seems to be worth risking these potential problems. Without conscious attention by leadership there might be a tendency, because the focus of the budget process is on numbers, to allow numbers to drive out attention to longer-term policy. Doug Holtz-Eakin discussed the challenge:

> They built a budget process where they tried to make sure that you counted costs and counted them subject to constraints, and if you let the constraints drive policy then CBO's going to drive the focus. . . . I don't think CBO can

be fairly criticized for short-term focus. It's pioneered looking long-term . . . but the process of scoring . . . has had that effect on occasion. And I think the Medicare Modernization Act is a classic example. Four hundred billion dollars over this window and we're going to tailor this legislation to fit it. And there were certainly times in the midst of that when I would talk to people and they would say that's bad policy and I would think 'do something else' . . . but they were driven by the score.[61]

Striking organizational balance on this front clearly poses problems. A reasonable question is whether there might be bigger problems if CBO did not do policy analysis, but only did budget analysis. The answer to this question would clearly be yes. A second question is whether it would be more of a problem if CBO had been organized by function, rather than product. Evidence appears to indicate that the answer to this question is also yes. In the end, it is extraordinarily difficult for information to create its own demand. This is most true when the information is perceived as discretionary, as sometimes is the case with CBO policy analysis work. What CBO can do is provide the information, and provide it in a timely manner and in a useable form, and let the chips fall where they may.

There is no question, however, that product-based organization had its internal costs—mainly manifested in sometimes strained relations between the BAD and the program divisions. Michael O'Hanlon noted that, from the perspective of his perch in the NSD, clearly the NSD needed BAD more than the latter needed the former. It was the BAD cost analysts who had access to the cost data who were often necessary to round out the NSD studies. If NSD staff could not get BAD staff interested in those studies, the necessary budget data might be hard to access.[62] Certainly this tension has been repeated across other divisions over the history of CBO, despite the almost universal view that Rivlin's organizational vision was fundamentally correct.

CBO's Educational Influence

There is no indication in the record of debates surrounding the creation of the congressional budget process that a goal of creating CBO was to educate either Congress (except about operation of the process itself) or the public. However, clearly one effect of CBO (and the process in general) has been to educate both sets of stakeholders. One reason for this has been the substantial attention CBO itself has paid to the readability and marketing of its reports and analyses.

Educating Congress

Before there was a congressional budget process, there was very little knowledge in Congress about budgeting—beyond members of the leadership and the tax and appropriations committees. In fact, it was not at all unusual to find members of Congress who had no idea what the difference was between authorizations and appropriations, or budget authority and outlays. This has improved substantially, as has general knowledge about what things cost and what accounts for that cost.[63] Van Ooms argued that "as CBO became more entrenched as the arbiter of the numbers and as members of Congress began to accede to that and accept that, I think they became more educable and educated on what was going on with the budget than they were before. . . . we went through fifteen years where no one was talking about anything but the budget."[64] Moreover, because membership on the budget committees turns over relatively frequently, more members have had an opportunity to learn about the larger budget issues and challenges facing the federal government.

In addition, there is the simple assistance that CBO provides to the committees. CBO does not formally draft legislation, of course, but it is constantly being asked to review legislation and offer informal opinions on the budgetary significance of the legislation. As members of Congress and congressional staff gain experience with this, they become better versed in the details and nuances of budgeting.

CBO and the Public

Although a role in educating Congress was not discussed at the inception of CBO, it is not much of a stretch to argue that this function is perfectly consistent with the intent of the congressional budget process. It is fair to say, however, that the role that CBO has come to play in educating the broader public was almost completely unanticipated.

This does not mean to suggest that it happened unintentionally. Certainly we have seen how Alice Rivlin cultivated relationships with the press, often irritating Congress in the process. There is certainly evidence that this extended to the *Washington Post*, in particular (recall the editorial that opened this chapter), having some inclination to protect CBO when it was threatened. This occurred when the agency was without a director for two years after Penner left, or when Gingrich was threatening to clean the place out after the Republicans took control of the Congress in 1994. In 2003, when Crippen was replaced by Holtz-Eakin, a *Post* editorial exhorted the Congress to avoid making "dynamic scoring a litmus test for Mr. Crippen's successor. They need a CBO director whose allegiance, like Mr. Crippen's, is to the credibility of the budget office and its projections."[65]

Van Ooms pointed to Reischauer, in particular, as a deft handler of the media: "I think Reischauer was just extraordinary because he combined a tremendous knowledge not only about the budget . . . but on economic policy, but he also has a way of dealing with the media. Even when he was director and had to play a somewhat subdued role, he did it very skillfully. And I think that as a result of that it really enhanced the credibility of the organization and gave it more visibility. Because Bob always had a ten-second sound bite and the reporters loved that."[66]

At first this public education role was a bit under the radar and a bit self-conscious. Recall the primary criticism of CBO in the early days was that the agency maintained too high a profile. Over time, however, it has become much more overt in serving the public and the media. Constraints are still substantial—CBO staff generally do not speak to the media for attribution and CBO staff never make policy pronouncements unless they are about arcane issues of budget concepts or procedure—but it seems to be accepted by members of Congress that CBO is going to get attention, that it has a public education role, and that this is acceptable. Acceptance of a public education role appears so pervasive as to be "one of the clearest effects" of the creation of CBO.[67] Perhaps the most unambiguous indicator of how wide acceptance of this role is is the existence of a CBO director's blog (started by Peter Orszag). Notably, there was not just congressional outcry but also equally public outcry regarding the appearance of partisanship that accompanied Elmendorf's visit to the Oval Office in July 2009.

This is not to say that the attention never causes difficulties. There is some suggestion that CBO can forget who the client is, and that at times it may have "forgotten that its primary purpose is to serve and feed Congress, and instead felt its primary purpose was to serve the public or the academic community within the public. And I think occasionally they've lost sight of who they serve. They serve the Congress. The Congress serves the public. CBO doesn't directly serve the public."[68] Whether this might be the desire of some in Congress or not, it seems clear at this point in time that CBO does directly communicate with—if not serve—the public. It is, in that sense, less like the Congressional Research Service, much of whose work is not even publicly available,[69] and more like the GAO, which works hard to garner attention for its analyses.

Efforts to Make CBO Products Accessible

CBO has, since early in its history, invested a lot of effort in making its products accessible to the user. This may have started because of a relatively early (and negative) experience: CBO produced a 392-page report on the economy that was not viewed as at all useful by members of Congress. With the objective of ensuring usability of its products, CBO has invested great effort in the editorial process. According to Roy Meyers, a CBO staffer for eight years but a consumer of CBO products since 1990, "one of the underrecognized great contributions of CBO is that there is such an organizational pressure to communicate clearly."[70]

Dick Emery, who also has experience on both sides of CBO reports, agrees:

> I think that CBO's written products—the reports—have been consistently of very high caliber. And I give Alice Rivlin personally a great deal of credit for that. I think Alice's standards for the quality of the written product were very high, and the result was that CBO has traditionally produced useful, readable documents that contributed to the debate. Now, I think it would be much

more difficult to say that a report was the cause of a legislative action one way or another, but I think that there clearly is a significant quality to those reports. That also applied to the annual budgetary volumes, the quality of the writing was again very high quality, straightforward writing on budget issues. I think the readership has actually gotten quite small outside of academia, but by the same token having that information has been very important—particularly in the U.S. system, where you have an independent Congress.[71]

CBO has had a publications office from the start, which gives significant attention to customer service. One CBO director observed that Linda Schimmel, the long-tenured head of CBO publications, was perhaps the most valuable CBO employee, and (particularly in the days before the internet) perhaps the only one many people actually interacted with.[72]

The rise of the internet enhanced accessibility of CBO products. Most reports produced by CBO are available online, and the CBO website permits users to easily search for reports by topic and year. Letters CBO writes to members of Congress are released immediately on the CBO website. Many of the data underlying CBO economic and budget reports are increasingly available as well.

Finally, there are the cost estimates. In the past, anyone could request a cost estimate, but estimates were not otherwise explicitly published. Potential readers needed to know precisely what they were looking for to obtain such a report. Now, however, all cost estimates are published on the CBO website. As a result, anyone with access to a computer can obtain estimates at virtually the same time Congress does. Thus when a particularly newsworthy issue arises—say the potential cost of the 2009–10 health care reform bill or the 2003 Medicare prescription drug bill—the CBO cost estimate can be easily found. It should be noted that, consistent with both the function of public education and the agency's profile as a source of neutral analysis, CBO is typically very careful to detail the assumptions used in developing these estimates.

Putting all of this together—the public reports, the availability of cost estimates, the attention to accessible writing—it is hard to escape the conclusion that CBO and its leaders have not accidentally, but intentionally, democratized the availability of nonpartisan information on the economy and the budget. Given the importance of an informed electorate to the efficient operation of democracy, it is hard to overstate the significance of this development.

What CBO History Tells Us about the Role of Expertise

CBO would appear to have been a spectacular success in terms of the quality of information produced. On the basis of the criteria Alice Rivlin laid out at the beginning—that the organization would be credible and nonpartisan, that it would be respected, and that it would deliver products in an accessible form—it can hardly be judged to have been anything but successful. It is nothing short of remarkable that a nonpartisan institution such as this could have been preserved in an increasingly partisan environment in which contentious policy and resource issues are sometimes addressed. It is a tribute to the initial vision of Rivlin and the sustained effort of her successors and CBO staff that the agency has maintained and enhanced its credibility.

What of the effects of that information? First, there is little question that people pay attention, from members of Congress, to presidents, to the media, to members of the general public. Recall Hird's suggestion that legislators in states with NPROs valued nonpartisan information more as their own political environments became more partisan.[73] There is little doubt that the congressional policymaking environment has grown much more partisan, but CBO's influence has also grown over this same period. State NPRO directors told Hird that a higher value was placed on their information not in spite of being nonpartisan, but because of it.[74] Consider the health care reform debate. The president cared about the fiscal effects of health care reform, at least in part, because he needed to obtain majorities to pass the legislation in both houses. And he cared about CBO because the only way to convince some members of Congress that the bill actually reduced the deficit was for CBO to certify that it would. If he had simply asked them to believe OMB's analysis, he might have had less success in influencing their views.

Given the cacophony of information available as inputs to policymaking, the ascendancy of political spin, and the decline in the depth of media reporting, a neutral analysis function appears even more important today than it was in 1975. This is particularly true given the complicated set of problems the country faces—rising health care costs, uncertainty of retirement provisions for many, challenges to the global financial system, crumbling infrastructure, energy sector uncertainties—that will likely involve a costly government response. Any such response, in turn, is likely to intensify longer-term federal budget challenges (i.e., the deficit). Certainly having a source of nonpartisan information as we face these problems increases our chances of coming to effective policy solutions. This is the point made by Esterling, who could have been talking about CBO when he said that "Congress's capacity to use expertise to reform public policy depends heavily on the quality of debate among interest groups, and the quality of debate in turn depends critically on the state of knowledge for the policy that has been socially constructed among experts."[75] Objective information is necessary not simply to inform Congress so they can place themselves above politics and make "good decisions." It is also necessary for them to understand the likely impacts of their political choices. A democracy, in short, needs not just argument to survive: it needs reliable information. If all stakeholders (policymakers, media, citizens) in a policy discussion do not share the same information, progress is difficult (at best), and outcomes are at risk.

The type of information CBO provides, then, is necessary to effective policymaking. Alas, it is only necessary, not sufficient. Many of CBO's experiences—from its work on GSE reform, to its admonitions to Congress to address the nation's long-term fiscal challenges—suggest that only external political imperatives result in progress toward solutions. CBO was raising concerns about the problem of large federal deficits consistently from the time of the Reagan tax cuts in 1981 through the end of that administration. It was not until 1990—when the George H. W. Bush administration and Congress agreed on a package of tax increases and spending cuts, and a budget process reform that enforced compliance with those actions—that those warnings were heeded. At that point, CBO information—on the distributional effects of policies and on appropriate means of budget enforcement—was used in the process of working out the details.

At a more micro level, on the other hand, there is no question that information provided by CBO on the costs of policies can have a substantial effect on the design of those policies. Sometimes the effect may be to stop legislation from moving, such as reportedly happened particularly during the BEA period. On at least as many occasions, the effect is to change the structure of the policies to make them fit within some prescribed fiscal limit.

It is also important to note, as Hird argues, that as is true at the state level, it is not just the production of written products that matters. It is the existence of a nonpartisan institution that can forge relationships, advise committees and staff, respond to letters, testify before Congress, and generally become part of the "nervous system" of Congress. He contends that assessing the influence of policy-analytic organizations by simply looking at whether their products are used potentially misses the most important part of the story. Certainly that would be true with CBO. CBO has been most effective when Congress does not simply wait for the cost estimate or the report to come, but instead engages in ongoing dialogue with CBO staff about policies. The highest-profile example of that was the Obama health care reform, as the informal give-and-take appears to have had the largest effect on the ultimate content of the legislation.

Examples discussed in this book suggest that the main influence of CBO on policy comes as it informs the design of that policy after decisions have been made to pursue it (not by forcing policy change to happen). Although CBO has often been blamed for killing particular policy ideas, such as the Carter welfare reform or the Clinton health care reform, it seems more likely that these ideas died of other wounds, and CBO was simply a convenient scapegoat. So the notion, as advanced by Skocpol in chapter 1, that CBO is somehow an extraconstitutional source of independent power, seems extreme to say the least. Like many administrative institutions, CBO does exercise power, but largely power delegated to it under the law—that Congress could recapture easily if it so desired.

Whatever the failings of the congressional budget process, it seems clear that it could never have even gotten off the ground without the assistance of CBO. Moreover, given that the goal of the 1974 Budget Act was to make the Congress a stronger player in the budget process, CBO was central to making it happen. It has done this by providing the legislative branch with an independent source of information. Starting with its challenges to the Ford and Carter budgets, becoming more prominent with its analyses of the Reagan economic program, and reaching its zenith in the confrontation between Congress and President Clinton in 1995 and 1996, CBO has given Congress an ability to challenge the president. This simply could not happen without a set of alternative—arguably credible—economic and budgetary numbers.

Challenges for the Future

What, if anything, does this tell us about the future? Is there anything CBO might do to be more effective? Is there anything Congress might do to make better use of the resource? The research in this book suggests at least some options.

Future Challenges for CBO

Given the number of problems that affect the budget confronting Congress, there is a constant struggle within CBO to apply sufficient resources to inform policymaking for each of these problems without sacrificing capacity to address other problems. For example, the recent shift of resources to analyze health care reform needs and options might conceivably leave the agency relatively weak in other areas, such as its ability to analyze the problems of financial institutions.

Even though the organization of CBO by product, separating policy analysis from budget analysis, may deliver benefits in terms of enabling CBO to look at the broader effects of policies, it continues to create an internal management challenge of getting the two arms of CBO to work together. The burden of mitigating this risk should reasonably be on the program divisions. Program divisions are more well placed to take the lead in communicating and promoting collaboration with BAD, because the latter is heavily involved in deadline-driven work.

A continuing challenge, and one that came into immediate focus once again under unified government (the Democratic Congress and President Obama), involves remaining nonpartisan when all of the institutions of government are controlled by one party. An example of this surfaced in early 2009, when House Republicans reacted to the Democratic economic stimulus by basing their reservations on a CBO study suggesting that much of the money would not be spent fast enough to make a difference while the economy was still in recession. It expanded even further with the consideration of health care reform language. In such a situation, CBO can find itself with few friends, and under implicit or explicit threat, particularly in the congressional appropriations process.

Future Challenges for Congress

Thus far Congress has, sometimes unintentionally, selected leaders for CBO who have been committed to maintaining the institution as the strong, nonpartisan voice that Congress intended it to be. Although it would be difficult for a director of CBO to do great long-term damage to the organization without getting rid of a lot of people, it is important to have a director who is committed to the mission of the organization. It was just luck in 1995 that the House Republicans did not get what they bargained for in June O' Neill. On the other hand, the same House Republicans intentionally selected Doug Holtz-Eakin in 2003 not because he had worked in the White House, but because he could effectively lead CBO. The same was apparently true in 2009 when Doug Elmendorf was chosen. Democrats may have had control over who was on the list, but substantial attention was paid to choosing a director both parties could support. It is important, therefore, to give appropriate credit to the budget committees and their leaders for the success of CBO.

Because Congress has a great many problems on its agenda, it needs to develop a strategy to most effectively prioritize the CBO agenda in providing necessary analysis and estimations. This may be a particular challenge for an institution as decentralized as Congress. Not only will many committees have issues that require CBO assistance, but each also has both a majority and minority—each of which in turn may desire this assistance. It may be most effective for the majority and minority leadership to take an active role in priority setting, as they did on the 2009–10 health care reform legislation.

There will certainly be occasions in the future when Congress is tempted to lean on CBO to produce a particular answer, and to exact retribution if this answer does not come. This would indeed be short-sighted and destructive behavior. A strong CBO is not simply a tool for the congressional majority. It is a tool Congress can also use to strengthen itself in interactions with the executive branch. In the end, a weaker CBO means a stronger executive branch. Many believe that desirable. The point is that this would be the outcome if CBO were to be marginalized or made more partisan. Short-run political gains might accrue to such a strategy. In the long run, however, a weaker CBO would result in Congress cutting off its institutional nose to spite its budgetary face.

Neutral competence shines light on alternatives. In complicated public policy choices, transparency about assumptions is the foundation of neutrality. Alice Rivlin established a standard, reinforced by subsequent directors, requiring disclosure of the specific assumptions underlying CBO analyses. Over its thirty-five-year history, the agency has modeled precisely the transparency indispensible to reasoned debate and deliberation. In the prevailing environment—in which analysis often involves clear disclosure of the results, but scant attention to the assumptions (which may even be intentionally obscured)—CBO standards on this front are conspicuous. Given the complexity of and uncertainty associated with many problems facing the country, it is inevitable that different analysts will reach different conclusions based on diverse assumptions. Reasoned debate is not possible if only conclusions are aired: it requires revelation of assumptions to draw those conclusions. If Congress is interested in improving the effectiveness of public policy, it can demand that all analyses used to inform decisions explicitly specify assumptions used. Only then can we have a reasonable chance of finding the most effective solutions to public policy problems.

In the end, the future success of CBO will largely depend on two things. The first is the desire of CBO leadership and staff to produce quality nonpartisan information in a timely manner. The second will be the desire of Congress to make use of these data to make decisions that are in the long-term interest of the country, rather than their own short-term interests. Although this particular skunk may be a necessary guest at the picnic, it does not change the fact that those in attendance might want to either shoot the unwelcome intruder or—if they think this will work—ignore it entirely. At this moment, however, given the broad credibility and demonstrable influence of the institution—as well as the severity of budget issues likely to dominate on the national stage for the foreseeable future—it seems unlikely that the agency will be ignored on any issue that has substantial economic or budgetary significance any time soon. This, by the way, describes most of them.

Notes

1. "An Excellent Skunk," *Washington Post*, February 17, 1995, A24.

2. Ibid.

3. Ad Hoc Advisory Committee meeting.

4. Hugh Heclo, "CBO as a Professional Organization," unpublished manuscript.

5. As a counterargument, one might observe, Paul Posner noted in an interview that Elmer Staats once told him that "it is easier to be nonpartisan when you have 535 masters than when you have one!" (July 15, 2004).

6. Heclo, "CBO as a Professional Organization."

7. This point was made by a congressional staff member (who preferred to remain anonymous) in an interview with the author.

8. Lew, interview.

9. Susan Irving, interview with the author, July 15, 2004.

10. Joseph Minarik, interview with the author, October 27, 2004.

11. Primus, interview.

12. Ooms, interview.

13. It also must be acknowledged that many of them may not care which are correct, but select between options based on the ones they want to be right.

14. Horney, interview.

15. Emery, interview.

16. Ibid.

17. Blum, interview.

18. Emery, interview.

19. Senate Committee on the Budget, *Congressional Budget Office Oversight*, 94th Cong., 1st sess., October 6, 1975, 35.

20. Blum, interview, November 2004.

21. Marvin Phaup, interview with the author, March 2, 2004.

22. Rivlin, interview.

23. Meyers, interview.

24. Irving, interview.

25. Thomas Kahn, interview with the author, October 27, 2004.

26. Phaup, interview.

27. Primus, interview.

28. Bates, interview.

29. Rivlin, interview, 2003.

30. Meyers, interview.

31. This assessment was confirmed in interviews with Emery, Phaup, Rivlin, and Van de Water.

32. Emery, interview.

33. Phaup, interview.

34. Blum, interview, February 2004.

35. Kahn, interview.

36. Bates, interview.

37. Austin Smythe, interview with the author, April 30, 2010.

38. Observation made by a congressional staff member (who preferred to remain anonymous) in an interview with the author.

39. Holtz-Eakin, interview.

40. Meyers, interview.

41. Roy Meyers, "Late Appropriations and Government Shutdowns: Frequencies, Causes, Consequences, and Remedies," *Public Budgeting & Finance* 17, no. 3 (1997): 25–38.

42. Robert Lee, Ronald Johnson, and Philip Joyce, *Public Budgeting Systems*, 8th ed. (Sudbury, MA: Jones and Bartlett, 2008). 296.

43. Congressional Budget Office, *The Budget and Economic Outlook* (Washington, DC: GPO, 2010).

44. Government Accountability Office, "Fiscal Wake-Up Tour," www.gao.gov/special .pubs/longterm/wakeuptour.html.

45. Irene Rubin, "The Great Unraveling: Federal Budgeting, 1998–2006," *Public Administration Review* 67 (2007): 608.

46. Ibid., 610, 613.

47. Ibid., 610–11.

48. Louis Fisher, "Federal Budget Doldrums: The Vacuum in Presidential Leadership," *Public Administration Review* 50 (1990): 693–700.

49. Senate Committee on Government Operations, *Federal Act to Control Expenditures and Establish National Priorities*, 93rd Cong., 1st sess., November 28, 1973, 31.

50. Kogan, interview.

51. Ehrlich, interview.

52. Posner, interview.

53. Lew, interview.

54. Bates, interview.

55. Smythe, interview.

56. Anderson, interview.

57. Holtz-Eakin, interview, 2004.

58. Primus, interview.

59. Lew, interview.

60. Rivlin, interview.

61. Holtz-Eakin, interview, 2004.

62. Michael O'Hanlon, interview with the author, June 23, 2006.

63. Kogan, interview.

64. Ooms, interview.

65. "Needed: A Skunk," *Washington Post*, November 20, 2002, A24.

66. Ooms, interview.

67. Marcuss, interview.

68. Bates, interview.

69. Recently, more CRS products have been made public.

70. Meyers, interview.

71. Emery, interview.

72. Robert Reischauer made this point to me when I was a staff member at CBO in the early 1990s.

73. John Hird, *Power, Knowledge and Politics* (Washington, DC: Georgetown University Press, 2005), 73.

74. Ibid.

75. Kevin Esterling, *The Political Economy of Expertise* (Ann Arbor: University of Michigan Press, 2004), 249.

Index